MARKETING SCIENCE INSTITUTE SERIES

# Consumer Behavior

# Marketing Science Institute
## 1033 Massachusetts Avenue
## Cambridge, Massachusetts 02138

The Marketing Science Institute was established in 1962 as a nonprofit organization to contribute to improved marketing performance through research designed to provide objective information about marketing practices and their effects. MSI's program includes studies aimed at developing more reliable research procedures; explorations of consumer behavior; and investigations of public policy issues related to marketing.

In October, 1968, the Institute's Board of Trustees approved the establishment of a new association between MSI and the Harvard Graduate School of Business. MSI retains its status as an independent research organization, but it can now benefit from the Business School's facilities, such as the computer center and the various libraries, and from working closely with Harvard faculty.

MSI is supported by member companies representing leading U.S. industries. The Institute's bylaws also permit acceptance of grants or gifts from foundations, associations, and governmental agencies.

# Consumer Behavior
## Theory and Application

**JOHN U. FARLEY**
Columbia University

**JOHN A. HOWARD**
Columbia University

**L. WINSTON RING**
University of Wisconsin — Milwaukee

ALLYN & BACON, INC.    BOSTON

# Contributors

GEORGE S. DAY, Graduate School of Business, Stanford University

JOHN U. FARLEY, Graduate School of Business, Columbia University

MORRIS BALDWIN HOLBROOK, Graduate School of Business, Columbia University

JOHN A. HOWARD, Graduate School of Business, Columbia University

SHLOMO I. LAMPERT, The Eliezer Kaplan School of Economics and Social Sciences, The Hebrew University of Jerusalem

PAUL F. LAZARSFELD, University of Pittsburgh

TERRENCE V. O'BRIEN, University of Arizona

PAUL A. PELLEMANS, Departement d'Economie d'Enterprise, Facultes Universitaires de Namur

MICHAEL PERRY, Graduate School of Business, Tel Aviv University

L. WINSTON RING, University of Wisconsin, Milwaukee

JAGDISH N. SHETH, University of Illinois

# Contents

# Preface

The present volume deals with a topic of great importance to social scientists in all fields. The decisions that a buyer in the market makes are bound to have parallels with, for example, a voter making up his mind about a candidate, or a high-school boy deciding whether to re-enlist. It will be helpful to provide a short inventory of social science literature that parallels the contributions in the present collection.

As to the general schema developed by Professors Howard and Sheth, a very pertinent and close parallel was written by psychologist Tolman[1] for a joint enterprise published in 1951 by a group of Harvard social scientists.

The general design of the buyer behavior research project as described by Mr. Day was based on repeated interviews. Under the name of panel studies, this design has acquired increasing importance throughout the social sciences. Not surprisingly, the new *International Encyclopedia of the Social Sciences* includes a detailed description of the technique, written by Levenson,[2] a Columbia sociologist.

Anyone concerned with social interaction will, of course, be interested in the contribution by Mr. Lampert on "Word of Mouth." Similar work by social psychologists and sociologists is reviewed and discussed in the book *Personal Influence*, written by Elihu Katz and myself.[3]

An important aspect of effective use of panel studies is the use of so-called cross-lagged correlation, which involves causal influences based on time series data. Cross-lagged correlation is skillfully applied to buying behavior in Mr. O'Brien's contribution. His work can be compared to similar efforts made elsewhere, for example, *Problems in Measuring Change*, edited by Harris.[4]

The relations among attitudes, intention, and behavior are probably the most vexing in the whole survey field. The literature is so vast that the only advice for the reader looking for comparison is to look into the new *Hand-book of Social Psychology*, edited by Lindsey and Aronson.[5] The index of every volume containing pertinent references from now on will include the contribution of Mr. Sheth.

The use of simulation in the social sciences, represented by Mr. Perry's contribution, is quite new. Probably students of man–machine systems have been most active in this field, and a good review can be found in the book by Arthur Siegel and Jay Wolf.[6]

Problems of definition and measurement are, of course, common to all the social sciences, and the Social Sciences Research Council convened a conference on the history of quantification, including representatives of the natural sciences. The report of this symposium, edited by Harry Woolf,[7] will show where business research stands in relation to its sister sciences. The contribution of Mr. Ring and Mr. Pellemans in the present volume clearly belongs in this tradition.

Mr. Day raises the question of the stability of responses in studies where subjects were re-interviewed. This is an important problem for the following reason: change can be due to the actual experience of subjects but it can also be due to the unreliability inherent in measurement. The tradition of psychometrics has focused mainly on the error problem. Sociologists are more concerned with how real the phenomenon of true change is. Concrete experiments on this point have been reported by Patricia Kendall in her monograph *Conflict and Mood.*[8] George Katona and his group of psychological economists have also made valuable contributions to the issue.

The concluding contribution by Messrs. Farley and Ring can also be looked upon as an overture to a next volume. They give a mathematical formulation to the Howard scheme through a set of simultaneous linear questions. This is a technique that connects authors in a large variety of fields, including economics, and the work comes close to what some other social scientists call *path analysis*. A broad view of this interesting new development can be found in a recent collection edited by Blalock,[9] titled *Causal Models in the Social Sciences*. The contributions to that volume are mainly concerned with situations where only a few variables are related to each other. The Howard scheme represents a complex flow chart where a number of variables interact with each other over time. Further mathematization and testing with such a broad approach are challenges opened up by the work reported here.

A twofold unity is apparent in the present volume. One derives from the conceptual scheme and the other from the fact that all contributors base their analysis on the same pool of data. Both the theory and the amount of factual information collected are very large indeed. To make his work manageable, each author in this volume could select only a limited amount of the ideas and results available to the whole group. It is, therefore, most fortunate that Mr. Holbrook has provided a third kind of integration. He has analyzed each paper after the fact and given it its place in the total enterprise. The reader is well advised to move back and forth between the individual contributions and Mr. Holbrook's guide. This will make it much easier for him to see the interconnections.

Paul F. Lazarsfeld
University of Pittsburgh

### References

1.  Tolman, Edward C., in Talcott Parsons & Edward Shils (eds.), *Toward a General Theory of Action*, Part 3 (Cambridge, Mass: Harvard University Press, 1951).

2.  Sills, Davis (ed.), *International Encyclopedia of the Social Sciences* (New York: The Macmillan Co. and the Free Press, 1968).

3.  Katz, Elihu, and Paul F. Lazarsfeld, *Personal Influence* (New York: Free Press of Glencoe, 1955).

4.  Harris, Chester W. (ed.), *Problems of Measuring Change* (Madison, Wisconsin: University of Wisconsin Press, 1967).

5.  Lindsey, Gardner, and Elliot Aronson (eds.), *Handbook of Social Psychology* (Reading, Mass.: Addison Wesley Publishing Co., 1968).

6.  Siegel, Arthur I., and J. Jay Wolf, *Man-Machine Simulation Models* (New York: John Wiley & Sons, Inc., 1964).

7.  Woolf, Harry, *Quantification* (Indianapolis: Bobbs-Merrill Company, 1961).

8.  Kendall, Patricia, *Conflict and Mood* (New York: Free Press of Glencoe, 1953).

9.  Blalock, Herbert, *Causal Models in the Social Sciences* (Chicago: Aldine-Atherton, Inc., 1971).

# The Genesis of Applied Buyer Behavior Theory

This book deals with development and application of integrated buyer behavior theory and evaluating the results of a specific test market.

The combination of solidifying the relatively abstract theory and solving very concrete problems in evaluating a test market project is natural, and the blending of these two major streams of marketing research activity illustrates many aspects that have characterized progress in market analysis in the last decade. Some of this progress has been theoretical—partially borrowed from the social sciences, to which marketing is so indebted, and partially new. Some of this progress has been methodological, both in terms of data collection technology and techniques of analysis which make better use of bodies of complex data. The development of this combination, though, is in several ways greater than the sum of the parts. In this regard, the book constitutes a logical step in the development of marketing systems analysis and may also prove to be an important step in the development of marketing information systems for the analysis of test market results.

## THE BOOK'S GENESIS

The book is composed of twelve different chapters by ten authors. The chapters are tied together by two major themes: (1) the thrust of the theoretical frameworks in which the papers are cast and (2) the specific field research project that all the papers deal with.

The theoretical underpinnings are provided by a theory of buyer behavior. The most comprehensive version of this theory, developed over nearly a decade, appeared in *Theory of Buyer Behavior*, by John A. Howard and Jagdish N. Sheth, three years after the test market was run. The book was published in its full form in 1969, although earlier and less detailed versions of various aspects of the work appeared over a period of seven years. The theory is concerned with the factors that govern consumers' decisions of what

1

products and which brands to buy, and it attempts to describe and explain important marketing phenomena. This allows prediction, delimits areas of concern for the marketer in specific problems, and integrates in a manageable form the themes of the basic disciplines to which the study of consumer behavior owes such a lavish debt.

These goals are very close to those of practicing marketers, so as the theory of buyer behavior began to take form and started to gain attention, it was not surprising that practicing marketers began to ask its authors whether the theory could help them with their problems. One such inquiry led to planning and executing a complex information-gathering project in connection with a test market of a convenience food product in 1966. The data collection project involved a number of phases sometimes used in evaluating test markets, but it had a unique characteristic—it was planned roughly in the context of the then-developing buyer behavior theory. Since that time, it has become increasingly clear that it is feasible to meld conventional market research and development of buyer behavior study by careful preplanning of data collection and methods of analysis.

The six-month data collection project, described in detail in Chapter 3, resulted in a large and very rich set of data, consisting of panel reports and a series of intensive mail and telephone interviews conducted with panel members. These data were, in combination with elements of the emerging theory, the genesis of a wide variety of research projects dealing with various aspects of both the buyer behavior model and the test market. In fact, development of the model and the empirical work were so intimately related throughout this research that they were for practical purposes inseparable.

Some of the individual research pieces involved cross-sectional analysis of the behavior of individual purchasers, and some involved time series analysis of behavior of individuals or groups of individuals. Some of the work studied particular aspects of buyer behavior, while other studies dealt with a larger model more globally but in less detail. Methodology included techniques drawn from systems analysis, models and methods from the social sciences, multivariate statistics, and econometrics. Some of the work was done in connection with doctoral dissertations, and some was done by faculty members, who played a variety of roles in the project. Many of the studies built upon earlier ones.

Plans for further field testing of the model using other kinds of markets and products required synthesis of earlier results. A pattern of related development of theory and application came out in this synthesis, so it appeared that it would be useful to gather these results in a coordinated form. Thus the nine authors whose original work is presented here were asked to prepare a description of their part in the project. Each author was told the plan of the book and the part that others in the project were asked to play in its creation. With the exception of the last chapter, all the material has been specially prepared for this volume, although some of the basic results have been reported elsewhere in different form. After all the individual pieces were collected, a final synthesis was prepared, which attempts to combine the results over both time and constructs into an integrated whole.

## ORGANIZATION OF THE BOOK

The book is organized into six interrelated parts:

1. *The System and the Study.* This set of three papers provides the basic description of a buyer behavior model and of the design of the test market that form the central core of this book. Included are "The Structure of Buyer Behavior," by John A. Howard, which presents theoretical underpinnings of the buyer behavior structure that emerged at the end of the project; "A Description and Evaluation of the Design of the Buyer Behavior Research Project," by George S. Day; and "Some Measurement Effects in Purchase Panel Data from the Test Market," by L. Winston Ring, which deals with some methodological questions about an experimental panel as compared with a control panel.

2. *Subsystem Analysis.* This section is composed of papers that are smaller-scale studies that ultimately developed into sections of the system laid out in the Howard paper. The papers are very much in the tradition of the behavioral sciences, in both approach and methodology. They constitute the interface between mainstreams of traditional marketing research methods and newer theoretical and methodological material, and they also exemplify the partial piece-by-piece research that is required to translate abstract ideas into an operational model. For example, in "Word of Mouth Activity during the Introduction of a New Food Product," Shlomo Lampert examines word-of-mouth communications patterns involved in adoption of the product and in diffusion of information about the product through the test community. Jagdish N. Sheth examines in detail the characteristics and dimensions of the attitudinal structure related to the new product. This theme is expanded in terms of stability and prediction in George S. Day's examination of attitudes in "Attitude Stability, Changeability, and Predictive Ability," and in Paul A. Pellemans' "Investigation on Attitude and Purchase Intention toward the Brand."

3. *System Stability.* Two quite different approaches to the study of the dynamic characteristics of the interrelationships are included. Michael Perry, in "Simulation of Buyer Behavior," constructs a computer

analogue of a simplified version of the buyer behavior model and analyzes behavior of the model over time. Terrence V. O'Brien, in "Information Sensitivity and Brand Choice," uses cross-lag correlational techniques to identify and sort out causal relationships among many of the variables that ultimately appeared. Establishment of causal direction has been a consistently difficult problem for market researchers and is also an important step toward development of the system in its entirety.

4. *Full System Analysis.* About three years after the original project started, John U. Farley and L. Winston Ring cast a then-current version of the buyer behavior model as a set of linear relationships in "A Simultaneous-Equation Regression Test of the Howard-Sheth Model." By this time, a fairly complete picture of the entire model was available, so a more global test seemed appropriate. Using techniques borrowed from econometrics, they attempt to evaluate the explanatory power and predictive usefulness of this model in terms of implications for buyer behavior theory, the test market results, and research methodology.

5. *A Synthesis of the Results.* Recognizing that the sequence of earlier studies involved substantial development over time, Morris Holbrook attempts to tie these results together into a comprehensive framework describing a later version of the buyer behavior framework.

6. *A Glimpse into the Future.* In "Buyer Behavior and Related Technological Advances," John A. Howard looks forward to the changes that can be expected for the marketing manager, market researcher, and market model builder as a result of developments like those described in this book.

7. *Combined Bibliography.* This combination of references from all the papers provides a convenient bibliography of various applications of buyer behavior theory.

## BACKGROUND NEEDED TO USE THE BOOK

The methodologies used by the various authors reflect the obvious increased sophistication of marketing research over the last decade. While cross-tabulation has been and will continue to be important to marketing research, the complex interrelationships implied by the buyer behavior model force use of rather advanced model-building techniques and statistical thinking. Some of these are used at various points throughout the book, not for their own sake but because they are needed. On the other hand, relatively little background is required to be able to read the book and absorb the major ideas. Ability to read and understand a flow chart is important, since the flow chart is a most convenient language for communicating both the basic model and the technology used in several specific applications. Some background in multivariate statistics is also needed and an appreciation of multiple regression and correlation. An awareness of factor analytic techniques is also useful, though not necessary.

## THE BOOK'S ROLE

Of what use is a book like this? Who might use it?

For one thing, the book helps answer the gnawing question asked repeatedly by both marketing practitioners and market researchers, "What can I do with buyer behavior models?" The answer to this question is multifaceted. The theory is useful in planning studies and experiments, in suggesting what data to collect and when to collect it, and in indicating appropriate tools of analysis for empirical work.

Second, the book offers a kind of road map for planning, executing, and controlling market research projects with multiple goals to be served from a single data base. This, in turn, means that the book may play a useful role as an intermediate guide to the development of a structure for an integrated marketing information system.

Third, the book is a useful companion piece to any of the growing volumes of literature for a course on buyer behavior or consumer behavior. This means that the book can provide the student of marketing with a picture of the integration of theory and application that does not emerge so clearly from descriptions of results or collections of papers less closely related to one another than those included here.

Fourth, for readers who want a relatively quick, comprehensive view of the field, the book provides a useful introduction to buyer behavior theory and its applications. For example, if a week or two of a marketing management course or marketing seminar are devoted to buyer behavior models, this volume (or appropriately selected sections) provides integrated coverage of the topic.

Finally, market research courses need concrete examples of (1) a variety of research techniques as applied to marketing research problems and (2) integration of theory with every phase of the research process. The book provides material to meet both of these needs.

# I

## The System and the Study

# 1. The Structure of Buyer Behavior

## John A. Howard

## 1. INTRODUCTION

Marketing executives are finding more and more that they are expected to provide quantitative support for their marketing plans. Change in the nature of the company organization has much to do with this trend. First, line relationships are less firm, and lateral relations are becoming more common. A brand manager must get the cooperation of a number of people—sales manager, advertising manager, merchandising manager—and these people all want evidence before they agree to the marketing plan that grows out of his creative ideas.

Second, planning procedures do not only generate plans. The marketing plan serves also as a splendid instrument of corporate control, which permits the major delegation of marketing decision making that we observe. The plan of the brand manager contains a detailed description of what he and others involved in marketing his brand will do and the results they expect to achieve. Higher management then achieves control of the brand operation by later comparing the brand's actual performance with this expected performance.

This is a condensed summary of J. A. Howard and J. N. Sheth, *The Theory of Buyer Behavior*, New York: John Wiley and Sons, 1969, which was a major extension and elaboration of the ideas that appeared in Howard, *Marketing Management*, 2d ed., Homewood, Illinois: R. D. Irwin, Inc., 1963, particularly Chapters 3 and 4. All page references will be to this 1969 source unless otherwise indicated. A few further developments of the theory are made here mainly to link it more explicitly and operationally to information in the market. The concept of stimulus-as-coded is incorporated as a construct, for example. Also, by distinguishing between goals and motives, and between personal and professional goals, it is possible to clean up some loose ends and to avoid using the term "inhibitor" which sometimes misleads the reader. The author is indebted to Professor L. Winston Ring for his incisive criticism and to the Foundation of the American Association of Advertising Agencies for financial support.

Because of its importance as a control device, higher management evaluates the plan carefully. An unsupported assertion by the brand manager can become suspect. The fewer of these unsupported assertions in his plan, the more likely it is to be accepted.

Stimulated by consumer concerns, legislators at all levels of government are increasingly raising questions about the social desirability of a range of marketing practices, some of which have not been previously questioned. Currently, the evidential support for proposed legislation tends to be meager, and quantitative data about consumer response would do much to clarify the issues and suggest solutions.

By far the largest amount of the supporting evidence required for both private and public issues has to do with why the buyer buys a brand or product class. This is true regardless of whether the buyer is a consumer, industrial, or institutional buyer. Further, this evidence is very difficult to acquire. The following discussion will attempt to throw light on the question as it pertains to any kind of a buyer—consumer, industrial, or institutional— although the terminology here does not fit these organizational buyers as well. For example, "brand" is less meaningful for them than "product-supplier."

"Why does the buyer buy?" is a surprisingly subtle question and it requires equally subtle answers. There are many levels at which it can be asked and answered. Willie Sutton was asked why he robbed the bank. Willie replied, "That's where the money is!" From Willie's view of the world—his frame of reference—this was a perfectly honest answer. To him the issue was not whether to rob, but instead, given that you are going to rob, which is the best place to rob—a home, a filling station, or a bank? The moralist would wish to have the question answered at the first level.

In the following pages we will ask at a number of levels why the buyer buys, and attempt an answer at each level. We can say, for example, that he buys the brand because he likes it. Then the next level question is, "Why does he like it?" etc. in almost infinite regress.

Unfortunately, like all human behavior, buying behavior is complex, as any brand manager will vouchsafe. This complexity is show in Figure 1.1, which is a complete picture of a system which describes buying behavior. It may appear horrendously complex but the reader should bear in mind the truly enormous variety in buying situations: the purchase of chewing gum versus the purchase of an automobile versus the industrial buyer purchasing electric motors in a factory that produces refrigerators. This variety must be encompassed within the system if it is to make even a pretense of generality.

To simplify the description of the different levels of why a buyer buys, let us group the reasons into three categories by setting up three different buying situations based on how much information the buyer needs to make

Figure 1.1
Structure of Buying Behavior

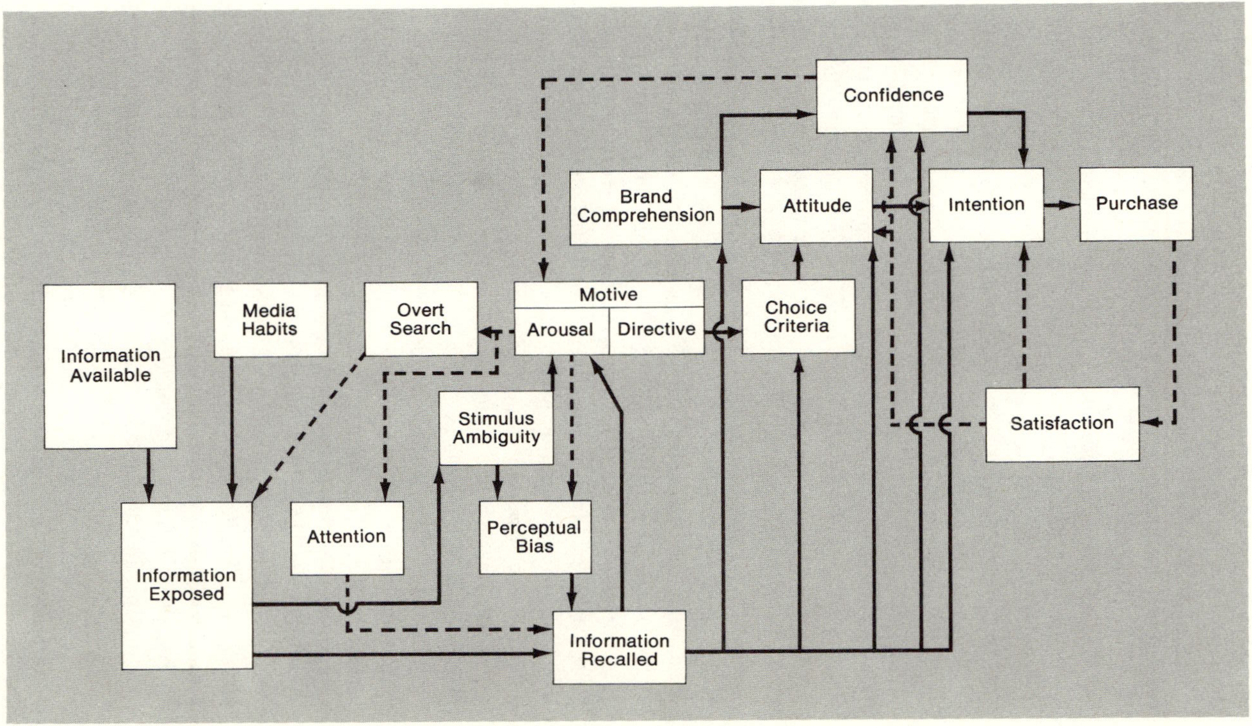

his decision. The policy maker—private or public—can fit his particular problem into the appropriate case and proceed to analyze it with those concepts. In the first situation, which involves only six of the variables in Figure 1.1, he needs relatively little information. We call this Routinized Response Behavior (RRB). The second situation, which involves changes in all but one of the variables—Choice Criteria—in Figure 1.1, and in which the buyer needs considerable information, is called Limited Problem Solving (LPS). Finally, in the third case, which is Extensive Problem Solving (EPS) and involves all the variables in Figure 1.1, he needs a great amount of information. Let us define these terms.

Routinized Response Behavior (RRB) can be viewed as a preference equilibrium position for the buyer, and the other two positions—LPS and EPS—can be viewed as explaining (1) what pushes him off the equilibrium position and (2) how he returns to it. RRB does not imply, however, that the buyer's brand choice is fixed and automatic when action is triggered by an intensified need. The choice can still be influenced by the information that is available at the time of purchase. Although the outcome of his choice is not fixed, his brand and product-class concepts are fixed. He understands each brand that he considers and has a definite degree of preference or predisposition for it. There will be some conditions of his environment, such as whether the brand is available in his retail store, which will obviously influence his purchase irrespective of his brand preference. Thus, he needs some information even for this decision. We would expect this case to exist with a frequently purchased item where the period between purchases is short enough for the buyer to avoid significant loss of memory of facts related to the brand between purchases.

Limited Problem Solving applies to the situation where a buyer is being confronted with a new, unfamiliar brand and has a need for an item in that familiar product class. Hence, he can be thought of as being in product-class equilibrium. By "product class" we mean those brands that are closely substitutable in the buyer's mind in satisfying a given set of his needs. He must form a concept of the brand. To form the brand concept he needs more information than he does to choose when the concept is already formed, as in Routinized Response Behavior.

Extensive Problem Solving occurs when the buyer is confronted by a brand in an unfamiliar product class, and so he is in complete disequilibrium. In this situation he not only must judge a new brand but also develop new criteria by which to judge it: he must form a new product-*class* concept. Development of new criteria requires still more information than judging a new brand by familiar criteria. Thus, product class can be operationally defined in terms of these criteria. The buyer can be said to have a product-class concept well formulated when he has acquired (learned) the criteria by which to evaluate all brands in that product class. Still more information is needed in Extensive Problem Solving than in Limited Problem Solving.

Beginning with RRB, each situation incorporates additional elements of the theory of buyer behavior and the relations among them as portrayed in Figure 1.1. The elements for the most part are internal to the buyer's nervous system; they are in his "head." The input to the system is Information Available, which is all the information relevant to the alternatives of choice to which the buyer might be exposed, and it is the same for all buyers in the market. The output is Purchase. The large number of constructs connecting Information Available and Purchase suggests the complexity of the purchase event: the great number of influences that can cause the buyer to buy one brand instead of another or even buy nothing at all.

With this perspective on the theory, let us proceed to examine each of the three buying situations in order to delineate the various levels at which we can ask and answer the question, "Why does the buyer buy or not buy your brand?" The reader should bear in mind that the answers at different levels serve different purposes. The earlier levels as presented here are more appropriate for control purposes in either a public or private policy sense. In planning, the earlier levels are more appropriate for prediction and the later levels are more appropriate for explaining *why* a particular course of action was or was not successful.

## 2. ROUTINIZED RESPONSE BEHAVIOR

The first level of "why the buyer buys" is his *need* level. On his way home from the office, for example, he accidentally passes a bakery shop and the odor of freshly baked pastries assails his nostrils, which contain his olfactory sensors. Suddenly he is hungry and this causes him to think that his wife would appreciate having him bring home some dessert. Why did he buy? The odor triggered certain psychological and physiological processes that caused him to be hungry—to have a real need. In psychological terms, it stimulated his Motives (pp. 99–118) which can be written as $M^a$ where "$a$" denotes the "arousal" or the intensity aspect of Motives as opposed to the content of his Motives ($M^c$). This effect would be to increase the probability that he will buy a unit of the product class but would not increase the probability that he will buy a particular brand in that class. Presumably, in an advanced society where finer discriminations are necessary, a number of motives operate in any given purchase situation.

Empirically, an important question is, "How can you distinguish a motive from a habit?" A motive is a driving force; it has the capacity to accentuate other responses. The reduction of a motive leads to learning a new habit. Thus, habit is merely a regular pattern of behavior, with no driving force. Extremely intense motives, however, cause vacillation if a simple habit pattern of behavior has not been learned and stereotyped behavior if it has.

Knowing that a buyer experiences a need tells us when he will buy, but it does not enable us to predict with accuracy just *what* brand he will buy, but with more information we could. What is this additional information?

We must know his Intention (to buy) (pp. 132−145). As he enters the door of the shop we ask him, "What do you intend to buy?" He replies, "Spice cake!" He *intends* to buy spice cake either because he has eaten it in the past and found it tasty or because he has heard, especially from friends whom he trusts, that it is tasty. Tying in Figure 1.1, each line that connects any two boxes there represents a relationship that can be stated in an equation. To simplify we refer to Purchase as $P$, and Intention as $I$ with a particular brand being denoted by $x$ in subscript form.

$$P_x = f(I_x) \tag{1}$$

Thus, Intention is positively related to Purchase but not perfectly related because conditions of purchase may be different when he buys than what he anticipated they would be when he earlier said he intended to buy. Throughout this paper, this general functional form will be used. It merely states that the variables are related but does not suggest even whether that relationship is positive or negative, much less a more precise statement. When the equation is discussed in the text, however, whether it is positive or negative will, with a few exceptions, be stated. In a few cases the relation is known to be nonlinear.

For some purposes it is more useful to know what part of the buyer's decision process underlies his Intention than it is to know his Intention; for example, perhaps some of the elements in that process may be influenced. Figure 1.2 is a diagram describing the decision process of a driver buying gasoline for her car. Most of the boxes imply a condition that will affect the purchase and so the driver needs information about each of these conditions. Hence, the boxes represent *information-processing* rules. In Box 3, for example, she compares the time when she will need to have her car serviced with the time by which her gasoline tank is likely to be empty. Further, a *decision rule* is implied between each of two boxes, for example, between Box 2 and Box 3: ask myself whether my car will be serviced before it needs gas. An explicit decision rule is contained in Box 6.

Still another concept in the decision process is that of a *stop* rule: a decision rule that says "Buy nothing!" If the answer to the information-processing rule in Box 2 is "Yes," the implicit decision rule is a stop rule. The

**Figure 1.2**

**Motorist Buying Gasoline**

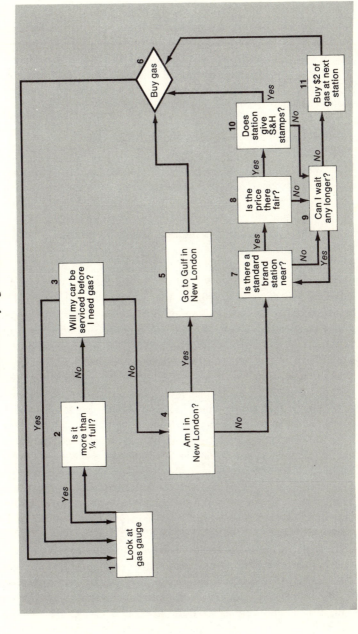

From J. A. Howard and J. N. Sheth, *The Theory of Buyer Behavior*, New York: John Wiley & Sons, Inc., 1969, Figure 4.6.

stop rule concept is especially important. It explains why a person may buy nothing—no brand—in a product class. The reason for this—the market condition that causes it—is, of course, important information for forecasting the total purchases of a product class as well as for market planning purposes. Let us suppose, for example, that between Boxes 5 and 6 there was an information-processing rule that asked: "Is gasoline more than 60¢ per gallon?" Presumably one of the boxes out of it would ask about prices at competing stations. If all were greater than 60¢ per gallon, then a stop rule could operate: the driver would cease using her car, for example. Here we see price of the brand in its role as a constraint on action.

These rules—information processing, decision, and stop—can be viewed as imbedded in an ongoing pattern of broader behavior, and in this way brand buying can be systematically related to shopping behavior, for example, and store selection. Finally, knowing the conditions specified by the information-processing rules not only helps us predict the buyer's behavior, but allows us to change some of the conditions and thus change his behavior.

These conditions specified in Figure 1.2 should be viewed as criteria upon which the buyer partially evaluates brands. From Figure 1.2, for example, we can infer that this buyer prefers (has a favorable Attitude toward) Gulf gasoline and so will use the Gulf station in New London. The conditions specified in this picture of her decision process, however, can cause her to go contrary to her Attitude and buy some brand other than Gulf. These conditions or criteria, called impersonal or professional goals, serve Motives only indirectly, whereas the dimensions of Attitude discussed below are personal goals, which serve Motives directly. Her personal goals could be to obtain a brand of gasoline that gives good mileage, does not cause the motor to knock, and whose filling stations provide quick service and clean restrooms. As indicated by Figure 1.2, her impersonal or professional goals could be to minimize her effort (buy at the nearest standard brand), to buy gasoline at a fair price, and to obtain S & H stamps. Here we are, of course, defining goals at an operational level, but it is often useful to define them at a more general level. Illustrating with an industrial buyer will clarify the distinction between personal and impersonal goals: an industrial buyer finds that interacting with Salesman A is more satisfying to his affiliation motive than interacting with Salesman B, and so his Attitude toward A's product is more favorable. A's price is higher, however, and the buyer's achievement motive is satisfied by pleasing his boss, who wants him to buy as cheaply as possible. Hence, if the buyer chooses B over A, his professional goal is dominating his personal goal. To a consumer buyer, the level of price is per se irrelevant, but its implications are quite relevant. To the extent that our lady pays more for gasoline at one station than another, she will have fewer financial resources available to further her other needs or Motives. In the same way, if she receives S & H stamps, she could have more resources for other purposes. In summary, Intention is a function of the buyer's expectations about the values of the conditions specified in his information-processing rules.

Implied here is the obvious point of a means–end chain. The industrial buyer chooses from A to satisfy his goal of associating with "pleasant" people, which in turn satisfies his affiliation motive. A longer chain is implied in the next instance. Buying from B satisfies his price goal, which is a means of meeting his goal of pleasing his boss, which in turn is a means of satisfying his achievement motive. One could further pursue this analysis by hypothesizing that his achievement motive was learned, because by learning it he was better able to satisfy his innate motives of hunger, sex, etc. Also, especially for industrial buying behavior, it is probably very useful to view his personal goals as the criteria by which he decides which alternatives to consider seriously—his *evoked set* (p. 33)—and his professional goals as the criteria he uses to choose from among the alternatives in this evoked set.[7]

Now that we have discussed how Intention determines purchase, let us drop to a more fundamental level of explanation and ask: "What causes Intention?" The answer is

$$I_x = f(F_x^C, A_x, C_x) \tag{2}$$

where $F_x^C$ is Facts Coded (pp. 152–153): the knowledge of, or the prediction about, the facts specified by the buyer's information-processing rules; $A_x$ is Attitude (pp. 127–132) toward $x$ (Gulf in Figure 1.1); and $C_x$ is Confidence in ability to evaluate $x$. The "$C$" in $F_x^C$ refers to "coded" information, an operational measure of which is recall of the information. $F_x^C$ incorporates the information that $x$ exists, that it has certain denotative characteristics, and that it has certain connotative (favorable or unfavorable) characteristics. The net favorable information is positively related to Intention. Attitude $(A_x)$ indicates evaluation of $x$ in terms of its perceived capacity to satisfy needs directly.

We speak here as though Attitude is only a unidimensional concept, but when we want to deal with the causes of Attitude change, it is fruitful to think of it as being the resultant of a number of dimensions. A consumer likes—has a favorable Attitude toward—a car, but he likes it for particular reasons: economy, acceleration, comfort, etc. Hence, if we are interested in *why* Attitude changes, as we usually are, we investigate the extent to which each of these dimensions changes since some can change and others cannot. Further, Attitude is like Intention in this respect: both have an underlying set of dimensions. As mentioned earlier, we can think of the Attitude dimensions as being personal goals and Intention dimensions as being impersonal or professional goals. This view may seem more reasonable if you stop to consider that the buyer logically could, if he wished, choose on one of the dimensions and attempt to maximize it subject to the constraints of the other dimensions, as in a linear programming problem.[7] In Figure 1.2, the conditions specified in the driver's decision process were professional goals and there she appeared to be "satisficing"—achieving on a satisfactory level—on all of them instead of maximizing on one. Thus, lying behind Intention is Attitude (personal goals) and impersonal or professional goals.

Finally, Confidence ($C_x$) is her confidence in her ability to judge the quality of the brand (pp. 143−145). Both $A_x$ and $C_x$ are positively related to Intention. Hence, if both $A_x$ and $C_x$ are high and none of the information about the market conditions is unfavorable to $I_x$, there is a very high probability that she will buy the brand.

In Routinized Response Behavior, we say that the buyer is in *preference equilibrium*; he is brand loyal as indicated by his high Attitude, but he will buy some other brand if it is sufficiently more favorable to his professional goals. If the brand is constant with respect to both his personal and professional goals, he will continue to buy the same brand repeatedly and so be in *purchase equilibrium*.

The economic literature on buying behavior, by its assumption of "given tastes," is confined to Routinized Response Behavior. For this reason, traditional economic analysis has serious shortcomings in understanding buying behavior where technological change creates a continuous flood of new products that require adjustment of "tastes." Recently, however, Baumol[1] and Lancaster[3,4] have separately suggested modifications of economic demand theory that incorporate the idea that people judge consumption items on more than one criterion, or to put it in Lancaster's terms, people do not judge apples on "appleness" but on the underlying attributes of taste, juiciness, texture, etc. These modifications permit closer intellectual interchange between economic theory and the point of view expressed here. Nevertheless, the mechanisms of change are still left unarticulated and even the static case allows for no distinction between personal and impersonal goals.

## 3. LIMITED PROBLEM SOLVING

### 3.1 Introduction

When a buyer is confronted with a new brand in a familiar product class, his choice process becomes more complicated. More variables are required to explain why he buys.

One of the major complications is that perceptual effects often enter in because the buyer is taking in more information, and the information is often ambiguous because he has less understanding of the problem than in RRB. Let us first deal with the nonperceptual effects and then incorporate the perceptual.

### 3.2 Nonperceptual Effects

In the previous section, Attitude and Confidence were introduced. To get to a more complete explanation of buying behaviors, we must ask what determines them. If we denote the *new* brand by $y$:

$$A_y = f(B_y^C, S_y, F_y^C) \qquad (3)$$

where $A_y$ is the buyer's Attitude toward the brand. $B_y^C$ is Brand Comprehension (pp. 96–99), his understanding of the denotative or descriptive features of the brand, such as how he identifies it, the aspects or dimensions of it that he discusses with his friends, and those aspects from which he can make evaluative inferences. These aspects are not evaluative in themselves, however. A high level of Brand Comprehension is associated with a favorable Attitude. This follows because he bothers to be well informed only about his preferred brand. $S_y$ is the Satisfaction that he received from prior purchases of $y$ and it is positively related to Attitude. $F_y^C$ in this case is the evaluative facts the buyer has perceived about $y$. By "evaluative" is meant information stating or implying that $y$ is good or bad for him, effective or ineffective in serving his needs. We emphasize "perceived" or coded information because, as will be discussed later, the human mind sometimes modifies information in processing or coding it. This information could come from salesmen, advertising, the buyer's friend, a newspaper story, *Consumer Reports*, etc. Again, the net favorable information is positively related to Attitude. These variables are thus a summary of the forces that determine Attitude.

How about Confidence? It is the third element in the triad of factors making up the buyer's brand concept or brand image; $B_y^C$ is the descriptive element, $A_y$ is the evaluative element, and $C_y$ is the strength or firmness of that image. What determines its level is an important question since it is one of the determinants of Intention:

$$C_y = f(B_y^C, S_y, F_y^C) \qquad (4)$$

$S_y$ is the Satisfaction the buyer receives from the product's use (pp. 145–150). All the variables relate positively to Confidence. It might appear that $C_y$ is redundant because it has the same determinants as $A_y$. The difference is that different aspects of $F_y^C$ are involved. In one case, $F_y^C$ may contain an evaluative statement from advertising that will influence $A_y$ but because of its low credibility will not affect $C_y$; whereas if $F_y^C$ contains a statement from a friend, $C_y$ will be influenced.

Now that we have delineated the forces that lie immediately behind Intention, how about the more basic influences of $B_y^C$, $S_y$, and $F_y^C$? What shapes them?

$$B_y^C = f(F_y^C) \tag{5}$$

Brand Comprehension is determined by those aspects of the perceived information which have to do with how the buyer descriptively conceptualizes the brand and decides into which product class it fits. It is especially important because it represents the buyer's capacity to discuss the brand with his friends. If $B_y^C$ is low, he has not yet acquired a grasp of its underlying characteristics and of the words that are labels necessary for these characteristics so that he can discuss the brand with his friends. Worse yet, he has not acquired the words even to *think* about it with and to *remember* it. His ability to discuss it with his friends is central to his behavior because his evaluative judgments are strongly shaped by these conversations. The descriptive elements of $F_y^C$ are positively related to Brand Comprehension.

Because we have examined $A_y$, $C_y$, and $B_y^C$, we are now in position to define more carefully what is meant by a brand concept or brand image. $B_y^C$ is the denotative or descriptive aspects of a brand concept; $A_y$ is the connotative or evaluative aspects of it; and $C_y$ is a measure of its firmness.

How rapidly and easily does a buyer learn about the new product? Assuming that he is exposed to adequate information, the task is one of learning a concept, and he must not only learn the concept but also learn to associate the word—the brand name—with the class concept of the brand. A concept is a representation of experience with the object acquired either directly by significative means or indirectly by symbolic means. A number of conditions influence this rate of learning. One major determinant of how easily a person learns about the new brand is how similar it is to those brands he is already familiar with: the more similar it is, the more easily he will learn. Similarity can be either physical or semantic. $B^C$ incorporates physical dimensions of the brand, and the semantic aspects associated with these physical dimensions can be captured in $B^C$, $A$, or $I$ depending upon their psychological nature. A second determinant of the speed of learning is the complexity of the brand: the greater the complexity, the slower the learning. A brand can be complex in two ways, one of which supplements the other. The greater the number of dimensions on which the buyer conceptualizes, the greater the complexity. Also, the greater the degrees of discriminability on each dimension, the greater the complexity. It may be helpful to remind the reader here that in LPS the buyer knows these dimensions and need only judge the brand in terms of them. A third determinant is the salience of these dimensions: the extent to which they command attention and are perceivable. The greater the salience, the easier and faster the learning. The fourth determinant is the nature of the information-handling task. Obviously, as the magnitude of the information load decreases (as indicated by the complexity of the concept), the easier it is to learn. Also, as the ratio of the negative and positive instances of the concept decreases, learning becomes easier. Negative instances are dimensions that do not fit the concept and positive instances are those that do. The more prevalent the positive instances in the information load, the easier the learning. In addition, the order in which the information is presented makes a difference. Understanding a concept sometimes requires understanding subsidiary concepts. If these subsidiary concepts are not presented first, one will have difficulty understanding the main concept. Finally, it is generally agreed that a combined deductive and inductive approach will facilitate learning more than either method alone. An inductive approach emphasizes experience; the buyer is exposed to positive and negative instances of the brand. The buyer is shown the brand and permitted to experience it, whereas the deductive approach describes its dimensions verbally and thus presents a formal definition of it.

Returning to the general line of discussion, what determines Satisfaction?

$$S_y = f(P_y) \qquad (6)$$

There is a feedback from the consumption of the brand ($P_y$), which yields varying degrees of pleasure ($S_y$) to the buyer. Further, the mere act of purchasing may also yield pleasure. The nature of this relation is complex and depends upon the extent of pleasure received, its recency, its ambiguity, and its periodicity.

A discussion of the source of $F_y^C$ (the coded facts) introduces us to the somewhat complex area of perceptual effects. Before we examine $F_y^C$, let us set a background for the understanding of these effects.

### 3.3 Perceptual Effects

These still more fundamental reasons for "why the buyer buys" arise because the new brand is unfamiliar to him and any information about it, therefore, is also unfamiliar, necessarily ambiguous, and subject to misinterpretation.

To provide perspective on the perceptual problem, we can look at it on each of three levels. First, there is a certain amount of information available to a consumer in the market, such as the advertising, what the people he might talk with who know something about the brand would say, all the retail displays of the brand, etc. This we call Facts Available ($F_y^A$), which is the total information available in a given market about the brand. Second, the buyer is exposed to only a small part of this information. Hence, the amount of exposure is due partly to the available information, partly to the accident of encountering it in carrying out nonpurchasing activities, and partly to his overt effort to obtain buying information. An important determinant, but certainly not the only one, of what he is accidentally exposed to is his Media Habits ($M^H$), his tendency or habit of looking at some media (broadly defined) and not others, such as newspapers and TV, or whether he belongs to organizations. Overt Search ($O^S$) is the intensity of the buyer's overt effort to seek information, and, of course, it should affect the amount of information he is exposed to. The specific information to which he is exposed is identified by Facts Exposed ($F^E$).

Finally, of the information to which he is exposed, he takes in only a small portion. His information-processing capacities are limited as is true of all persons. The information he does take in and retains or remembers is "coded facts," $F_y^C$.

$F_y^C$ has been used in a number of equations, and to get to a still more fundamental level of understanding we must explain it:

$$F_y^C = f(F_y^E, A_y^n, P_y^B) \tag{7}$$

As indicated above, Facts Exposed ($F_y^E$) is the information about the brand to which the buyer was exposed (pp. 63–68). $F_y^E$ and $F_y^C$ are positively related. Attention ($A_y^n$) is the buyer's receptivity to information. This receptivity regulates the quantity of information that flows into the buyer's nervous system via any or all of his five senses, usually the auditory or visual senses (pp. 154–155). Because the senses are interrelated, affecting one of them tends to affect the others. $A_y^n$ can be operationally conceptualized in terms of the eye–camera research: recordings of the extent to which the pupil of the buyer's eye is dilated as the result of viewing an interesting ad. The technique has been applied to evaluating advertising. Attention and $F_y^C$ are also positively related. $P_y^B$ stands for Perceptual Bias, the tendency of the buyer to distort the information, which affects its quality as he processes it (pp. 168–183). No relation is hypothesized for reasons described later.

We have already discussed the determinants of Facts Exposed:

$$F_y^E = f(F_y^A, O_y^S, M^H) \tag{8}$$

where $F_y^A$ is the information available in the buyer's environment about the brand. Overt Search $(O_y^S)$ is effort expended by the buyer to acquire information, such as talking with people he ordinarily would not have about the brand, reading additional advertising, obtaining a copy of *Consumer Reports* from the public library, etc. (pp. 155–156). It is distinguished from the effects of $A_y^n$, in the previous equation, which is merely the opening or closing of his receptors. In $O_y^S$ he exerts overt effort to obtain information upon which to base his purchase. $O_y^S$ and $A_y^n$ together constitute total search effort. Both variables are positively related to information exposed.

What determines $A_y^n$? It happens that $A_y^n$ and $O_y^S$ are determined together:

$$A_y^n, O_y^S = f(M^a) \tag{9}$$

where $M^a$ refers to the arousal or energizing aspect of Motives. When introducing RRB—the buyer has a firm concept of the brand—back in Section 2, we referred to an awakening of the buyer's need as a result of smelling the odor of baking pastries on his way home from the office. $M^a$ is the intensity of the motives satisfied by the product class of which $y$ is a member. When we speak of intensity of a motive, we are, of course, implying a given motive content that can take on varying degrees of intensity. It might be one of the innate motives such as hunger or sex, or it might be one of the learned values such as achievement, affiliation, or power.

This relation between arousal and the two search variables is at first positive, but it becomes negative as arousal becomes so intense as to cause stereotypy or maladaptive behavior. Also, Attention is affected first, and then, if it fails to provide adequate information, Overt Search begins to operate.

Perceptual Bias, $P^B$, is not a state variable but a collection of mechanisms, each of which is made up of a number of state variables. A state variable is one that represents a single condition. Thus, $P_y^B$ needs more elaboration for us to understand the causality involved. The variables contained in the mechanisms are fairly well worked out (pp. 168–179). First, one of the major influences in $P_y^B$ is the ambiguity of the brand information $(F_y^E)$ confronting the buyer, which is called Stimulus Ambiguity $(S_y^A)$ (pp. 156–167). $S_y^A$ plays a central perceptual role as shown below.

Second, the contextual cues surrounding $F_y^E$ also matter. An ad about sports equipment is a "different" ad in the sports page than when it appears elsewhere in the newspaper. Third, the intensity of Motives—the motives relevant to this product class $(M^a)$—influence $P_y^B$, as does the content of these motives $(M^c)$. Finally, the buyer's Attitude $(A_y)$ also makes a difference. Although by no means a complete picture, these forces give some idea of the complexity of the relations affecting $P_y^B$. We will leave it as an unelaborated process variable.

The role of memory must be mentioned. Information Recalled clearly implies long-term memory, material that the buyer remembers for several hours and longer. Much of the information $(F^C)$ that enters the buyer's nervous system is retained only in short-term memory, which is a matter of a few seconds. Think, for example, how many times you remember a telephone number only long enough to dial it, and then forget it. At least some of the same forces that influence $P^B$ also determine whether the input will be stopped at short-term memory or permitted into long-term memory and so cause the buyer to respond negatively or positively to a recall question.[6]

Since arousal plays a central role, knowing its determinants is important:

$$M^a = f(S_y^A, C_y, F_y^C) \tag{10}$$

The ambiguity $(S_y^A)$ of the information $(F_y^E)$ leads to conflict in the buyer's mind because of the varied interpretations he can make, so ambiguity increases arousal. $S_y^A$ is related to $M^a$ in a complex way, as shown in Figure 1.3. The principle is that buyers like some ambiguity but not too much. When the buyer encounters (is exposed to) an ad that is extremely unclear, either physically or in meaning, he tends to ignore it. This ad would be on the extreme right of the $S_y^A$ axis. An ad or salesman's story can be ambiguous in meaning, for example, either because the buyer doesn't trust the motives of the ad writer or salesman, or because he thinks the ad writer or salesman is

Figure 1.3

Stimulus Ambiguity—Arousal Relation

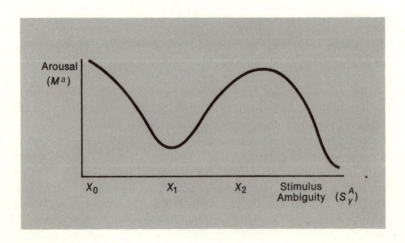

incompetent and simply doesn't know what he is writing or talking about. If the ad is not too ambiguous, he looks at it and he will come to understand it. The value of $S_y^A$ will move to the left. The $X_2$ position creates the most interest. As he learns more and more about the ad from repeated exposure, however, he begins to close it out because he already knows the content. Thus, he reaches the $X_1$ position on $S_y^A$. Still more exposure will bore him, he approaches $X_0$, and he will begin to look around ($M^a$ increases) for something different, perhaps another ad, to relieve his boredom. Thus, $X_1$ is his optimum level of stimulation: he strives to achieve it and when it is achieved he avoids achieving less ambiguity of the current stimulus by looking at something else.

The brand concept itself is subject to the same boredom phenomenon. Confidence ($C_y$) is the brand analogue of the ambiguity of the information about the brand ($S_y^A$) except, of course, that $C_y$ is stated in an inverse manner to $S_y^A$. You can visualize the effect of $C_y$ as affecting the level of the curve in Figure 1.3. Thus, as $C_y$ increases, the level of the curve in Figure 1.3 declines so that a given ad will reach the position of limited arousal ($X_1$) more quickly.

Finally, we can use this mechanism to explain why buyers use a brand for a period and then for no apparent reason shift to a new brand. Thus, we have the recurring cycles of sensitivity to market information that we observe in a stable market by buyers of some product classes. Executives report they have observed this cyclical behavior among detergent buyers. On the other hand, some product classes may be inherently complex enough that the boredom stage is never reached. Here, the buyer would reach full information, tend to close out any further ads, and continue to buy the same brand: to remain loyal.

Information about the brand ($F_y^C$) also affects $M^a$, for instance, when it tells him about a food in such a realistic way that he becomes hungry sooner than he otherwise would have. It exerts a positive effect depending upon the content.

What determines Stimulus Ambiguity? As indicated earlier, it is the ambiguity (complexity or uncertainty) of the stimulus to which the buyer is exposed:

$$S_y^A = f(F_y^E) \qquad (11)$$

We can see here how, as information and experience lead to brand evaluations, the buyer zeroes in on his preferred brand, and assuming he needs no information for his impersonal goals, information-purchase equilibrium is achieved as he closes out further information. Thus, we have a special case of RRB, one where *no* information is needed.

We have now completed the explanation of how the buyer buys when he is confronted with a new product ($y$) in a familiar product class. Our next problem is to explain his behavior when he is faced with a new brand that represents an unfamiliar class.

## 4. EXTENSIVE PROBLEM SOLVING

Here we discuss the most fundamental level of explanation for why the buyer buys. These changes are less frequent, more drastic, and require considerably more information because the buyer reexamines his whole choice process, though perhaps unconsciously. Put another way, he is in a state of complete disequilibrium, and Overt Search is intense.

The dimensions by which he evaluates the brand are called Choice Criteria ($C_z^C$), which include both personal goals and impersonal or professional goals. EPS is defined in terms of whether changes occur in these goals. The sources of change are:

$$C_z^C = f(F_z^C, M^{ca})$$

(12)

$C^C$ is Choice Criteria, $z$ is a new brand in an unfamiliar product class, and $M^{ca}$ is Motives, specified in terms of both content and level of arousal. Motives specified in this way are positively related to Choice Criteria. We hypothesize that with given Motives as the foundation, information about the new brand ($F_z^C$) will give content and intensity to Choice Criteria.

The intensity of the buyer's motivation ($M^a$) is likely to increase as he acquires the necessary information and approaches the purchase of $y$. His anticipation of the Satisfaction that the purchase will yield increases. In EPS particularly, however, there are likely to be negative features of the product class that must be reconciled with the positive ones, and these negative ("avoidance") features increase more rapidly as he comes nearer to the decision in space or time than do the favorable ("approach") features. This relative increase of the negative influences can lead to conflict (pp. 289–291). The buyer's purpose for obtaining information is to reduce the conflict. The tendency for $M^a$ to increase as he approaches the purchase is a central tenet of Nicosia's conceptualization of the buyer, although Nicosia defines attitude and motive differently and postulates a different causal sequence than is advanced here.[5]

Another way of looking at Choice Criteria is to say that they connotatively identify the product class, the class of brands that the buyer views as being closely substitutable in satisfying his needs. The product class concept is important because it identifies who your competitors are. The product class concept can be said to change whenever the weighting of the dimensions of Choice Criteria change. The extreme case is, of course, when a dimension's weighting drops to zero, that is, when it becomes completely irrelevant.

The learning problem is immensely greater in EPS than in LPS. The same brand in this setting is a much more complex concept. In EPS the buyer has little framework with which to begin thinking about the "thing." A typically sophisticated adult will obviously have many associations to draw upon in his attempt to conceptualize this new "thing," but he will probably not have great faith $(C)$ in the correctness of any evaluative dimensions that he may infer from these associations.

On the other hand, because he has fewer preconceptions in EPS, it will be easier to influence him to conceptualize it in a particular way. In LPS his framework—his brand concept—is set and it is difficult to get him to perceive a brand as anything much different than other brands in this product class. To the extent that this flexibility exists, marketing management's concern with "positioning" a new product is a justified one.

Since we hypothesize that any change in the buyer's Motives, either content or arousal, will cause a change in the Choice Criteria content and intensity, what changes Motives? Our belief is that brand-related information can affect the intensity aspect $(M^a)$ of Motives, as in Equation (10), but not the content.

Finally, another complication must be admitted. Up to this point we have said little about how Motives shape the information-processing and decision rules associated with Intention. What is the nature of this relation between Motives and the professional goal component of Intention? The relation is more obvious and probably often more relevant in industrial buying than in consumer buying. Assume an industrial buyer purchasing small electric motors that come in different colors. Presumably, the buyer would be personally indifferent as to which color he bought. His criteria, then, for choosing among the colors would be strictly professional. His Motives, for example, would be to please his boss, which could involve achievement and power motives. This would be the pure case where Attitude is irrelevant in the purchase. On the other hand, he may be buying something where the brand choice would be affected by his nonprofessional Motives, and we could refer to his relevant Choice Criteria in that case as *personal goals*. Also, each professional goal will be weighted according to its contribution to the achievement and power motives.

## 5. EXOGENOUS FORCES

### 5.1 Introduction

So far we have, with two exceptions, dealt only with endogenous variables—variables whose changes we explain. In addition, there is a class of variables whose changes we do not explain. These we call exogenous (pp. 68–91).

One of the exceptions was the information available $(F_x^A)$, which we took as given. The other was Motives Content $(M^c)$, which we do not believe is influenced by brand-related information, and so we called it an exogenous variable. As we will see, exogenous variables fall into two classes: informational and demographic-sociopsychological. The latter are general market-segmenting variables, not unique to any particular market.

In doing empirical work, the researcher may wish to treat only part of the system, and if so, any endogenous variables that are inputs to this subsystem can, of course, be treated as exogenous variables, that is, as unexplained. He may, for example, wish to take Facts Coded as given and treat it as exogenous.

### 5.2 Content of Exogenous Variables

From a variety of literature, we have found at least suggestive evidence for seven types of exogenous variables. Each type really involves several possible measures and the measures described below are illustrative. In Section 5.3 the relationships will be enumerated.

Importance of Purchase $(I^P)$ is variously labeled degree of involvement, importance of purchase, importance of the task, or seriousness of the consequences (pp. 72–75). It is a measure of the relative intensity of Motives that governs the buyer's activities relating to the given product class relative to other product classes.

Personality Traits $(P^T)$ are the buyer's enduring dispositions or qualities that account for his relative consistency in emotional, temperamental, and social behavior, which explain differences in behavior among buyers (pp. 75–77).

Financial Status $(F^S)$ is the quantity of funds a buyer has or expects to have available for expenditure on goods and services during some specified time period (pp. 78–81). It is a function of current income and saved past income (assets).

Time Pressure $(T^P)$ is the inverse of the amount of time the buyer has available both for the purchase and consumption acts associated with a particular product class and the information seeking that is associated with the purchase act (pp. 77–78).

Social and Organizational Setting $(S^{OS})$ refers to the loose social arrangement, implied by "reference group," that the buyer *identifies* with or compares himself with to such an extent that he tends to adopt its standards, attitudes, and behavior as his own (pp. 81–87). It provides a *social anchoring* for the buyer whereby his brand judgments and purchase and consumption acts are influenced by this relationship, and so the self-concept is probably a useful tool here. $S^{OS}$ includes the somewhat tighter social arrangement implied by "formal organization," which is much of the social environment of the industrial, institutional, or distributor buyer. Just how people in a company relate to each other and affect each other's behavior is dealt with by organization theory.

Social Class ($S^C$) is a description of the condition that society is divided into classes (pp. 87–89). These classes can be ranked according to the views of their members as to the value of each class in terms of its contribution to society as a whole.

Culture ($C^u$) is a selective man-made way of responding to experience, consisting of patterns of behavior transmitted from person to person (pp. 89–91). Its essential core is traditional ideas and especially their attached values; it consists of a system of subcultures that influence the behavior of its members, but in time, they determine the subcultures.

### 5.3 Relationships of Exogenous Variables

Although one purpose here is to describe the relationships among the exogenous and endogenous variables, this discussion will also afford the opportunity to summarize the complete system. The reader, as in the previous section, should bear in mind that there are probably several possible measures of each of these concepts. Each exogenous variable will be underlined so that it can readily be identified.

$$P_x = f(I_x) \tag{13}$$

$$I_x = f(F^C_x, A_x, C_x, \underline{C^u}, \underline{S^C}, \underline{S^{OS}}, \underline{T^P}, \underline{F^S}) \tag{14}$$

The three social variables—Culture, Social Class, and Social and Organizational Setting—are not well defined, and just how they influence Intention is not known. They are included, however, to encourage their elaboration and testing. Time Pressure and Financial Status are positively related to Intention. $T^P$ will affect the amount of search effort, and for $x$ the effect will be positive. $F^S$ will influence the buyer's willingness to spend money and, hence, will also be positively related to Intention.

$$A_x = f(B^C_x, S_x, F^C_x, \underline{C^u}, \underline{S^C}, \underline{S^{OS}}, \underline{P^T}) \tag{15}$$

Again, the relations involving the three social variables are left unspecified. The effect of Personality Traits depends upon the particular trait involved. The evidence is that extroversion, introversion, and neuroticism (degree of adjustment) are probably the most meaningful. It may be that these underlie more immediate traits, such as innovativeness, commonly used in buying research.

$$C_x = f(B_x^C, S_x, F_x^C, \underline{P^T})$$  (16)

The personality trait of self-confidence would be expected to affect the buyer's level of Confidence in judging the quality of a brand.

$$B_x^C = f(F_x^C, \underline{C^u}, \underline{S^C}, \underline{S^{OS}}, \underline{I^P}, \underline{P^T})$$  (17)

Importance of Purchase is positively related to Brand Comprehension, as is mental capacity, a Personality Trait. A dimension of Brand Comprehension is the evoked set—the number of brands considered. Anxiety, which appears to be an aspect of neuroticism, is negatively related to the width of (the number of brands in) the buyer's evoked set.

$$S_x = f(P_x)$$  (18)

$$F_x^C = f(F_x^E, A_x^n, P_x^B)$$  (19)

$$F_x^E = f(O_x^S, \underline{F_x^A}, \underline{M^H})$$  (20)

$$A_x^n, O_x^S = f(M^a, \underline{I^P}, \underline{P^T}, \underline{T^P})$$  (21)

Equations (18) and (19) contain no exogenous variables. In Equation (20), the amount of information the buyer is exposed to is positively related to the amount of information available and the extensiveness of his media habits. Importance of Purchase has a positive effect on Overt Search and presumably on Attention. We postulate that the Personality Traits of mental capacity and venturesomeness are positively related to search effort. Finally, Time Pressure is inversely related to search.

$$M^a = f(S_x^A, C_x, F_x^C, \underline{F^S})$$  (22)

Financial Status could influence the arousal or intensity of Motives in that downward shifts in financial capacity could cause frustration because of the required adjustment in reducing expenditures. Frustration would increase arousal.

$$S^A_x = f(F^E_x) \tag{23}$$

$$C^C = f(F^C_x, M^a, \underline{M^c}) \tag{24}$$

The reader will recall that $M^c$ is treated as an exogenous variable because we believe that brand-related information ($F^C_x$) has no effect on motive content.

## 6. SUMMARY

A structure intended to describe buying behavior has been set forth in three parts constituting three mutually exclusive categories to simplify the exposition: EPS (complete disequilibrium), LPS (product-class equilibrium), and RRB (brand equilibrium and even information-purchase equilibrium). A policy maker, private or public, can fit his problem into one of the three categories and proceed to analyze it with those respective concepts. The evidence for the structure and its implications have been but little touched upon in this paper. The specific nature of the functional relations has not been spelled out. For many of them a linear approximation will probably be satisfactory, but the fact that the empirical counterpart of the total system—buying behavior in the market place—appears to be so stable suggests that they are by no means all linear. Buyers do not exhibit explosive behavior. Some evidence on the more specific shapes of the functions is available in the following pages. The timing of the changes in the system—the dating of the variables—is not touched upon, although there is some slight evidence on this issue, too.

## References

1. Baumol, William, "Calculation of Optimal Product and Retailer Characteristics: The Abstract Product Approach," *Journal of Political Economy* 75 (1967): 674–685.
2. Howard, J. A., and J. N. Sheth, *The Theory of Buyer Behavior* (New York: John Wiley & Sons, Inc., 1969).
3. Lancaster, Kelvin J., "A New Approach to Consumer Theory," *Journal of Political Economy* 74 (1966): 132–157.
4. Lancaster, Kelvin J., "Change and Innovation in the Technology of Consumption," *American Economic Review* 56 (1966): 14–23.
5. Nicosia, Franco, *Consumer Decision Processes* (Englewood Cliffs, N.J.: Prentice-Hall, Inc., 1966).
6. Norman, Donald A., *Memory and Attention* (New York: John Wiley & Sons, Inc., 1969).
7. Simon, Herbert A., "On the Concept of Organizational Goal," *Administrative Science Quarterly* 9 (1964): 1–22.

# 2. A Description and Evaluation of the Design of the Buyer Behavior Research Project

George S. Day

Mail diary panels have become an essential technique for evaluating new product introductions. Although the projectability of test market results has been subject to much controversy,[3] there is no doubt that measures of initial trial and depth of repeat are valuable guides to the health of new (and established) products. Such data is also essential as input to recently developed techniques for forecasting long-run market share.[5,6] Under the circumstances it is understandable that marketing researchers have been reluctant to risk biasing this source of data by making changes in the basic panel design.

Considering this context, the design of the Buyer Behavior Research Project was a risky and possibly unprecedented departure from usual practice. However, the achievement of the project goals required information that could only be obtained from an extensive mail questionnaire plus three telephone interviews of the sample, in addition to the usual screening questionnaire and biweekly mail diaries. These departures made it essential to have a parallel "Control" panel group, which was limited to the mail diary. The evaluation of the "Columbia" or analysis panel is largely in terms of the differences in purchasing activity measured by the two panels.

## SAMPLE SELECTION

Both panels were operated in the statewide region where a new brand of a convenience food product was being tested. The product class contained only

33

one brand prior to the introduction of the new brand. Also at the beginning of the test period another new brand was introduced into this market by a competing company. Both new brands were very similar to the old brand in packaging, price, and product attributes.

The first step in the selection of the sample was to draw at random 70,000 households from all the telephone directories in the region. In order to obtain dispersion throughout the region, 70 clusters of 1000 households each were drawn at regular sampling intervals. Because the counties were ranked in order of descending size, the larger counties were sampled first and contained as many as 20 clusters, while some of the smaller counties did not fall into any cluster.

The next step was the mailing of a recruitment letter and a "classification quiz" to each of the selected households. The letter described the work of a panel member in interesting terms and emphasized how helpful and necessary the information would be, but an incentive was mentioned only in passing. In fact it had been decided to award panel members with various pieces of a kitchen-utensil set as they continued to participate. By de-emphasizing the incentive it was hoped that the responses would not be overweighted in favor of "money" or "price" conscious respondents who might reflect this bias in their brand choice behavior.

Over 8000 households responded to the recruitment letter by returning the classification quiz. This quiz provided standard demographic and recent product-usage information for subsequent analysis. The response rate of 11.4 percent compares well with mailed questionnaires in general, but of course is much poorer than the kind of response obtained by personal interview recruitment. The big advantage of mail recruitment is the much lower cost. The drawbacks are that the sample is in one sense "self-selected," and better educated housewives tend to be over-represented.

Two matched panels of 1100 households each were selected from the overall pool of 8000 responses, one arbitrarily becoming the "Columbia" panel, the other, the "Control" panel.* The membership of the panel was not completely representative of the population. It had been previously decided that there would be 50 percent more users of the product class in which the new brand was entered in the panel than in the population. Because present

---

*The following comparisons are illustrative of the success of the matching. Note that the "Columbia" panel figures are based on the subsample of 955 that responded to the mail questionnaire. Thus the differences also reflect the characteristics of nonresponders.

|  | Columbia Panel | Control Panel |
|---|---|---|
| Proportion in cities of more than 250,000 | 34.1% | 35.2% |
| Average age of housewife | 45.6 years | 44.6 years |
| Proportion in families of five or more | 23.1% | 23.4% |
| Proportion with working housewife | 57.3% | 60.0% |

users of the product were expected to be the main source of the triers and repeaters of the new brand, the decision to over-represent users was really an attempt to increase the analysis base. Of course this modification of the sample would have no effect on the relationships being studied, although it would have to be taken into account in any projection of the results.

Before discussing cooperation and attrition it is useful to review the sequence of contacts with the Columbia panel. It had been assumed that the extra work load of one mail questionnaire and three telephone interviews, plus additions to the diary form, would increase the dropout rate in the Columbia panel over the usual rate, as represented by the Control panel. However, there was no relevant previous experience available that would give any insights into this problem.

## SEQUENCE AND TIMING OF CONTACTS

(After the respondent had been assigned to the Columbia panel.)

(1)   Week 1. One week prior to the introduction of the new brand, an eighteen-page mail questionnaire was sent to 1100 households and returned by 955 households. The excellent response rate, 86.8 percent, was attributed to the interesting nature of the questionnaire, and the fact that a gift was sent to each household four days after the questionnaire was mailed, regardless of whether the questionnaire had been returned by that time.

(2)   Week 2 to Week 21. At the end of every two weeks during this five-month period each household sent in a purchase diary, reporting the details of purchases in five major food-product categories. Only three of the five products were of interest; the other two served as disguises. Each diary included a series of general questions designed to identify the first time the household became aware of any new brand in the five product categories, the source of the awareness, the reason for the first purchase of the brand, and satisfaction in the event of usage.

(3)   Week 6. First telephone interview (868 interviews completed). The sequence of telephone interviews was primarily designed to measure changes in awareness and attitudes toward the test brand. The switch from mail to telephone at this point was dictated by (a) the need to compress all interviews into the shortest possible time, so that individual responses were comparable, and (b) to qualify people as either aware or not aware of the test brand, and several other brands, before asking further questions. In this way it was hoped that the interviews would not serve as a source of information about the test brand.

Each telephone interview asked a series of questions about sources of information concerning the new brand, as well as other brands, and attitudes and intentions toward these brands. However, when a brand was not of central importance to the study it would be included only once in the first two interviews.

(4)  Week 11.  Second telephone interview (757 interviews completed·). The drop in the number of completions was due to refusals and/or panel dropouts, an unusual number of moves out of the test market region, and vacationing households, which put respondents out of reach. (See Table 2.1.)

### Table 2.1

### Analysis of Reasons for Non-Response

|                                    | Telephone Interview | | |
|------------------------------------|------|------|------------|
|                                    | 1    | 2    | 3          |
| Starting sample size[a]            | 955  | 914  | 831        |
| *Less*                             |      |      |            |
| Refusals[b]                        | 25   | 46   | 42         |
| No answers                         | 39   | 49   | 35         |
| Panel member on vacation           | N/A[c] | 22 | N/A        |
| Miscellaneous incomplete (moves out of market area, telephone disconnected, or sick in hospital) | 23 | 40 | 22 |
| Completed interviews               | 868  | 757  | 730[d]     |

[a]Those who refused to be interviewed were not contacted again.

[b]The figure for refusals in interviews 2 and 3 includes those who had dropped out of the panel before the telephone contact. There were 13 in this category in the second interview.

[c]N/A = data not available.

[d]Actual usable questionnaires from interview 3 were 718.

(5)  Week 22.  Third telephone interview (730 interviews completed). This interview came immediately after the wrap-up of the diary panel. Refusals by panel members were the highest in this interview, because some respondents thought their participation was finished and others

felt that three rather dull interviews were too much of an imposition when there had been no warning of any interviews at the beginning of the panel.

## INITIAL COOPERATION AND ATTRITION

One criterion of attrition, which permits comparisons of the Columbia panel with the Control panel, or any other panel, is the number of households returning diaries. (See Table 2.2.) This figure tends to be unstable within any particular two-week period, as diaries are often late and have to be included in the next period's tabulation. Also, it is not entirely descriptive of the *total* attrition of the Columbia panel, as households may have continued to send in diaries even though they did not return the mail questionnaire or were missed by one or more telephone interviews.

### Table 2.2

#### Attrition of Columbia and Control Panels over a Five-Month Period

#### (Both panels started with 1100 households.)

| Period | Number of Households Returning Diaries | | Cumulative Difference in: Columbia Minus Control Panel |
|---|---|---|---|
| | Columbia Panel | Control Panel | |
| 1 | 832[a] | 808 | + 24 |
| 2 | 934 | 930 | + 28 |
| 3 | 891[b] | 865 | + 54 |
| 4 | 859 | 915 | − 2 |
| 5 | 768[c] | 786 | − 20 |
| 6 | 825 | 866 | − 61 |
| 7 | 701 | 770 | −130 |
| 8 | 742 | 819 | −207 |
| 9 | 718 | 770 | −259 |
| 10 | 678 | 707 | −288 |
| | Average difference over the ten periods | | − 28 |

[a]Influence of mail questionnaire felt here.
[b]Influence of first telephone interview felt here.
[c]Influence of second telephone interview felt here.

The actual performance of the Columbia panel can be seen from Table 2.3, which compares the initial and continuing attrition, as a proportion of the initial panel size, to the average performance of eight panels, as reported in Bucklin and Carman.[1] The similarity of the performance of the Columbia panel to other published panels is encouraging. The initial dropout rate is lower in the Columbia panel primarily because of different recruitment procedures. There is a tendency in panel recruitment by personal interview for respondents to want to be agreeable, or perhaps to succumb to momentary pressure to participate. This increases the chance that second thoughts, after the departure of the interviewer, will lead to a decision not to participate, despite having agreed previously. The somewhat higher continuing attrition rate is a combination of vacationers deciding to drop out during the summer, and the effect of the unannounced extra work load of two telephone interviews during the first two and one-half months. Had the Columbia panel been continued for another few months, without further interference, it is probable that the continuing attrition rate would have approached 3.0 to 3.5 percent per month.

Table 2.3

Initial and Continuing Attrition—Columbia Panel
Versus Average of Eight Other Panels

(Percent of initial panel size; after refusals eliminated.)

|  | Columbia Panel | Average of Eight Published Panels |
|---|---|---|
| Dropout during first 3 to 6 weeks | 19.4% | 20.2% |
| Continuing attrition rate (percent per month using running average number of returns) | 4.3 | 2.7 |

When the Columbia and Control panels are compared, it appears that the extra work load initially encouraged a high level of cooperation. Perhaps the mail questionnaire increased the level of interest, while the two telephone interviews served as reminders to return the purchase diary that was on hand. These positive effects were short-lived indeed. In the three biweekly periods following the second telephone interview "reminder," the cumulative difference in the return rates of the two panels was 65 percent of the total cumulative difference in ten periods. It is difficult to say whether this is due to (1) the release of pressure on the panel members, (2) a manifestation of resentment at the unexpected work load, or (3) a reflection of some intrinsic difference in the two panels.

## SENSITIZATION DUE TO PANEL MEMBERSHIP

By sensitization we mean that membership in the panel as well as the interviews made the respondent more aware of and interested in the products and brands being studied. Although there was probably some sensitizing of those in the Control panel, we were most concerned with the differential effects of membership in the Columbia panel versus the Control panel. This analysis is limited to purchasing data, inasmuch as independent but comparable cross-section surveys of attitudes and awareness were not available.

The first question is whether usage of the three products being studied was influenced by panel membership. The relevant data is shown in Table 2.4 for three product classes; product 1 is the class into which the new brand was introduced; 2 and 3 are similar to 1 in terms of purchasing characteristics, although cross-elasticities of demand between products are low. From these results it is clear that the telephone interviews, in particular, served a reminder function. The extent of the effect is exaggerated with these products because they are all "discretionary" food products for which a number of alternatives exist. So it is not surprising that some members of the Columbia panel bought these products when they had been alerted to the interviewers' interest in them.

**Table 2.4**

**Differences between Panels in Proportion of Total
Households Using Product**

| | $\left(\dfrac{\text{Columbia panel}-\text{Control panel}}{\text{Control panel}} \times 100\%\right)$ | | |
|---|---|---|---|
| | Product 1 | Product 2 | Product 3 |
| Period 1 | +14% | + 8% | +15% |
| Period 3 (after interview 1) | +64 | +16 | +39 |
| Period 5 (after interview 2) | +47 | +31 | +59 |
| Period 7 | +26 | +15 | + 6 |
| Period 10 (before interview 3) | +43 | +36 | +26 |

The question remains whether brand shares were also biased by the interviews. Two pieces of evidence are available to answer this question. The first deals with the trial and repeat rates for the newly introduced brand (2), being tracked by the two purchase panels, as well as a competing brand (3) of the same product, which was introduced at virtually the same time. Table 2.5 shows a significant upward bias in the trial rates reported by the Columbia panel. There is reason to believe that the trial rates in the two panels would have converged over the long run. Although the trial data for Brand C appears inconsistent with this hypothesis, it should be realized that this brand was literally reintroduced in period 8. Thus the data for Brand C in period 10 does not reflect a steady-state market situation.

**Table 2.5**

**Differences in Trial and Repeat Rates between Panels**

$$\left( \frac{\text{Columbia}-\text{Control}}{\text{Control}} \times 100\% \right)$$

|  | Brand B | Brand C |
|---|---|---|
| *Trial* | | |
| Period 1 | + 16% | + 3% |
| Period 3 | + 76 | +21 |
| (after interview 1) | | |
| Period 5 | + 48 | +27 |
| (after interview 2) | | |
| Period 7 | + 38 | +24 |
| Period 10 | + 33 | +27 |
| (before interview 3) | | |
| *Repeat* | | |
| Period 1 | N/A | N/A |
| Period 3 | + 48 | N/A |
| (after interview 1) | | |
| Period 5 | + 39 | N/A |
| (after interview 2) | | |
| Period 7 | + 6 | N/A |
| Period 10 | − 08 | N/A |
| (before interview 3) | | |

The repeat data in Table 2.5 are more encouraging because of the rapid convergence of the two panels. The early disparity in repeat rates is a result of the shift of the trial rate forward in time, since early triers are likely to repeat their purchase earlier. The convergence is reasonable, since the decision to make a repeat purchase should depend on the degree of satisfaction with the usage experience and thus be independent of information provided by the panel interviews.

If the usage trial and repeat rates measured by the two panels converge, there should be no difference in long-run market share measures. Given the slow rates of convergence of two of the three basic parameters, it is somewhat surprising to see in Table 2.6 that the market shares showed rapid convergence. The most likely reason is that those who were attracted to the product class because they belonged to the Columbia panel were less interested in the two new brands (B and C) than were the regular buyers of the product. Otherwise the market shares for brands B and C would have always been higher in the Columbia panel, because the trial and repeat rates were higher.

**Table 2.6**

**Difference in Share of Dollar Volume between Panels**

$$\left( \frac{\text{Columbia–Control}}{\text{Control}} \times 100\% \right)$$

| Month | Brand B | Brand C |
|-------|---------|---------|
| 1 | +48% | − 47% |
| 2 | +17 | − 12 |
| 3 | − 3 | + 53 |
| 4 | −18 | − 27 |
| 5 | − 4 | + 13 |
| Weighted average share for 5 months | − 3% | − 7% |

## CONCLUSIONS

There is no question that the interviewing did sensitize panel members to the three product categories included in the Buyer Behavior Research Project. The most extreme and lasting bias was found in the usage rate. This in turn influenced the trial rate and the market share. Yet from the point of view of the objectives of the project, this bias is a small price to pay for the data that was collected. It is also encouraging that the bias in absolute levels of purchasing activity did not appear to disturb essential *relationships*. This point was first made by Kosobud and Morgan[4] under somewhat different circumstances. In this study the confirming evidence for this hypothesis is (1) the fact that the bias did not influence the repeat rate (after the first three months) and (2) an internal analysis that found that the shape of the attitude–subsequent-behavior relationship was independent of the purchasing rate.[2] This latter result is important in view of the likelihood that light buyers were those most influenced by the interviews.

Nonetheless, few researchers would be satisfied with biases of the magnitude that are reported here. There are, however, significant opportunities for improvement in the design of this study. These would take the form of (1) starting the panel at least four to six weeks before the new product is introduced and disregarding the purchase data collected during the run-in period; (2) operating the panel for at least eight months following introduction, in order to spread out the telephone interviews; (3) asking about more brands and product categories in order to disguise the researchers' interest; and (4) avoiding specific brand evaluation questions on the initial mail questionnaire whenever there is a possibility that large proportions of the sample are not aware of the brand. With these and other improvements the basic design used in this study merits consideration by any researcher who wishes to learn about the structure and response of a market in detail.

**References**

1. Bucklin, Louis P., and James M. Carman, *The Design of Consumer Research Panels: Conception and Administration of the Berkeley Food Panel* (Berkeley: Institute of Business and Economic Research, University of California, 1967).
2. Day, George S., *Buyer Attitudes and Brand Choice Behavior* (New York: Free Press, 1970).
3. Gold, Jack A., "Testing Test Market Predictions," *Journal of Marketing Research* 1 (August 1964): 8-17.
4. Kosobud, Richard F., and James N. Morgan, eds., *Consumer Behavior of Individual Families over Two and Three Years* (Ann Arbor: University of Michigan Press, 1964).
5. Massey, William F., "Forecasting the Demand for New Convenience Products," *Journal of Marketing Research* 6 (November 1969): 405-412.
6. Parfitt, J. H., and B. J. K. Collins, "The Use of Consumer Panels for Brand-Share Prediction," *Journal of Marketing Research* 5 (May 1968): 131-146.

# 3. Some Measurement Effects in Purchase Panel Data from the Test Market

## L. Winston Ring

### I. INTRODUCTION

Consumer purchase panels are traditionally used for many purposes in marketing. Two common uses are for forecasting purchase behavior of the universe of consumers and for evaluating or refining elements within the market mix. These two uses are quite distinct, and they have been to a large extent incompatible. Furthermore, these restricted individual uses do not necessarily represent the most efficient nor the maximum potential usage of panels.

To obtain accurate estimates of purchase behavior if test market conditions were to be extended to further areas, it has usually been regarded as necessary to disturb as little as possible the behavior of purchase panel members within a test market. It is fairly common not to probe deeply into attitudes, to avoid altering respondents' state of brand awareness, and not to utilize the reported purchase data until, say, six weeks have elapsed after beginning of panel membership.

Contrarily, to refine the marketing mix it is necessary to evaluate consumers' responses to the attributes of products, and it is desirable to measure panel members' attitudes before and as they purchase and evaluate new brands. The alternative of omitting measurement of panel members' attitudes and intentions is to formulate inferences based upon their reported purchase actions. This can be very misleading as it requires the assumption that the analyst measures product attributes in the same manner as consumers, and that he places the same degree of importance upon the attributes as consumers. The usual disparity between the manufacturer's language and the consumers' language is widely recognized.

This chapter reports the results of a comparison of the reported purchase behavior of the interviewed panel and that of the noninterviewed panel. The information used is that common to both panels: the screening questionnaire and the biweekly purchase diaries. No use is made either of the information obtained in the mail questionnaire or of the telephone interviews. The first general intention of this research is to determine who is affected, and in what way, by interviewing. From this the intention is to derive evidence previously not available regarding whether the two common uses of panels mentioned above are necessarily incompatible and whether better or more innovative use of panels is feasible.

The primary conclusions are:

1.   The act of measurement as performed did not affect the basic framework, which determines how respondents make purchase decisions, but it did affect the speed of informational input and processing.

2.   Certain categories of persons were affected by interviewing so that permanent or very long-term differences in reported purchase behavior were created. This is not necessarily in conflict with (1) above or (3) below.

3.   It is possible to utilize reported purchase data from heavily interviewed panels and obtain accurate forecasts of some of the most important aspects of purchase behavior in the noninterviewed panel.

## II. METHODOLOGY

The primary approach used was to segment the panels based upon the demographic data obtained in the screening questionnaire and compare reported purchasing between panels by corresponding segments. The segments used are:

aggregate

1-member households
2-member households
3-member households
4-or-more-member households

housewife age 15—30
housewife age 31—45
housewife age 46—60

no children
some children

housewife has 1–9 years of education
housewife has 10–12 years of education
housewife has 13–16 years of education

housewife is employed
housewife is unemployed

housewife reports use of brand A within the last 6 months
housewife reports that she never purchases A

The measures of purchase activity used for the single prior existing brand A and the newly introduced competitive brand B are:

total units purchased per day

total trial units purchased per day

total purchase instances per day (a respondent might purchase two or more units in one purchase instance)

Repeat purchase units were not measured directly but were obtained by comparison of total and trial units.

The values of these purchase variables were computed for brands A and B for days 1 to 140 for each of the ten categories of reporting respondents. The average values by weeks were plotted on purchase–time axes and the comparative purchase behavior of each category determined by superimposing the graphs from the two panels.

This technique of straightforward comparison by segments does have several limitations, the main one being that it does not reveal the net effect upon purchasing of each category while holding constant the effects of other segmentation variables. It is, however, the only technique known to the author that is readily interpretable, operationally feasible, and that permits interpanel comparisons.

The use of Automatic Interaction Detection[4] seemed desirable, but was rejected because it did not seem operationally feasible. It is difficult enough to compare four measures of purchase activity for two brands, two panels, ten categories of panel members at twenty different times, without having a different set of categories included and excluded in the analysis for each panel at each time, which the author envisioned as the result of using AID.

Another approach that has many potential benefits is the use of a linear model, with each measure of purchase activity as the dependent variable and each segmentation category as a zero–one independent classificatory variable. This has been performed, but only a few of the results are reported here. The disadvantages of this approach are that within a panel only differences between categories can be estimated, and the conditions necessary for parameter estimates to be comparable between panels have not been completely determined.

## III.  DETAILED RESULTS

### Mail Questionnaire

The 18-page questionnaire was mailed to each member of the Columbia panel one week prior to the introduction of brand B and one week prior to the beginning of purchase recording by the two panels. These Columbia panel members were asked many questions about general homemaking, nutrition, and eating habits. They were asked *regarding brand A and a prominent brand in two similar product classes*: who in the house used the brand, the respondent's attitudes regarding fourteen attributes of the brand, her opinion of how likely thirteen different types of persons were to use the brand, and how likely the respondent was to purchase the brand within the next month. The new brand B was not mentioned in the questionnaire.

We would expect this measurement to add little exposure to new information, because A has been on the market with wide distribution for over two years. However, the arousal state of motives would probably be affected. Other things being equal, we would predict that respondents would tentatively reexamine their choice criteria as they relate to the respondent's store of brand information, and sales of A would increase as both prior users and nonusers tentatively tried A to determine if it might satisfy currently unsatisfied needs or might serve as a previously unconsidered substitute means for satisfied needs. This conclusion cannot be fully tested, because B (and unexpectedly, C) was then introduced into the test market. It would be expected that the prior interviewing increased the average attention level so that the presence of B on the shelves of grocery stores would be noted, and sales of B would be increased. Sales of A may decrease as prior users of A try B, or sales of A may increase as prior nonusers try A rather than B, which seems more likely.

As expected, reported total units of B purchased were higher in the interviewed panel during the following four weeks, but the purchase rate was only 10 percent higher than in the control panel. The reported total units purchased of A were affected much more: the purchase rate was 25 percent higher than in the control panel.

One-member households were most affected by the mail questionnaire. These persons doubled their unit purchase rate of A and purchased less than one-half as many units of B as similar persons in the noninterviewed panel.

The next most affected category was prior nonusers of A. These interviewed persons purchased approximately 70 percent more units of A than similar persons in the control panel, but their purchasing of B seemed unaffected. These large increases in usage of A were partially offset by the purchasing behavior of prior users of A: such persons in the interviewed panel decreased their units purchased of A relative to the control panel and increased their purchases of new brands B and C as expected.

These differences between panels in total units were apparent from the beginning of purchase reporting. The differences between panels for A decreased, so that four weeks later they were noticeable in only two categories—in the interviewed panel, two-member households were then purchasing 35 percent less of A than such households in the control panel, and 4-or-more-member households were purchasing 35 percent more of A. Any remaining effects upon total units of B are uncertain and statistically insignificant due to the small number of purchases.

The above discussion refers to total units purchased. For brand A these were primarily repeat rather than trial purchases (except, of course, for the category of prior nonusers); for brand B they were obviously almost all trial purchases. So few persons made repeat purchases of B that no conclusions are possible regarding measurement effect.

### First Telephone Interview

This interview occurred approximately 35 days after the questionnaires were mailed and about three days after the second biweekly report of purchases. Columbia panel respondents were asked to recall brand names in the product class of interest and two similar product classes. For each of the brands A, B, C and the two foremost brands in each of the two similar product classes that were not recalled by respondents, the brand name was stated, and respondents were then asked if they had heard of it. If A, B, C and the leading brand in each of the two related classes were recalled or recognized, respondents were asked regarding each brand: (1) if they had discussed the brand with anyone; (2) if they had seen the brand advertised; (3) how they would rate their attitude on eight product attributes; (4) what was their degree of confidence in judging the brand; and (5) how likely they were to purchase the brand in the next month.

This differed substantially from the mail questionnaire. The mail questionnaire asked similar questions, but the other types of questions also asked in the telephone interview (such as reasons for using the product class) very probably caused respondents to consider their personal needs and the degree of need satisfaction. The telephone interviewing seems much less of an active agent in affecting need arousal and evaluation; but awareness, or

Information Exposed and Information Coded, is now probably greatly affected. Every respondent who had not heard of brands A or B was informed by the interviewer of its existence.

This leads us to expect that in the interviewed panel sales of A will decrease and sales of B and C will increase. Prior users of A are informed of B and C and will purchase them on a trial basis. Prior nonusers of A have been encouraged in the mail questionnaire to consider the use of the product class as a means of need satisfaction, and they are now informed of two relevant brands.

After the telephone interview, reported total units of A purchased by the interviewed panel decreased approximately 15 percent below the level in the control panel. This depressed level of purchasing continued for approximately two weeks. This decrease was followed by an increase, so that over the next three weeks the average reported total units of A purchased in the interviewed panel was almost 50 percent higher than in the control panel.

The overall pattern of response to brand B of the interviewed panel members was opposite to the pattern for A. As might be expected, because B was new and had only a small market share, the percentage differences for B between panels were larger than for brand A. During the first two weeks after the interview, the average reported units of B purchased were almost 150 percent higher in the interviewed panel than in the control panel. This effect was reversed over the next three weeks: the average sales were 25 percent lower than in the control panel.

These interviewed individual categories constituted the aggregate lower—higher total purchase pattern for brand A:

2-, 3-member households
housewife age 46–60
no children
housewife has 13–16 years education
prior user of A

These same categories followed the opposite higher—lower pattern for B, as did all other categories except one-member households and housewives with 1–9 years education, each of which had low product purchase rates. There were under 70 such households in this sample.

A second distinct pattern in total sales was apparent: higher sales of A in the interviewed panel than in the control panel for the two-week period and also in the subsequent three-week period.

Those categories that followed the higher—higher total purchase pattern for A are:

4-or-more-member households

housewife age 31–45

housewife has 10–12 years education

housewife is employed

prior nonuser of A

The first three of these categories also followed the high–high pattern for brand B. The last two categories followed the high–low pattern, as stated before.

These aggregate sales are of course made up of two very different purchase components: first or trial purchases and repeat purchases. These sales components also followed distinct patterns as shown in Table 3.1.

Table 3.1

Categories of Purchasers Following Distinct Purchase Patterns

Brand A

| Trial Purchases | | Repeat Purchases | |
|---|---|---|---|
| Low–High | High–High | High–Not Lower | Low–Not Lower |
| 4 or more members housewife 15–30 housewife 46–60 housewife 10–12 yr. education prior nonuser of A | 2 members 3 members no children housewife 13–16 yr. education housewife employed | 4 or more members housewife 10–12 yr. education prior nonuser of A | 2 members 3 members no children housewife 13–16 yr. education prior user of A |

Brand B

| Trial Purchases | | Repeat Purchases |
|---|---|---|
| High–Low | Not Lower–Not Lower | Not Lower–Low |
| housewife 15–30 prior user of A | (all categories except those listed at left) | 2 members 3 members housewife 15–30 housewife 46–60 no children some children housewife 13–16 yr. ed. housewife employed prior user of A prior nonuser of A |

Two distinct consumer types were quite apparent. They are:

| I | II |
|---|---|
| 4-or-more-member household | 2-, 3-member household |
| housewife age 31–45 | no children |
| housewife 10–12 years education | housewife 13–16 years education |
| prior nonuser of A | |

These two groups appear to be behaving in quite opposite systems. In some ways, of course, they are, if this behavior is viewed in isolation. However, a large part of this difference is due to a speeding up of interviewed consumers' trial and evaluation of the new brand, especially group I persons who were not prior users of the product class. Members of group I who had not purchased A by the time of the screening questionnaire and did not do so after the mail questionnaire seem not to have altered their dispositions toward this old brand. Therefore, when they are stimulated by interviewing, they are more prone to make trial purchases of the new brand. Persons also in group I who had not made a purchase of the old brand by the time of the classification quiz but who did so after the mail questionnaire now tend also to make a repeat purchase of the old brand.

Group II members seem to regard the product in a similar manner, but the reaction to the mail questionnaire was different from that of group I. Two-member households who had not used brand A at the time of the mail questionnaire had lower than average rates of trial purchases of A, and prior users then increased their repeat purchase of A. After the telephone interview, group II members increased their trial rates of A (as group I does two weeks later) and B. Group II members who had prior use of A at the time of the screening questionnaire decreased their repeat rate of A after the telephone interview and increased their rate of trial purchases of B.

At the end of the five-week period, total units purchased by aggregate panel members were approximately the same in the two panels for both brands A and B. The primary exception is the category *prior nonuser of* A. These persons in the interviewed panel continued to purchase brand A at a rate almost twice that of noninterviewed persons. So the number of purchased trial units of A continued to be larger, whereas repeat units of A were purchased at a slightly decreased rate. As prior purchasers outnumber nonprior purchasers by four to one and purchase more frequently, this produced a total purchase rate in the interviewed panel comparable to the control panel.

**Second Telephone Interview**

This interview occurred five weeks after the first telephone interview and approximately nine weeks after the mail questionnaire. The questions asked in this interview were very similar to those in the first telephone interview.

The characteristic effects of this interview are difficult to isolate by categories as the magnitudes of effects were smaller than those from the first interview. Of course, any effects discussed below are confounded with any lingering effects from the earlier interviewing.

The high—low and low—high, two week—three week patterns so dominant after the first telephone interview also occurred, but the pattern was so much less distinct that it might well have been due to random fluctuations. Therefore only the results of the following five weeks as a whole and the subsequent six weeks are discussed.

During the five weeks after this interview, the only categories in the interviewed panel with reported units of A differing from the control panel by more than 25 percent were:

1-member households          (interviewed = 2 X control)
nonuser of A                       (interviewed = 1.6 X control)
prior user of A                    (interviewed = 0.7 X control)

The number of purchase instances reported is about 20 percent higher in the interviewed panel and is not decreasing except for one-member households. The number of trial units of A purchased remains almost 50 percent higher on the average in the interviewed panel; repeat purchases are about 20 percent lower and are decreasing except for one-member households and nonusers of A.

In the subsequent six-week period only two categories differ on the average by more than 25 percent from the same categories in the control panel for total reported units of A:

1-member households          (interviewed = 2 X control)
3-member households          (interviewed = 0.5 X control)

The number of purchase instances reported remains about 20—25 percent higher than in the control panel, trial rates are 10 percent higher, repeat rates are about 10 percent lower, and total units are almost the same.

By the end of the six-week period (the end of data collection) all aggregate measures of purchase activity for A were comparable (within 15 percent) between panels; and, except for one-member households, all categories were comparable or were close and interpanel distances were decreasing.

The total units purchased of B were approximately the same in both panels during the five weeks after the second telephone interview. Opposing differences between categories were present, but their magnitude was smaller than after the first telephone interview, and no new meaningful patterns were present. Group IA in the interviewed panel purchased less of B, and group IIA purchased more.

| IA | IIA |
|---|---|
| 4-or-more-member household | 2-member household |
| housewife age 31−45 | housewife age 15−30 |
| some children | no children |
| housewife employed | housewife unemployed |
| nonuser of A | prior user of A |

These two groups are very similar to groups I and II referred to in the discussion of the first telephone interview, and they are maintaining the purchase pattern established then.

On the average, from the telephone interview until the end of data collection eleven weeks later, total units reported purchased of B were comparable between panels, the number of purchase instances reported was about 20 percent higher in the interviewed panel, units purchased in a purchase instance were about 20 percent lower, trial units were about 20 percent higher, repeat units were about 20 percent lower.

More importantly, the distances between similar categories in the two panels were decreasing, and at the end of the data-collection period all categories were roughly comparable between panels in their reported purchasing of the new brand.

## IV. SUMMARY MEASURES

Figure 3.1 shows the changes over time of the number of reported purchase instances of the product class in the interviewed panel relative to the control panel. The beginning differential is attributed to the mail questionnaire, as the two panels were carefully selected and matched by frequency of product-class usage. The effects of the two telephone interviews are clearly discernible in the greatly increased number of purchase instances in the interviewed panel.

Of primary interest here is the trend at the end of the data-collection period. The panels' rates of purchase instances definitely seem to be converging. The final higher rate of purchasing in the interviewed panel is

Figure 3.1

Relative Rates of Purchase Instances

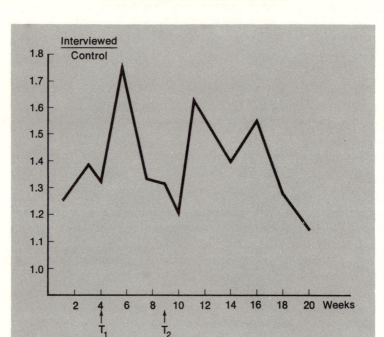

offset by decreased units per purchase instance as the final trend market shares are comparable between panels (Day, Chapter 2 of this book).

Figures 3.2 and 3.3 show the aggregate cumulative trial and repeat purchase rates for brand B in the two panels. Cumulative trial at a point in time is measured as the percent of panel members who by then have made a purchase of B. Cumulative repeat is measured as the percent of current purchasers of B who have made a prior purchase of B. The effects of the mail questionnaire on the cumulative repeat rate are uncertain because there were so few persons making repeat purchases of B in either panel. However, the effects of the first telephone interview are clearly seen in the higher repeat rate for the interviewed panel. If the second telephone interview had any net effect on this aggregate measure, it is difficult to discern. Most interesting is the continuing virtual identity of cumulative repeat rates between panels only three weeks after the second telephone interview.

The total effects of interviewing on the cumulative trial rate of B are clear, although the separable effects of the telephone interviewing are

Figure 3.2

Cumulative Trial Rates of B

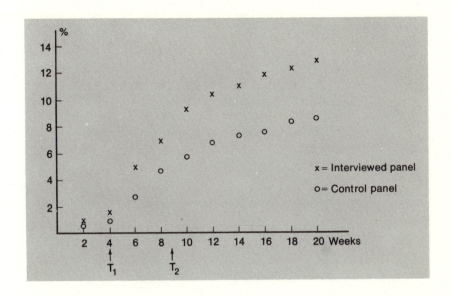

Figure 3.3

Cumulative Repeat Rates of B

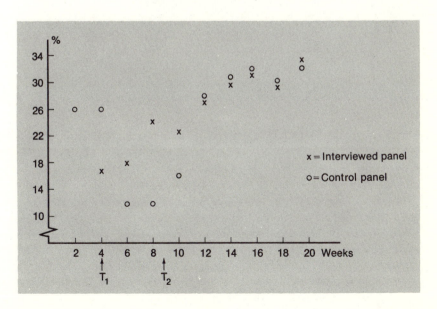

obscured in this aggregate cumulative measure of purchasing. The ratios of trial rates in the interviewed panel to the control panel are shown in Figure 3.4. Note there that the interpanel differences in trial rates, while declining very slightly, are for all practical purposes stable three weeks after the second telephone interview.

Figure 3.4

Relative Cumulative Trial Rates of B

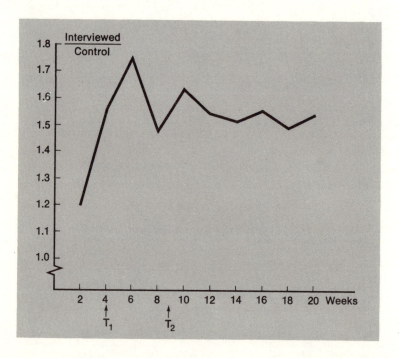

As discussed in the Detailed Findings, the cumulative trial rates differed by categories, and the categories were affected differently by interviewing. The average trial rates (terminal cumulative trial rates divided by the elapsed number of days) are shown for each category in Table 3.2.

The usefulness of this measure of penetration in evaluating test-market performance is shown by the trial rates for the categories of prior user and nonuser of A. In both panels prior users of A were about four times as apt to make trial purchases of B than were nonusers of A, which shows that the primary source of customers for B was brand switching rather than market expansion. Ominously, in spite of heavy advertising by TV, radio, and

Table 3.2

Average Daily Trial Rates by Category[a]

| Category | Control Panel | | Interviewed Panel | |
|---|---|---|---|---|
| | A | B | A | B |
| aggregate | .0007 | .0006 | .0011 | .0010 |
| 1-member households | .0005 | .0007 | .0006 | .0005 |
| 2-member households | .0006 | .0006 | .0008 | .0008 |
| 3-member households | .0007 | .0004 | .0012 | .0010 |
| 4-member households | .0008 | .0006 | .0014 | .0012 |
| housewife age 15–30 | .0008 | .0007 | .0011 | .0008 |
| housewife age 31–45 | .0007 | .0005 | .0015 | .0011 |
| housewife age 46–60 | .0007 | .0005 | .0009 | .0009 |
| no children | .0007 | .0006 | .0008 | .0009 |
| some children | .0007 | .0006 | .0014 | .0011 |
| housewife 1–9 yr education | .0006 | .0003 | .0009 | .0006 |
| housewife 10–12 yr education | .0007 | .0006 | .0011 | .0010 |
| housewife 13–16 yr education | .0007 | .0006 | .0011 | .0011 |
| housewife employed | .0007 | .0006 | .0010 | .0009 |
| housewife not employed | .0007 | .0006 | .0011 | .0010 |
| prior user of A[b] | – | .0013 | – | .0019 |
| nonuser of A[b] | .0012 | .0003 | .0019 | .0005 |

[a]Terminal cumulative trial rates may be obtained by multiplying these values by 140. For the aggregate category, the cumulative trial rate of B is .0006 × 140 = .084 in the control panel and .14 in the interviewed panel.

[b]As indicated on the screening questionnaire.

newspaper for brand B,* during the 140 days of purchase reporting in each panel the old brand attracted customers new to the product class at a rate four times as great as did the new brand.

## V. CONCLUSIONS

Many effects of interviewing on different categories of consumers have been presented. More effects have been observed than can be fully summarized without much further study and research. Therefore the concluding remarks

*Unfortunately, advertising was not monitored in the test market, so precise comparisons are not possible. It is fairly safe to assume that the intensive advertising level aimed at attracting customers to B was greater than the normal advertising level for A.

are limited to the three primary questions with which the research was most concerned.

1.  Did the interviewing affect the structure which determines how consumers make purchase decisions?
2.  Were categories of persons affected to such an extent that permanent or very long-term differences in purchasing behavior were created?
3.  Can the reported purchase data from interviewed panel members be used to obtain accurate predictions of the purchase behavior of noninterviewed consumers?

The evidence for question (1) is inherently inferential, for it cannot be proven how consumers would have behaved if they had not been interviewed. The various pieces of evidence do, however, point to the conclusion that the structure has not been changed; consumers process bits of information in accordance with their already existing systems of decision rules, even though they are subjected to input stimuli by interviewing which they otherwise would not have been or which would not have occurred at such an accelerated rate.

a.  The mail questionnaire did not greatly modify the tendency of prior nonusers of A to try the new brand. It would have been indicative of an altered structure if persons almost all of whom were aware of the product class but had not tried it rushed out to buy a new brand with no new distinguishing characteristics. Instead prior nonusers tried the old brand that they had seen or heard of before but had not yet tested!

b.  After the first telephone interview, which primarily affected awareness, prior users of A decreased their repeat purchasing of A, temporarily increased their trial purchasing of B, but then switched back to A. This is to be expected if the structure of brand evaluation is unchanged among prior users of a brand who try a "me too" brand that offers no price advantage.

c.  Prior nonusers of A who were not stimulated by the mail questionnaire to try A did not then try A after being exposed to information regarding the existence of a new competing brand. The altering of an implied prior decision not to purchase A because of an irrelevant opportunity to purchase B would indeed be suspect!

d.  The second telephone interview affected purchasing to a much less marked degree than the first telephone interview. This is as expected if a primary effect of the telephone interview was accelerated awareness of the new brand. The second instance of informing consumers of the existence of B should have less effect on purchase decisions than the first if the primary content of the second communication is redundant information.

e.  The cumulative repeat rates in the two panels converged rapidly. This is an important piece of supporting evidence, as it indicates that the evaluation of a brand and the resultant tendency to repurchase it are not dependent upon whether the consumers were interviewed.

f.  The ratio of cumulative trial rates between panels rapidly stabilized to a slightly decreasing trend. This is consistent with the assumption that the decision process had been accelerated, but that the structure had been maintained. The ratio decreased slightly as noninterviewed consumers gradually became aware of the new brand and made trial purchases that they would have made earlier if they had been interviewed.

g.  The ratio of brand A to brand B cumulative or average trial rates within a panel is very similar to the ratio between panels for almost all categories of consumers. In particular, the ratio of aggregate trial rate in the control panel is $.0007/.0006 = 1.17$ and the ratio in the experimental panel is $.0011/.0010 = 1.10$. The difference is well within the range of round-off error. This indicates that while trial of the product class had been encouraged and trial of B had been accelerated, the long-run tendency to try the old brand relative to the new brand had not been affected.

An important possible exception to the above comments is the category of one-member households. As shown in Table 3.2, this was the only category of consumers in the interviewed panel who tended to try B at a rate less than that of noninterviewed panel members. This could be due to many reasons, one of which is that for these persons the initial mail questionnaire focused upon a topic these persons usually do not have an opportunity to discuss. As a result of this communication they tended to purchase quickly the brand involved in the communication—the old brand. Having tried the brand, they became somewhat loyal to it. It is consistent with this interpretation that in the noninterviewed panel, one-member household was the only category in which consumers made more trial purchases of the new brand than the old. This would result from the hypothesized sensitivity of these persons to communication on this topic, but the source for these persons in the noninterviewed panel was the high level of advertising accompanying the introduction of the new brand.

The second question is similar to the first, but it is primarily descriptive rather than analytical. Whatever the cause, are any changes in purchasing behavior so persistent and pervasive that once panel members are interviewed the reported purchasing will not converge, or will converge only after a very long time, to approximate that of noninterviewed panels? This cannot be answered conclusively in the present case, because new brand B had only about a 10 percent market share when data gathering from the experimental panel ceased. This makes interpanel comparisons by categories hazardous, because sample sizes of purchasing by categories were very small.

Some significant terminal differences do exist between panels for some categories of consumers. Almost all of these differences are for total units and repeat purchase units. There are almost no differences for trial purchases. It is not clear whether all of these differences are permanent, but some appear to be. This is really to be expected, because brand loyalty will usually result even for almost identical products.[3] In any case, the terminal differences between categories are sufficiently small and self-canceling that the net effect is judged to be negligible.

It was pointed out that aggregate repeat purchase rates for B are comparable between panels, the ratio of cumulative trial rates of B shows a stable and almost constant trend, and terminal market shares are comparable.

The answer to the third question is potentially very important for applied marketing research. It is possible to interview panel members and still obtain accurate generalization of aggregate purchase behavior!

Frequently, the most important estimate desired from a purchase panel is the repeat purchase rate. As stated by Mr. Pearson, Director of Market Planning, Bristol-Myers Products, "In fact, repeat purchase is the real name of the game in market testing."[1] Figure 3.3 shows that the interviewing as performed had only very short-term effects on the aggregate cumulative repeat purchase rate. This fact by itself permits much more innovative and efficient use of panels. One such recent innovative use by Market Insights, Inc., is to pass out full value coupons for the test product to panel members and obtain accurate and most rapid estimates of repeat purchase rates.[2]

Another frequent estimate desired from a purchase panel in a test market is the trial rate, and interviewing does accelerate and magnify this. However, if the interviewing is unbiased, as it was designed to be in this project, it appears that the effects upon trial rates can be adjusted for. Admittedly, the specific method illustrated below is a first approximation and would not work for all types of interviewing and all types of products. When interviewing, the researcher should communicate to the respondent only protocol instructions for answering except where creation of brand name awareness is implicit in the asking of a question. Modifications would probably have to be made for very inexpensive products and different purchase-to-purchase cycles.

The recommended first step is to record the terminal cumulative trial rate in the interviewed panel. In the present case this is 13.4 percent. This is the upper limit for the trial rate in a noninterviewed panel.

The next step is to ignore all trial purchases that occur prior to two weeks after the second telephone interview affecting awareness. This use of a two-week period is based upon the detailed analysis which showed that after the first telephone interview, prior users of A tried B at an increased rate for only two weeks. Also, incidentally, the ratio of trial rates in the two panels is stable two to three weeks after the second telephone interview, and the cumulative repeat rates are then also comparable between panels. The terminal trial rate of 13.4 percent minus the trial rate of 10 percent two weeks after the second telephone interview yields 3.4 percent. As some trial purchases would have occurred even without the heightened arousal and awareness due to interviewing, this forms the lower limit for the estimate of the normal trial rate.

In some instances it may be sufficient to know the upper and lower limits of the expected cumulative trial rate. However, a more precise single-valued forecast is frequently needed. This can be obtained by use of the two rules below.

The first rule suggested is to decrease by 20 percent the trial purchases that occur during the month following an initial questioning which is judged to affect the arousal state of motives and examination of choice criteria but not directly to affect awareness. The actual interpanel difference was only 10 percent, but that is subject to substantial sampling error due to the small number of trial purchasers of the new brand during the first month.

The second rule is to ignore all trial purchases occurring two weeks after questioning that is unbiased regarding brands except that it informs unknowing respondents of the existence of the new brand. The detailed analysis showed this to be the time period when most interviewing-caused trial purchases occur.

Application of these two simple rules yields a reasonable, conservative estimate of 7.7 percent for the cumulative trial rate of B if it had not been affected by interviewing. This is sufficiently close to the actual figure of 8.6 percent in the control panel that no managerial decisions are likely to be affected by the difference.

It has been shown above that it is possible to interview panel members and still obtain accurate estimates of these aspects of purchase behavior usually desired from consumer panels in test markets: brand shares, cumulative trial rates, and cumulative repeat purchase rates.

Further refinements of the suggested rules for adjustment of trial rates are obviously needed, and the role of judgment by experienced marketing researchers and marketing managers can never be eliminated; but the implications of these initial results are sufficiently important that these refinements will hopefully soon be provided by subsequent research projects.

These results suggest the possibility of greatly reducing the cost of using consumer panels, and therefore increasing the efficient use of test markets. If the trial rate were doubled by increasing brand awareness through interviewing, the panel size necessary for accurate predictions would be reduced by 50 percent. By adjusting the purchase data from interviewed panels, the market researcher need not prolong the existence of the panel while waiting for the effects of interviewing to disappear. This is important for cost benefits but also because the results of test markets are frequently monitored closely by competitors, and the longer the panel and test market are used, the more opportunity of immediate competitive retaliation.

The final two implications below are perhaps most important. These concern the use of information obtained by interviewing. Test markets should not always be used just to obtain purchase data but also used to refine the planned marketing mix. This cannot be done without asking consumers to evaluate the competing brands. This could be done by interviewing users of the brand who are not panel members, but the greater difficulty is usually not in asking the questions but in locating the users. Clearly one dual purpose panel is less expensive than two single purpose panels. More importantly, full use of attitudinal data requires knowledge of the purchase behavior of the respondents.

Finally, use and refinement of general models of consumer behavior can be incorporated into the test market. This is academically desirable for the resulting contribution to knowledge of consumer behavior, but it also builds the ability of managers to improve the current marketing mix and to formulate strategic decisions regarding optimal target product markets that are based upon empirically defensible models of consumer behavior.

**References**

1. The National Industrial Conference Board, *Market Testing Consumer Products*, Experience in Marketing Management, No. 12 (New York: NICB, n.d.).
2. ORC Findings, "Accelerated Purchase Panels," A report by the Opinion Research Corporation, Princeton, n.d.
3. Sheth, Jagdish N., "An Investigation of Relationships among Evaluative Beliefs, Affect, Behavioral Intention, and Behavior," Chapter 5, this text.
4. Sonquist, John A., and James N. Morgan, *The Detection of Interaction Effects*, Monograph No. 35 (Ann Arbor: Survey Research Center, University of Michigan, 1964).

# II

# Subsystem Analysis

# 4. Word of Mouth Activity during the Introduction of a New Food Product

Shlomo I. Lampert

## INTRODUCTION

This study* examines word of mouth (WOM) activity about the new brand that was introduced to the test market during the period in which the Buyer Behavior project was undertaken. WOM is defined as an oral and informal transmission or exchange of information among people, none of whom is assumed to have any commercial interest when he participates in this activity.[4]

Investigation of WOM activity may have several aspects such as: who are the people that are most likely to engage in it, what is the information content distributed through this activity, how intense is this activity at various time intervals, how influential is WOM as compared with other information media, etc. This study investigates WOM activity at three time intervals during the introduction of the new brand B. The aspects studied are the level of WOM activity and what people are most likely to engage in this activity.

The underlying assumptions for this study are: (1) WOM activity is not a spontaneous activity, i.e., it is independent neither of personal differences nor of other happenings in the market place. (2) The product type has an influence on which personal differences and which happenings in the market place are related to WOM activity. Personal differences and happenings in the

*This chapter is a summary of an unpublished doctoral dissertation, Columbia University, Graduate School of Business (1971).

market place, which are hypothesized in this study to be related to WOM activity, are referred to as *factors*.

To be more explicit, this study examines first the level of WOM activity at three time intervals. Second, it investigates the relationship of various factors to WOM activity, and, where previous research is available, indicates the conformity as well as the relevance of the previous research to this study. It is worthwhile to mention at this point that the findings of this study differ from previous findings, since B is a brand that does not seem to fall within the same product classes cited in the previous research. Third, since WOM activity is an integral part of the buyer's behavior, the findings are discussed in the context of a theory of buyer behavior, specifically, the one suggested by Howard and Sheth.[14] Finally, the possible implications of the findings for the marketing practitioner are pointed out.


## THE IMPORTANCE AND THE CONTRIBUTION OF THIS STUDY

WOM activity is one of the information channels used by consumers in the process that leads them either to accept or reject a product. A notable example is the success of the Wilkinson Stainless Steel blades, which was attributed largely to WOM activity.[23] WOM is already recognized as a major source of information in many purchase decisions.[4,6] It is very likely that WOM activity will increase in importance as our society becomes more industrialized, new products are introduced into the market at increasing rates, and consumers become more and more overwhelmed by the information poured on them by commercial sources. A reasonable reaction may be a development of a defense mechanism that will limit potential buyers' perception of commercial sources, while emphasizing personal sources with which they interact regularly and whose judgment is of significance to them. It is therefore important to pursue research in this area in the hope of reaching a proven theory of WOM behavior. This study does suggest some new directions toward a more integrative theory, based on the findings here and elsewhere, which are likely to contribute to the discipline of marketing in theory as well as in practice.

In terms of the specific research presented here as compared with previous research this study has significant contributions. First, it studies WOM activity about a brand in a product class that was not studied before. Second, it studies all the people who engage in such activity, not just users of a product, as was commonly done before. Third, this study tests factors not tested before for relationship to WOM activity: i.e., unaided recall and attitude. Finally, the type of data—panel data selected from an almost statewide test market—and the type of analysis—$\chi^2$ analysis combined with regression analysis—were not used before in WOM studies.

## THE DATA

Since a detailed description of the data collection procedures is given elsewhere in this book, I shall refer only to some specific aspects that are relevant to the analysis. First, the investigation here concerned itself with WOM activity about *one* brand out of a number of brands within the specific product class and other closely related products. Second, B was a new brand, and only people who were aware of B could answer any questions regarding recall and judgment data about it. This resulted in a variable sample size as a function of the increase of awareness over time, which is substantially smaller than the total sample as a function of time. More specifically, the major source of data for this study was the three telephone interviews. *All* the respondents in each telephone interview represent the *total sample* of the specific telephone interview, while the *people who were aware of B* are a *subsample* of the specific telephone interview. The people who were aware are the sum of people who recalled the brand name either unaided or aided. Table 4.1 shows the respective total samples and subsamples.

Table 4.1

The Size of Total Samples and Subsamples in the
Three Telephone Interviews

| Period | Size of Total Sample | Size of Subsample |
|---|---|---|
| First telephone interview – T1 | 868 | 358 |
| Second telephone interview – T2 | 757 | 560 |
| Third telephone interview – T3 | 718 | 597 |

The distinction between the size of the total samples and the size of the subsamples is of major importance. The total sample is used only in the discussion of WOM activity as an information source. The subsamples are the ones that are the basis for the detailed analysis of who the people are who are most likely to talk. Only the subsamples include the people who *explicitly* indicate their action or inaction regarding WOM activity about brand B.

A final note about the data concerns the validity and the reliability of the data. Regarding the validity of the data, it can be said that since the purchasing panel that composes the sample is a self-selected one, it may have an inherent bias; thus the ability to generalize the results is questionable. Certain aspects of this are discussed by Day elsewhere in the book. As to the reliability, it seems that a repetition of the study under similar conditions can be expected to yield the same results since the product under study is one among several others surveyed, and the respondents do not seem to be preconditioned, a state that would cause a bias in their response.


## METHODOLOGY

The analysis of the data is composed of two parts, one regarding the level of WOM activity, the other regarding the testing of relationship of the various factors to WOM activity. The level of WOM activity is examined within the respective total samples as well as within the respective subsamples of the people aware of the brand. The level of WOM activity within the respective subsamples is also compared with individual patterns of behavior regarding this activity. The examination of the level of WOM activity within both the respective total samples and the respective subsamples is aimed at determining the importance of WOM activity as an information source within these populations. The comparison of individual patterns to the aggregate percentages within the respective subsamples is aimed at determining whether or not it is possible to detect a behavioral system regarding WOM activity.

The relationship of the factors to WOM activity is tested in two stages. The first stage is a $\chi^2$ analysis of contingency tables which consider WOM as a function of a certain factor: WOM $= f$(factor). The second stage is a regression analysis of the factors that show a consistent relationship in the $\chi^2$ analysis. By a consistent relationship of a factor we mean that two conditions are met: (1) the factor is related to WOM activity in each of three time periods; and (2) the relationship between the factor and WOM activity is in the same direction in each of the three time periods. In the regression analysis, the likelihood of engaging in WOM is the dependent variable and the factors are the independent variables. The regression analysis enables us to look at WOM activity and all the consistent factors at once, and indicates the contribution of each factor to the overall relationship between the factors and WOM activity.


## MEASUREMENT OF WORD OF MOUTH ACTIVITY

The measurement of WOM activity in this study is based on the question: "Within the last week or two have you talked with anyone in your family or anybody else about brand B?" A *yes* answer indicates engagement in WOM activity during the period, and a *no* answer indicates no engagement in WOM activity during the period. The above question was asked at each of the three telephone interviews; as can be seen, the reported WOM activity or inactivity is referred to a time interval of two weeks prior to the telephone interview.

This measure seems to underestimate the level of WOM activity in the population since it does not indicate (1) the number of people who participated in the reported activity, or (2) the number of times that each individual actually engaged in WOM activity. A possible overestimation of WOM activity can be a result of double counting of the same conversation; however, this is very unlikely since the sample is from a statewide test market, and any interaction among the sample members is a remote possibility. Thus, we conclude that the above measure does underestimate the actual level of WOM activity in the population.

## THE REPORTED WORD OF MOUTH ACTIVITY

The reported WOM activity is shown here in two contexts: first, as an information medium, where the total samples of all the respondents to the telephone interview are relevant; second, as an activity within the subsamples, i.e., people who are aware of brand B. These subsamples are examined thoroughly in this study, since only within these subsamples do we have an explicit statement of action or no-action as to WOM.

Table 4.2 shows the number of people who reported talking about brand B in each telephone interview, the percentage which these people represent in the total sample, and the percentage of the talkers within the subsample. (Table 4.1 shows the size of the total samples as well as the size of the subsamples.)

If WOM is an information medium, the low percentage of talkers shown in Table 4.2 seems to indicate that it is not a widely used one. However, if we compare WOM to any other single medium, as TV, newspapers, and magazines, which are the major sources for reporting advertising exposure (data not presented here), we see that WOM is an important source of

### Table 4.2

### The Number of People Who Reported WOM Activity, and the Percentage of These People within the Total and Subsamples

| Time of Reporting | Number of Talkers | % of Talkers in Total Samples | % of Talkers in Subsamples |
|---|---|---|---|
| T1[a] | 54 | 6.2 | 15.1 |
| T2[a] | 97 | 12.8 | 17.3 |
| T3[a] | 51 | 7.1 | 8.5 |

[a]T1, T2, and T3 represent telephone interviews 1, 2, and 3.

information. In the first and second telephone interviews, the number of those reporting WOM activity is around two-thirds of the number reporting exposure to TV and over four-fifths of the number reporting newspaper and magazine advertising exposure. Both ratios are for the same time period. The number of people who reported WOM during the third telephone interview was only about two-fifths of the number of people reporting TV advertising exposure and slightly over one-half of the number of people reporting newspaper and magazine advertising exposure. Thus WOM as reported here does seem to be an important source of information, despite the fact that WOM is underestimated in this study due to nonprecise measurement, as was pointed out before.

In order to determine who the people are who are most likely to talk about B, we first have to establish if there is any recognizable pattern of the respondents regarding this activity; second, if a pattern exists, can we relate the likelihood of talking to some factors? For this type of analysis only the respective subsamples, where an explicit statement regarding action or no-action as to WOM is given, can be the analysis base. As can be seen in Table 4.2, the percentage of talkers within the subsample is about the same for the first and second telephone interview, while the reported WOM activity in the third period shows a sharp decline as compared with the previous periods reported. A significant decline in WOM activity between the second and the third reported periods is also apparent in the percentage of talkers within the respective total samples. It is thus tempting to assume that there is a change in the WOM activity of the subsample between the second and third telephone interviews that led to the decline in this activity. However, since we examined only three points in time, and only aggregate figures are presented, it is questionable whether it is possible to determine a change in behavior, rather than assuming that these aggregate numbers are a result of random variation. In order to achieve more conclusive judgment, an examination of individual patterns regarding WOM activity was made. Each individual pattern is actually a sample of size one and thus we had many samples (of size one) that were examined over three points in time. These samples are sufficient either to prove or disprove a behavior pattern.

The analysis of individual patterns over two consecutive periods (between the first and second telephone interviews, and between the second and third telephone interviews), as well as for all three time periods, pointed out that the aggregate patterns were in fact indicative of a behavioral pattern. More specifically it was shown that: (1) the size of the subsample of a certain period is dependent on the size of the subsample of the preceding period; (2) the aggregate number of talkers are not random numbers, but rather conform closely to the sum of individuals' behavioral patterns over the three periods; (3) the talkers are also not a group of people who "always" talk (*no one* talked in all three periods); (4) most talkers confine their activity to one period; relatively few engage in WOM activity in two consecutive periods, i.e., a person who talked at any time period was likely neither to participate in this activity in the preceding period nor to engage in it in the following period. Thus, we suggest that a person who engages in WOM activity at a certain time is doing so due to some environmental and/or personal factors operating on him at, or close to, the time of the reported WOM activity. This leads us to the examination of factors, both environmental and personal, which will shed more light on the determination of who is more likely to talk at any given time, as well as lead us to suggest a more integrative theory regarding WOM activity.

## FRAMEWORK FOR HYPOTHESIS

Word of mouth activity has been cited before, in hypotheses as well as in actual studies,* as largely an information-seeking activity directed at reducing the risk perceived by a potential buyer prior to purchase of a product new to him. This led to testing in this study the relationship of four factors that have been commonly used to prove that the above statement is true. Thus, we first test whether people who seek friends' opinions prior to a purchase of a new product are more likely to engage in WOM activity than are nonseekers. Second, we test whether people who are more socially integrated will be more likely to engage in WOM than those who are not socially integrated. It was assumed that people who interact more with their fellows will be more likely to use this source for information gathering. Third, we test whether people who have less confidence in their ability to judge the product, i.e., less specific confidence, are likely to engage more in WOM activity than those with greater specific confidence. The assumption here is that the lack of specific confidence will induce the person to seek information through WOM. Specific confidence seems to be inversely related to the concept of perceived risk, i.e., the higher the specific confidence, the less is the perceived risk. Fourth, we test whether people with generalized self-confidence are more likely to engage in WOM than are those who lack it. The assumption here was that to seek information, a person who has a higher generalized self-confidence, which is a personality trait, will be more likely to use a personal source of information, thus engaging in WOM.

    Aside from information seeking, it was suggested that WOM is likely to be related to exposure to other information sources close to the time of

*Specific references will be cited later when findings of this study are compared with previous work.

engaging in WOM activity. This study tests three different sources of information: exposure to advertising, receiving a sample, and purchase of the product.

An extension to the concept of information exposure is the level of attention at exposure time as well as the comprehension of the product, which are indicated by unaided recall of the brand by a respondent. We thus test if people who recalled the brand (unaided) are more likely to engage in WOM activity than people who do not.

Attention and comprehension are followed by developing an attitude toward the product. Thus, we test whether people who like the product are more likely to talk about it than people who either dislike or are indifferent to the product.

## SPECIFIC HYPOTHESES AND THE MEASURES
## USED IN THE ANALYSIS

### Hypothesis 1

People who seek friends' opinions before trying a new product are more likely to talk about the brand than people who do not seek friends' opinions. Functionally:

$$WOM = f(\text{Seek Opinion}).$$

The measure of seeking friends' opinions is based on the respondent's answer to the question (in the mail questionnaire): "I like to wait to hear how my friends like something before I try it myself." An answer of *true* classifies him as a seeker of friends' opinions, while *not true* classifies him as a nonseeker.

### Hypothesis 2

People who are more socially integrated are more likely to talk about the brand than people who are less socially integrated. Functionally:

$$WOM = f(\text{Social Integration}).$$

Two measures are used in the study to determine social integration. One is the number of people the respondent talks to during an average weekday. The exact wording of the question (in the mail questionnaire) is: "Not counting members of your family, about how many people do you talk to in person or by telephone during an average weekday?" Classification of the people into categories of social integration on this basis must have some arbitrariness; however, alternative classifications were tried with no change in results.

The second measure is the size of the informal group to which the respondent belongs. The exact wording of the question (in the mail questionnaire) is: "Are you a member of a group of people who are good friends who get together fairly frequently just to be with each other? Answer 'Yes' or 'No'; if 'Yes,' about how many persons are there in your group?" A *No* answer was considered as zero people in informal group. A *Yes* answer was a numerical one. (Again the procedure of the previous measure was used to justify the classifications.)

The actual classification of both measures of social integration is composed of four categories: *Poor* (score of 0–3), *Fair* (score of 4–5), *Good* (score of 6–10), and *High* (score of 11 or more).

## Hypothesis 3

People who are less confident of their ability to judge the product are more likely to talk than people who have more confidence. Functionally:

$$WOM = f(\text{Confidence in Judgment}).$$

The level of confidence of a person regarding his ability to judge the product is based on the respondent's answer to the question (asked in each telephone interview): "I would like to know how confident you are of your ability to judge brand B." The person classified himself within five possible categories: Extremely confident, Very confident, Somewhat confident, Slightly confident, or Not confident at all. Since it is a self-classification, and the difference in the meaning between *extremely confident* and *very confident*, on one hand, and *somewhat confident* and *slightly confident* on the other does not seem to be distinct, the five categories were collapsed into three categories of High, Low, and No. *High* represents a self-classification either within the Extremely confident category or within the Very confident category; *Low* represents self-classification within the Somewhat confident category or the Slightly confident category; and *No* represents people who classified themselves as Not confident at all.

## Hypothesis 4

People with generalized self-confidence are more likely to talk than people with no generalized confidence. Functionally:

$$WOM = f(\text{Generalized Self-confidence}).$$

Generalized self-confidence is measured here by an answer of *Yes* or *No* by the respondents to the following question (in the mail questionnaire): "Do you often hesitate to speak up or express yourself in a group?" A *No* answer is assumed to indicate generalized self-confidence, while a *Yes* answer is assumed to show lack of it. This measure has two limitations: first it is based on one question, and second it does not enable us to determine the level of the generalized self-confidence.

### Hypothesis 5

People who were exposed to other information sources—advertising, sample, or purchase—would be more likely to talk about the product than people who were not exposed to other information sources. Functionally:

$$WOM = f(\text{Exposure to Information}).$$

Information exposure is determined by reporting exposure to at least one of the media: advertising, sample, or purchase. The information factor is, according to set theory, the union of the events of advertising exposure, sample receiving, and purchase of brand B. The time interval of the reported advertising exposure is two weeks prior to the telephone interview, which coincides with the time interval of the reported WOM activity. The time interval for sample receiving and purchase is about a month prior to the telephone interview. The use of the different time interval for each information source is based on the assumption that the strength of the exposure, in terms of the ability to remember it, is greater in sample receiving and actual purchase than in advertising. Also, in sample receiving and in purchase we have to account for a possible time delay between getting the product and using it. A methodological note is in place here. We first tested each information source by itself for its relationship to WOM activity. However, in some instances the sample size in a specific period was too small to allow us to make inferences. Second, even when the sample size was sufficient, there was no clear indication that reporting exposure to more than one source of information at the selected intervals affected the likelihood of engaging in WOM activity.

### Hypothesis 6

People who recall (unaided) the brand name are more likely to talk about the product than people who do not recall it. Functionally:

$$WOM = f(\text{Unaided Recall}).$$

Whether a person recalls (unaided) the brand or not is determined by the following question (asked on each telephone interview): "Can you think offhand—off the top of your head—of any brands of (a related product class)? Can you think of any brands of (a related product class)? Can you think of any brands of (the specific product class)? Are there any others you can think of?" If an answer to any of these statements includes B, the respondent is classified as a recaller (unaided). If B is not mentioned for any of these statements, the respondent is classified as a nonrecaller (unaided).

**Hypothesis 7**

People who like the product are more likely to talk about it than people who either do not like the product or are indifferent to it. Functionally:

$$WOM = f(\text{Attitude}).$$

The measurement of a respondent's attitude toward the product is based on a self-classification of the respondent (at each telephone interview) on a seven-interval scale between the extremes of In general I like it very much and In general I don't like it. Since the classification is subjective, and differences in the scale positioning are not certain, we collapse the seven-interval scale to three categories of Like, Indifferent, and Dislike. The middle interval represents Indifferent, and the three intervals on each side are classified as Like and Dislike.

## FINDINGS

Before we present the actual findings, it is desirable to indicate several points. First, only a consistent relationship (see *Methodology*) is the basis for accepting or rejecting a hypothesis. Second, when the findings here are compared with previous findings and hypotheses (where available), we mention the reference without indicating the product studied or the measure used in each study. It is important, however, to point out that no one in the references cited studied a product in the same product class to which B belongs. We shall see later that product classification is of major importance in suggesting an integrative theory of WOM activity. Third, the measurement of the different factors hypothesized here is mostly different from the measures used in the cited references. However, we feel justified in comparing the findings of this study to previous research, since we are concerned mainly with the concepts behind the measures rather than with the measures themselves. Finally, the findings are presented in three steps: First, we present the findings for each hypothesis by itself. Second, we integrate the findings of this study into a logical system. Third, we indicate why the findings in this study do, or do not, conform to previous research.

The hypothesis (Hypothesis 1) that people who seek a friend's opinion before buying a new product are more likely to talk about B than those who do not seek it is rejected. The contingency tables for all three time intervals show that the percentage of talkers among the people who classified themselves as opinion seekers is not significantly different from the percentage of people who classified themselves as nonopinion seekers.

This finding does not conform to previous hypotheses and findings of Ryan and Gross;[22] Lionberger;[17,18] Lionberger and Hassinger;[19] Menzel and

Katz;[20] Coleman, Katz, and Menzel;[7] Coleman, Menzel, and Katz;[8] Bauer (hypothesis only);[5] Cox;[9] Cunningham;[11,12] Arndt;[1,3] and Engel, Knapp, and Knapp[13]—all of whom stated explicitly or implicitly that WOM is an information-seeking activity, and thus it had been expected that people who classified themselves as seekers of friends' opinions, prior to a trial of a new product, would be more likely to engage in WOM activity than those who classified themselves as nonseekers.

The hypothesis (Hypothesis 2) that people who are more socially integrated are more likely to talk about B than those who are less socially integrated is rejected. Here again, the contingency tables for the three time periods (for the two measures used) indicate that the proportion of talkers among the more socially integrated does not differ significantly from the proportion of talkers among the less integrated.

This finding again does not conform to the findings of previous research done by Ryan and Gross;[22] Lionberger;[18] Lionberger and Hassinger;[19] Menzel and Katz;[20] Coleman, Katz, and Menzel;[7] Coleman, Menzel, and Katz;[8] and Arndt.[1] These studies do indicate that people who are more socially integrated are more likely to talk about a new product than those who are less integrated.

The hypothesis (Hypothesis 3) that the lower a person's confidence in his ability to judge the product the more likely he is to talk about it is rejected. However, in this case a strong relationship has been found in the *opposite* direction, i.e., the higher the person's specific confidence the more likely he is to engage in WOM activity.

This finding not only shows nonconformity with previous hypotheses and findings but actually is in conflict with them. As was mentioned before, the concept of confidence in the ability to judge is inversely related to the concept of perceived risk, which was first introduced by Bauer.[5] More specifically, it is inversely related to the component of uncertainty within the concept of perceived risk suggested by Cunningham.[11,12] To clarify this point it is worthwhile to elaborate somewhat on it.

The theory of perceived risk suggests that purchase decisions among product classes and within a product class can be viewed as decisions involving a perceived risk. The risk perceived stems, according to Cunningham, either from uncertainty measured by the subjective probability that the product will perform as expected, or due to the consequences, i.e., costs, that may result from making the wrong decision, or both. It is suggested by the theory that people behave so as to minimize their perceived risk, and thus that the greater the perceived risk the greater is the likelihood that a person will seek information that will enable him to reduce it. One way to seek information is through WOM. Thus it is suggested here that the lower a person's confidence in his ability to judge the product the greater is his perceived risk, i.e., uncertainty, about the expected performance of the product. We therefore expected that the lower a person's confidence in his ability to judge the product the more likely he would be to engage in WOM activity to seek information about the product. However, as was indicated before, this expectation did not materialize; in fact, the contrary was found to be true in this case. Even if we assume that the product is in a product class where perceived risk is generally low as compared with other product classes, e.g., drugs, the most we could expect is that no relationship would exist between the level of a person's confidence in his ability to judge the product and WOM activity. Yet the findings here show clearly and consistently that the higher the confidence in the ability to judge, i.e., the *lower* the perceived risk, the *higher* the likelihood of engaging in WOM activity.

Specific studies that either implicitly or explicitly indicated that the higher the perceived risk the higher the likelihood to engage in WOM are: Lionberger;[17,18] Lionberger and Hassinger;[19] Menzel and Katz;[20] Coleman, Katz, and Menzel;[7] Coleman, Menzel, and Katz;[8] Katona and Mueller;[15] Cox;[9] Cunningham;[11,12] Arndt;[1,3] Engel, Knapp, and Knapp;[13] and Bell.[6] It is worthwhile mentioning that some of the above studies were the basis for Bauer's hypothesis[5] regarding perceived risk.

The hypothesis (Hypothesis 4) that people with generalized self-confidence are more likely to talk than people with no generalized self-confidence is rejected. The contingency tables do not consistently show significant differences between the proportion of people who talked about brand B among those with generalized self-confidence and those without it.

The above finding does not conform to previous findings by Arndt[2] and Bell,[6] who show that the higher the generalized self-confidence of a person the more likely is he to be exposed to WOM activity. It should be indicated that my measure of generalized self-confidence may be less reliable than the measures used by the above studies due to limitations indicated before. However, I suppose that despite its limitations, it still enables us to make an inference regarding the relationship between generalized self-confidence and WOM activity.

The hypothesis (Hypothesis 5) that people who were exposed to other information sources—advertising, sample, or purchase—would be more likely to talk about B than those who were not exposed to other information sources is upheld.

This finding conforms to previous findings of Cox and Cunningham,[10] related to advertising exposure; Arndt,[2] related to sample receiving; Arndt[2] and Pessemier, Burger, and Tigert,[21] related to purchase of the product;

Farley and Ring (Chapter 10 of this book), related to recall of advertising. All the above studies showed that people who were exposed to an information source were more likely to talk about the product than those who were not.

The hypothesis (Hypothesis 6) that people who recall (unaided) the brand name are more likely to talk about it than people who do not recall it is upheld. The contingency tables show a clear and consistent relationship for all three periods. No previous studies dealt with this factor.

The hypothesis (Hypothesis 7) that people who like the product are more likely to talk about it than people who either do not like it or are indifferent to it is rejected. It should be indicated that there is a relationship between attitude and WOM; however, in each time period there was a different type of relationship. Since the finding does not meet the condition of consistent relationship it is rejected. Here, again, no previous studies dealt with this factor.

Table 4.3 presents all the specific findings in this study versus the findings of previous studies in a summary form.

## Table 4.3

**Comparison of Findings of this Study and the Previous Studies
as to the Relationship of Factors to WOM Activity**

| Hypothesis | Factor | This Study[a] | Other Studies[a] |
|---|---|---|---|
| 1 | Seek opinion | N.R. | + |
| 2 | Social integration | N.R. | + |
| 3 | Confidence in the ability to judge the product | + | − |
| 4 | Generalized self-confidence | N.R. | + |
| 5 | Exposure to information | + | + |
| 6 | Unaided recall | + | N/A |
| 7 | Attitude | Irregular | N/A |

[a]N.R.–no relationship; N/A–not available; (+)–positive relationship; (−)–negative relationship; irregular–no consistent relationship over time.

In summary, out of the seven factors that were tested for their relationship to WOM, only three show a significant and consistent relationship over time. The factors are: (1) Confidence in the ability to judge the product; (2) Exposure to information sources; and (3) Unaided recall. All the three are positively related to WOM.

We would like to add an important comment regarding the factor of confidence in the ability to judge the product. It seems that such confidence is a learned quality rather than a personality trait. Also, as was mentioned before, there is a positive relationship between the level of confidence at a particular time and WOM during an interval close to it. Thus, it is desirable to find out whether an increase in the individual's level of confidence between two consecutive telephone interviews has increased his likelihood to report WOM in the latter, as compared with a decrease in the level of confidence, or no change. We may call the confidence level at a point in time a *state variable*, while a change in confidence is a *process variable*. The analysis shows a much stronger positive relationship of confidence as a state variable to WOM activity than confidence as a process variable; that is, it is not the *change* in the confidence level that best explains the relationship between confidence in the ability to judge the product and WOM activity, but rather it is the confidence level at a specific point in time that does it.

Now that we have established that three factors are related to WOM activity, it is important to know how they all operate as a system: does each contribute to an overall relationship to WOM activity or are they redundant? To answer this question, two methods of analysis were applied. One, which is based on set theory, was an examination of whether an intersection of factors (of course within smaller sample sizes) increases the likelihood of engaging in WOM activity. The second was a regression analysis based on all observations of the subsamples, where WOM is the dependent variable and the three factors are independent variables. Both analyses indicate that each of the factors contributes to the likelihood of engaging in WOM activity, and none of them is redundant.

## CONCLUSIONS BASED ON FINDINGS OF THIS STUDY

Word of mouth activity is one vehicle by which information is either diffused or received by people engaging in it. A close look at the factors that were tested for relationship to this activity and findings presented indicate consistency in the behavior of the people studied. We found: (1) no relationship between seeking friends' opinions before trying a new product and WOM activity; (2) no relationship between the degree of social integration and WOM activity; (3) a high positive relationship between the level of confidence in the ability to judge the product and WOM activity; and (4) no relationship between generalized self-confidence and WOM activity. These findings seem to indicate that we cannot characterize WOM activity, in our case, as an activity aimed at seeking information about the product in order to reduce the risk perceived by a potential buyer, as was suggested in previous hypotheses and findings.

Looking at the other findings, we see that in addition to confidence in the ability to judge the product, exposure to other information sources and unaided recall of the product are also positively related to WOM activity. Reporting exposure to information sources indicates a certain level of attention that was given to the product at the time of exposure. Unaided recall of the product seems to exhibit a higher level of attention given to the product than is manifested by a mere exposure to information. Moreover, unaided recall shows a considerable familiarity with the product, which is related to the concept of comprehension offered by Howard and Sheth.[14]

The findings of this study do not suggest any apparent relationship between WOM activity and fulfillment of a specific goal by the people engaging in it. While we do not eliminate the possibility that part of the reported WOM activity was directed at information seeking, it appears that WOM is more likely a reaction to a cue triggered by giving attention to the product at a specific time, familiarity with the product, and a personal feeling of competence in passing judgment about the product. Thus, we conclude that WOM activity here is composed of two components: one is information receiving, possibly related to information seeking, and the other is information diffusion or exchange with no apparent goal.

## SOME NEW DIRECTIONS FOR UNDERSTANDING WOM ACTIVITY

The comparison between this study and previous research shows substantial differences in the findings (see Table 4.3). The question is how we can explain these differences. I think that the clue to an explanation may be found not by looking at WOM as an activity by itself, but rather by thinking of it as an activity related to certain product-related characteristics. What we mean is that each product can be viewed as having certain characteristics that are consequential in enhancing either type of WOM activity, information seeking or information diffusion. The product-related characteristics we suggest here are: personal consequences, social consequences (both related to the concept of perceived risk—see Lampert, Sections 3, 4),[16] importance of purchase, relative advantage, and complexity of the product. Thus, we suggest that different products, which have a different characteristic or a different combination of characteristics, may have different mechanisms that will lead to WOM activity. To clarify the aspect of product-related characteristics as related to WOM, consider car buying. Personal consequences of making a wrong decision may involve annoyance, inconvenience, loss of time, etc., when the car does not perform as expected by the buyer. Social consequences are related to the image the buyer wants to project on his peers. Importance of purchase is evident due to the outlay involved. Relative advantage in the technological sense or usage does not seem to have a bearing on this case. The aspect of complexity is apparent here in terms of the number of components composing a car as well as the various functions, wants, and needs that are to be satisfied by a car. Due to these characteristics, it is apparent that a person will be likely to engage in WOM activity as a source for seeking information within his family, peers, and others, before he makes a purchase decision.

Let us now examine brand B in terms of the product-related characteristics as they are likely to relate to WOM activity. Howard and Sheth[14] suggest that there may be some personal consequences to the housewife of buying this product class. They suggest that adopting a convenience food may reduce the role of the housewife as a homemaker, an outcome which may not be to the liking of the housewife. As to social consequences, since this food product is not likely to be used in the context of social affairs, like coffee or liquor, no social consequences seem to affect the purchase decision. Importance of purchase is minor in this case since several servings can be bought for less than a dollar. Relative advantage is also not apparent in this case since B is a new brand within an existing product class where most of the population was aware of this type product before, and there is no evidence to indicate any relative advantage of B over other brands. As to the complexity of the product, it is evident that B is neither complex in its composition (from the customer point of view), nor is it complex in its use. In view of the above product-related characteristics of B, it is evident that we cannot expect much information seeking by a potential buyer through WOM or otherwise. Even the housewife, who may fear a diminished role as a homemaker due to adopting a convenience food, is not likely to seek information through WOM to resolve her problem. The above discussion has direct support from the findings of this study.

## THIS STUDY WITHIN THE THEORY OF BUYER BEHAVIOR

WOM activity is an integral part of buyer behavior, and as it is, we present our findings within such a theory, more specifically the one developed by Howard and Sheth.[14]

The theory classifies product innovations into three categories: major, normal, and minor, according to the information requirements of the buyer prior to actual purchase. Since B was an additional brand in an existing product class of which most of the respondents (over 90%) were aware, B can be regarded as a normal or a minor innovation. It would be a normal innovation to people who were not sufficiently experienced with the product class and would therefore be likely to seek information from various sources, and it would be a minor innovation to those who had adequate experience with similar brands in the product class that includes B and therefore can generalize their information to B without the use of outside sources. An extension to classifying new products according to the information requirements of potential buyers can be an indication of which information channels are likely to be used by potential buyers to obtain the required information. It seems to me that the product-related characteristics, mentioned before, can be useful in determining those channels of information (Lampert, Section 6.2).[16] For this specific case, outside information sources are likely to be used mainly by people to whom B can be regarded as a normal innovation, and the product-related characteristics of B seem to suggest that impersonal rather than personal sources are likely to be the major source of information.

The specific findings of this study can also be discussed in the context of the theory. The theory suggests various concepts and also indicates the relationships among them. We thus relate the concepts of the theory to WOM and the factors that showed a consistent relationship over time and then compare the relationships suggested by this study to the ones suggested by the theory.

The concept of Attention in the theory refers to the magnitude of information intake by a person at specific times. It is thus evident that people who reported exposure to information indicate a certain level of attention to the product at the time of exposure. Similarly, a person who recalled the product (unaided) seems to give attention to the product, or get information about it, at some time. It is suggested here that the level of attention seems to be higher for recallers (unaided) than for people who merely indicated exposure to information.

The concept of Brand Comprehension in the theory refers to knowledge of the existence of a specific brand (or brands) as well as knowledge of characteristics of the brand (or brands). Unaided recall clearly indicates knowledge of B (but not necessarily knowledge of B's characteristics). Thus, we attribute part of the unaided recall to Brand Comprehension.

The concept of Brand Confidence in the theory is very closely related, if not identical, to the confidence in the ability to judge the product that was studied in this project.

The concept of Overt Search in the theory includes all the activities of a potential buyer that are directed at collecting information about a product. WOM activity is one of these activities. However, Overt Search deals only with receiving information related to the "Inputs" in the theory, while WOM activity is a channel both for receiving and disseminating information. The part of WOM that is directed at dissemination of information is not dealt with in the theory, and a possible amendment to the theory is to regard this part of WOM activity as part of the "Outputs."

As can be recalled, the specific findings of this study show a direct and positive relationship between confidence in the ability to judge the product, exposure to information, and unaided recall and WOM activity. Figure 4.1 presents these relationships using the concepts of the theory with one exception, where WOM activity is used as an intermediate variable to distinguish between Overt Search and "Outputs."

Figure 4.1

WOM Activity and Its Relationship to the Concepts of the Theory

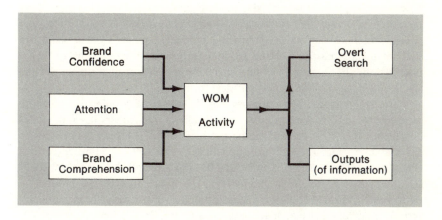

Comparing the relationships presented in the theory (shortening the concepts of the theory not dealt with in this study) and those indicated by the findings of this study, we see both conformity and nonconformity: (1) In both the theory and in this study there is a direct relationship between Attention and WOM activity—the part of WOM included in Overt Search. (2) The theory and this study are in conflict as to the relationship between Brand Confidence and WOM activity. The theory postulates a negative relationship as a feedback effect (related to the theory of perceived risk) while this study shows a direct and positive relationship. (3) The theory does not suggest any relationship between Brand Comprehension and WOM activity, while this study suggests a direct and positive relationship. (4) The theory omits the "Output" part of WOM activity, which seems to be of much significance in this study.

## THE IMPLICATIONS OF THE FINDINGS FOR MARKETING PRACTICE

This study cannot offer conclusive implications to the marketing practitioner since we only established relationships between WOM and some factors, and not a cause-and-effect type relationship. However, we can suggest alternative hypotheses based on the relationships found, and indicate the role the marketing man can play should one of the hypotheses be confirmed in future investigations. I shall indicate here only two virtually opposing hypotheses: (1) WOM activity is enhanced by scoring positively on each of the factors; (2) WOM activity enhances scoring positively on each of the factors.

The first hypothesis implies that if one desires to stimulate WOM activity about a product with similar product-related characteristics to B he should expose the market population to information that contains two major ingredients. First, the information has to be presented in a way that will facilitate remembering it (to achieve unaided recall), e.g., present stimulating advertising copy, a lovely jingle, etc.; second, the information has to be presented in a way that will enable the people exposed to it to build their confidence in passing judgment on the product, e.g., an advertisement can illuminate certain aspects of the product features that are of concern to the potential user but cannot be implied from the specific medium otherwise, like the flavor of the product, color, physical form, etc.

The second hypothesis implies that WOM makes people become more attuned to information about the product, remember it, and builds confidence in their judgment of the product. All these effects are of value to the marketer, since they all lead, hopefully, to an accelerated acceptance of the product. The question is then how to induce people to engage in WOM. I see one possible avenue in emphasizing the importance of the product in performing a needed function at the least cost (not necessarily in monetary terms), e.g., saving time, more convenient, etc. If the importance of the product can be conveyed, people will be more likely to talk about it because of the high information value they can distribute, which may enhance their social standing among their peers.

**References**

1. Arndt, J., "Word of Mouth Advertising: The Role of Product-Related Conversations in the Diffusion of a New Food Product" (Doctoral Dissertation, Graduate School of Business Administration, Harvard University, 1966).
2. Arndt, J., "Perceived Risk, Sociometric Integration and Word of Mouth in the Adoption of a New Food Product," in R. M. Hass, ed., *Science, Technology and Marketing*, Proceedings of the Fall Conference of the American Marketing Association, 1966 (Chicago: American Marketing Association, 1966), pp. 644—648.
3. Arndt, J., "Role of Product-Related Conversations in the Diffusion of a New Product," *Journal of Marketing Research* IV (August 1967): 291—295.
4. Arndt, J., *Word of Mouth Advertising: A Review of the Literature* (New York: Advertising Research Foundation, 1967).
5. Bauer, R. A., "Consumer Behavior as Risk Taking," in R. S. Hancock, ed., *Dynamic Marketing for a Changing World*, Proceedings of the 43rd National Conference of the American Marketing Association, June 1960 (Chicago: American Marketing Association, 1960), pp. 389—398.
6. Bell, G. D., "Self-Confidence and Persuasion in Car Buying," *Journal of Marketing Research* IV (February 1967): 46—52.
7. Coleman, J., E. Katz, and H. Menzel, "The Diffusion of an Innovation among Physicians," *Sociometry* XX (December 1957): 253—270.
8. Coleman, J., H. Menzel, and E. Katz, "Social Processes in Physicians' Adoption of a New Drug," *Journal of Chronic Diseases* IX (January 1959): 1—19.
9. Cox, D. F., "The Audience of Communicators," in S. A. Greyser, ed., *Toward Scientific Marketing*, Proceedings of the Winter Conference of the American Marketing Association, 1964 (Chicago: American Marketing Association, 1964), pp. 58—72.
10. Cox, H. B., and S. M. Cunningham, "Chicken Sara Lee Team Report" (Unpublished paper, Graduate School of Business Administration, Harvard University, 1961).
11. Cunningham, S. M., "Perceived Risk as a Factor in Product Oriented Word of Mouth Behavior: A First Step," in L. G. Smith, ed., *Reflections on Progress in Marketing*, Proceedings of the 1964 Educators Conference, December 1964 (Chicago: American Marketing Association, 1965), pp. 229—238.
12. Cunningham, S. M., "The Role of Perceived Risk in Product Related Discussion and Brand Commitment" (Doctoral Dissertation, Graduate School of Business Administration, Harvard University, 1965).
13. Engel, J. F., D. A. Knapp, and D. E. Knapp, "Sources of Influence in the Acceptance of New Products for Self Medication: Preliminary Findings," in R. M. Hass, ed., *Science, Technology and Marketing*, Proceedings of the Fall Conference of the American Marketing Association, 1966 (Chicago: American Marketing Association, 1966), pp. 776—782.

14. Howard, J. A., and J. N. Sheth, *The Theory of Buyer Behavior* (New York: John Wiley and Sons, Inc., 1969).
15. Katona, G., and E. Mueller, "A Study of Purchase Decisions," in L. M. Clark, ed., *Consumer Behavior: The Dynamics of Consumer Reactions* (New York: New York University Press, 1954), pp. 30–87.
16. Lampert, S. I., "Word of Mouth Activity during the Introduction of a New Food Product" (Doctoral Dissertation, Graduate School of Business, Columbia University, 1969).
17. Lionberger, H. F., "Some Characteristics of Farm Operators Sought as Sources of Farm Information in a Missouri Farm Community," *Rural Sociology* XVIII (December 1953): 327–338.
18. Lionberger, H. F., "The Relation of Informal Social Groups to the Diffusion of Farm Information in a Northeast Missouri Farm Community," *Rural Sociology* XIX (September 1954): 233–243.
19. Lionberger, H. F., and E. Hassinger, "Neighborhoods as a Factor in the Diffusion of Farm Innovation in a Northeast Missouri Farming Community," *Rural Sociology* XIX (December 1954): 377–384.
20. Menzel, H., and E. Katz, "Social Relations and Innovation in the Medical Profession: The Epidemiology of a New Drug," *Public Opinion Quarterly* XIX (1955): 337–352.
21. Pessemier, E. A., P. C. Burger, and D. J. Tigert, "Can New Buyers Be Identified," *Journal of Marketing Research* IV (November 1967): 349–354.
22. Ryan, B., and N. C. Gross, "The Diffusion of Hybrid Seed Corn in Two Iowa Communities," *Rural Sociology* VIII (May 1943): 15–24.
23. Sheth, J. N., "Perceived Risk and Diffusion of Innovation," in J. Arndt, ed., *Insights into Consumer Behavior* (Boston: Allyn and Bacon, 1968).

# 5. An Investigation of Relationships among Evaluative Beliefs, Affect, Behavioral Intention, and Behavior

Jagdish N. Sheth

Several researchers in social psychology have suggested a close relationship among *affect* (the individual's like or dislike of an object or concept), *beliefs* (cognitive structure representing bits of information related to that object or concept), and *behavioral intention* (tendency to respond to the object or concept by approaching or avoiding it). Rosenberg,[21] for example, hypothesized that affect is a function of beliefs related to the perceived instrumentality of an object or concept in attaining or blocking some valued states (motives, values, etc.), weighted by the relative importance of those valued states. Fishbein[10] considers affect and behavioral intention as the same thing, and very closely linked to beliefs about the object. Finally, Dulany,[5,6] in his theory of propositional control, has found behavioral intention as a function of (1) attitude toward the object defined in terms of beliefs about the object weighted by their reinforcing values, and (2) social and situational pressures, weighted by their reinforcing strengths. This resembles very closely the Rokeach[20] distinction between attitude-toward-the-object and attitude-toward-the-situation as two determinants of behavior.

Among all of these research propositions, the underlying objective is to search for some invariant linkage among the three broad areas of psychology that deal with cognitions, affects, and conations. Although extensive

I wish to thank Robert Rabin and Edis Erginler for excellent computational assistance. I am grateful to John A. Howard for providing research funds under the Columbia Buyer Behavior Project to carry out this study over a period of three years.

theoretical research is available in the area of attitudes on such linkage among beliefs (representing cognitions), affect and behavioral intention (representing conations),[15] there is considerably less empirical research. Furthermore, whatever empirical research is available so far is sketchy and heavily experimental, which makes substantive inferences difficult.

The present study attempts to provide a conceptual framework by which beliefs, affect, behavioral intention, and behavior are linked to one another. More importantly, it describes a large-scale empirical investigation of relationships among beliefs, affect, behavioral intention, and behavior related to buying and consumption of three brands of a convenience food product. The data for this study are based on a longitudinal study of 954 housewives, conducted at Columbia University under the leadership of John A. Howard.

## I. A CONCEPTUAL FRAMEWORK

Although several researchers have expressed pessimism about attitude's power to predict subsequent behavior,[3,8,14] attitude still remains a major hypothetical construct in social psychology. Unfortunately, attitude is defined in so many ways[2,16] that findings of various studies are not comparable.

Recently, attempts have been made, notably by Fishbein,[10] to sort out various components of attitude and suggest their interrelationships. However, there are some disagreements even in these attempts. For example, Fishbein would consider affect and behavioral intention as being equivalent, whereas Dulany[6] and Howard and Sheth[13] would consider behavioral intention as a *function* of affect *and* some other factors. Similarly, Dulany would consider behavior and behavioral intention as equivalent, but Howard and Sheth would think of behavior as a *function* of behavioral intention *and* nonpredictable (unanticipated) situational factors at the time of manifesting overt behavior.

In this section, an attempt is made to provide a conceptual framework that seems most realistic. It is based on the strengths of thinkings of researchers including Rosenberg, Rokeach, Dulany, and Fishbein. Figure 5.1 graphically represents the linkages among beliefs, affect, behavioral intention, and behavior.

(1) *Behavior (B)* is defined as a function of stated behavioral intention and those situational factors that could not be predicted by the individual at the time he expressed his behavioral intention. In most experimental studies, both behavior and behavioral intention are expressed contiguously in time and space so that there may be very few nonpredictable factors that would deviate behavior considerably from verbally expressed intentions. However, in naturalistic situations such as voting behavior or buying behavior, there is a

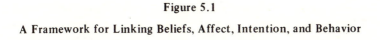

Figure 5.1

A Framework for Linking Beliefs, Affect, Intention, and Behavior

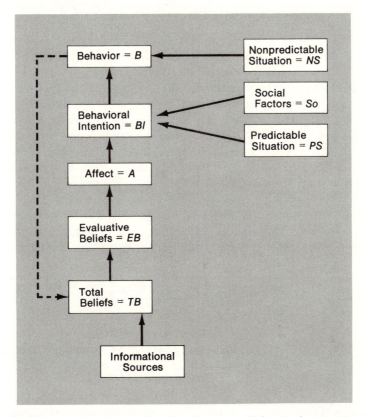

considerable gap in time and place between behavioral intention and behavior. Chances are very high that a number of nonpredicted situational factors enter into consideration when manifesting behavior that were not present when expressing behavioral intention. In consumer behavior, for example, numerous contingencies arise at the time of shopping and buying, such as unexpected store display of competitive products, experiencing time pressure due to other commitments, and sales pressures from the store personnel. Thus,

$$B_{ij} = b_1 [BI_{ij}] + b_2 [NS_{ij}] \qquad (1)$$

where $B_{ij}$ refers to individual $i$'s behavior toward $j$, $BI_{ij}$ is his verbal expression of intentions to behave toward object $j$, and $NS_{ij}$ are the situational factors related to object *j* that occurred at the time of behavior but were not predicted (anticipated) by the individual. This equation implies a two-factor theory of behavior. It should be pointed out that each factor (*BI* and *NS*) is presumed to be at least multivariate and possibly multidimensional.

(2) *Behavioral Intention* (*BI*) is hypothesized to be a function of (a) the individual's affect (*A*) toward the object, (b) social factors such as power (compliance) and attractiveness (identification) that impinge upon him at the time of expressing his intentions, and (c) those situational factors related to behavior that he could anticipate and therefore forecast at the time of expressing his intentions. Implicitly, therefore, behavioral intention is a *qualified* expression of behavior: given such and such things to happen in the future, I would or would not behave in such a manner. This is important, because it may be possible to predict behavioral intention but not actual behavior because both the anticipated and unanticipated factors may viciously deviate the individual's behavior from his behavioral intention. History has given numerous examples of this type, for example, in voting behavior where polls have gone significantly wrong. We can state this as follows:

$$BI_{ij} = b_3 [A_{ij}] + b_4 [So_{ij}] + b_5 [PS_{ij}] \qquad (2)$$

where $BI_{ij}$ refers to individual *i*'s intentions of behaving toward object $j$; $A_{ij}$ his affect toward $j$; $So_{ij}$ his social factors as they relate to object $j$; and $PS_{ij}$ his anticipated situation at the time of actual behavior as it relates to $j$. Affect (*A*) is hypothesized to be univariate, but both social factors (*So*) and anticipated situation (*PS*) are likely to be multivariate and possibly multidimensional.

It is possible that the three factors (*A*, *So*, and *PS*) that govern behavioral intention may act as opposing forces resulting in some sort of conflict. For example, an individual may very much like Rolls Royce but he cannot afford it; or an individual may like Cadillac, can afford it, but social factors may inhibit his expression of behavioral intention because Cadillac may be a socially unacceptable goal-object. In consumer behavior it is common among working housewives to find such a conflict toward many convenience (instant) foods.

(3) *Affect* (*A*) is defined as a function of evaluative beliefs (*EB*). Evaluative beliefs refer to cognitions (bits of information) about an object that portray a connotative meaning of that object as the goal-object. In other

words, evaluative beliefs represent the potential of the object to satisfy a set of relevant motives.[24]

Evaluative beliefs, as defined above, are only a small subset of total beliefs (*TB*) related to an object. Beliefs are cognitions or bits of information that are broadly classified as beliefs *in* the existence of an object and beliefs *about* that object.[11] The first type refers to an individual's awareness and knowledge of the existence of the object and its characteristics. In their theory of buyer behavior, Howard and Sheth[13] call this "Brand Comprehension." On the other hand, a belief *about* an object refers to the relationship of that object to some other object, concept, value, or goal. For example, a product such as Maxim freeze-dried coffee may be perceived as superior to some other product, say Nescafe, on taste and flavor.

Evaluative beliefs are part of beliefs about an object, but only those that portray the object as leading to or blocking the attainment of relevant goals or valued motivational states. For other categories of beliefs about an object, the reader is referred to Fishbein.[9] Evaluative beliefs as defined here can be considered equivalent to the perceived instrumentality component of Rosenberg's two-factor theory of attitude.[21]

In Equation (3) below, the relationship of affect (*A*) and evaluative beliefs (*EB*) is specified:

$$A_{ij} = b_6 [EB_{1ij}] + b_7 [EB_{2ij}] + \ldots + b_n [EB_{nij}] \qquad (3)$$

where $A_{ij}$ refers to individual $i$'s affect toward object $j$, and $EB_{kij}(k = 1, 2, \ldots, n)$ refers to the individual's $k$th evaluative belief about object $j$.

It will be noted that evaluative beliefs are not summed prior to relating them to affect, which is contrary to Rosenberg,[21] Fishbein,[9] and Dulany.[6] Based on a study of 30 products with a sample of more than 2000 respondents, Sheth[23] gives the following reasons:

a. Summing the beliefs is not theoretically explained by the advocates. There is no reason why we should not expect an individual to distinctly retain these beliefs in his cognitive map. On the other hand, there is enough evidence in multidimensional scaling of attitudes to suggest that the beliefs ought not to be summed.

b. Operationally, beliefs are obtained on a bipolar rating scale. Summing these beliefs entails deriving a compromise (average) value by aggregating extreme and moderate values of beliefs.

c. Beliefs can be positive or negative on a bipolar scale. Summing them assumes that one cancels out the other.

d. In regressing affect on beliefs, prior summing of beliefs consistently lowered their predictive power as compared to keeping them separate in a multiple regression.

(4) Evaluative beliefs are elements of total beliefs (*TB*) and hence they are shown to be derived from the latter in Figure 5.1. Also, total beliefs are acquired from informational sources and experimental sources.

(5) Finally, dynamics of change over time in total beliefs (and, therefore, possibly in evaluative beliefs, affect, and behavioral intention) are suggested in the feedback of consequences of behavior on the total beliefs. Underlying this feedback is a merger of cognitive consistency theories such as dissonance, balance and congruence, and reinforcement principles of learning theory. It should be noted, however, that this feedback operates simultaneously with learning of new beliefs from informational sources such as mass media, word of mouth, and books.

In this conceptualization, evaluative beliefs are fundamental to the determination of affect directly, and that of behavioral intention and behavior indirectly. However, this determination of the latter two is jointly with other factors: social and anticipated situation factors in the case of behavior intention, and also unanticipated situational factors in the case of behavior. This indicates that predictive power of evaluative beliefs should be less and less as we move from affect to behavior unless other factors are absent or held constant.

One additional point needs emphasis in examining the role of evaluative beliefs. It is that we must precisely define behavior and behavioral intention. Only then can we define and measure evaluative beliefs as representing perceived instrumentality of the object. In other words, to consider it as a goal-object, we must explicitly know the goals (motives, valued states, etc.) that impel a *specific* behavior and behavioral intention toward that object, for it is possible to manifest a variety of behaviors (correlated or uncorrelated) toward the same object. A parent, for example, behaves as father, hero, or friend with his child. Depending on a specific behavior, he would have evaluative beliefs about the child that are likely to differ from evaluative beliefs relevant to other behaviors. Even all of the supposedly strongly correlated behaviors called aggression, such as cursing, pushing, punching, and killing, may not be impelled by the same relevant motives, and, therefore, evaluative beliefs about the object toward which aggression is manifested may not be the same from one type of aggression to the other. It would appear that we have in the past committed mistakes in not identifying the appropriate behavior in predicting it from attitudes.

## II. DESCRIPTION OF DATA AND OPERATIONAL DEFINITIONS

The empirical investigation of the relationships among beliefs, affect, behavioral intention, and behavior is based on data collected in a large-scale study that attempted to test the Howard-Sheth theory of buyer behavior.[13] The theory of buyer behavior provides a description and explanation of consumer's brand-choice process and the development of brand loyalty over time. At the core of the theory is the concept of expectancy developed primarily by the process of learning from informational and experiential sources.

The data relevant to this study pertain to the three brands of the convenience food product; they will be called A (well-known brand), B (new), and C (new). This investigation examines the interrelationships among evaluative beliefs, affect, buying intention, and buying behavior toward the three distinct brands. Furthermore, for each of the brands, there are three separate sets of data collected in three telephone interviews.

The following are the operational definitions of affect, buying intention, evaluative beliefs, and buying behavior:

1. *Affect*—Overall like or dislike of a brand at the time of interview. The specific rating scale used was:

   In general, I like     □ □ □ □ □ □ □     In general, I
   it very much                                        don't like it.

2. *Buying Intention*—Verbal expression of intent to buy the brand within some specified time period from the time of interview. The particular scale used was:

   How likely are you to buy ____ in the next month?
   □ Definitely will
   □ Probably will
   □ Not sure one way or the other
   □ Probably will not
   □ Definitely will not

3. *Evaluative Beliefs*—Evaluation of a brand in terms of its certain characteristics, which are anchored to relevant criteria of choosing among several alternative brands in the product class.

   A set of evaluative beliefs was obtained from the respondent about each of the three brands in the three telephone interviews. The particular characteristics of the brands and the associated criteria of choice were based on a prior interview in depth of 100 housewives on milk additive products. A detailed description of the procedure followed is described in Howard and Sheth.[13]

The evaluative beliefs about a brand used here were obtained by the following bipolar rating scales.

| Delicious Tasting | ☐ ☐ ☐ ☐ ☐ ☐ ☐ | Not Delicious Tasting |
|---|---|---|
| Good substitute for meal | ☐ ☐ ☐ ☐ ☐ ☐ ☐ | Poor substitute for meal |
| Very nutritious | ☐ ☐ ☐ ☐ ☐ ☐ ☐ | Somewhat nutritious |
| Very good for a snack | ☐ ☐ ☐ ☐ ☐ ☐ ☐ | Not good for a snack |
| Very filling | ☐ ☐ ☐ ☐ ☐ ☐ ☐ | Not very filling |
| Good buy for the money | ☐ ☐ ☐ ☐ ☐ ☐ ☐ | Not a good buy for the money |
| Good source of protein | ☐ ☐ ☐ ☐ ☐ ☐ ☐ | Poor source of protein |

4.  *Buying Behavior*—Purchase of a brand of the product during the five months of panel operation.

   Buying behavior was operationally measured from the reported purchases in the diary that panel members filled out every two weeks. Two types of measures are used in this study. One is the number of purchases of a brand between two telephone interviews. The other is a classificatory measure of buying at least once or not buying at all.

There seem to be several advantages in using data from this large-scale naturalistic study compared to several experimental studies found in social psychology. They are:

1.  The study was conducted in a naturalistic environment that dealt with a real situation. It was conducted in cooperation with a large grocery company that was test marketing one of the new brands. It thus reduces the burden of substantive and statistical inference from a simulated laboratory type situation to the reality.* In short, all the differences that Hovland[12] pointed out between experimental and survey findings are absent here.

2.  The sample size of this study is large enough statistically to put faith in the findings. In addition the sample was based on standard probability sampling procedures.

3.  Due to the cooperation of the company, a unique situation was created

*This does not mean that simulated studies with atypical samples always imply impossibility of inference. See Sheth.[22]

in which measurement of beliefs, affect, and behavioral intention preceded actual behavior since the product was not even introduced in the market at the time of first interview and, therefore, no one could buy it.

4. This was a longitudinal study in which we could use time as a factor to build causation between attitude and behavior. It was, therefore, possible to measure prior attitudes for predicting subsequent behavior and also use prior behavior as a prediction of subsequent attitudes.

## III. RELATIONSHIP BETWEEN AFFECT AND EVALUATIVE BELIEFS

There are several compelling reasons to investigate the cognitive structure that underlies affect toward objects.[24] In marketing and consumer psychology, they can be summarized as follows: First, two buyers may both like a brand to the same extent but for different reasons. There is considerable literature on product differentiation and market segmentation to support this.[17] In fact, several companies have consciously avoided presenting a profile (image) of their products in the hope that *all* potential consumers would buy and consume them for their own reasons. Second, a brand is usually consumed in a variety of ways and situations even by the same buyer. Affect toward the brand may not reveal this.

Accordingly, in this section an attempt was made to examine the predictive power of the seven evaluative beliefs in explaining variance in affect toward each of the three brands. Based on the earlier discussion, the evaluative beliefs were kept distinct instead of being summed to a single constant prior to correlating them with affect. Multiple regression analysis was performed on nine sets of data (3 brands X 3 telephone interviews) in which affect toward the brand was the criterion variable and the evaluative beliefs were the predictor variables.

Table 5.1 summarizes the results of these nine multiple regressions. It lists the total predictive power as well as the relative importance of each of the evaluative beliefs in terms of standardized regression coefficients (beta weights).

a. In all nine cases, evaluative beliefs are significantly related to affect beyond the .01 level. The amount of variance in affect that could be explained by the evaluative beliefs ranges from a low of 41 percent (in the case of brand B-Telephone 1) to a high of 71 percent (in the case of brand A-Telephone 3). Considering the sample size and naturalistic aspects of the study, these percentages are very high. Therefore, we can state that evaluative beliefs are consistently capable of predicting variance in affect.

### Table 5.1

### Prediction of Affect by Evaluative Beliefs

| Beta weights | A | | | B | | | C | | |
|---|---|---|---|---|---|---|---|---|---|
| | $T_1^a$ | $T_2$ | $T_3$ | $T_1$ | $T_2$ | $T_3$ | $T_1$ | $T_2$ | $T_3$ |
| Taste | .57 | .61 | .63 | .52 | .58 | .49 | .43 | .59 | .59 |
| Substitute for meal | .05 | .13 | .06 | .14 | .16 | −.02 | .24 | .20 | .03 |
| Nutrition | .05 | −.03 | .01 | −.09 | .01 | .03 | .23 | −.14 | .06 |
| Snack | .04 | .09 | .16 | .06 | .24 | .10 | .14 | .08 | .02 |
| Filling | .12 | .05 | .04 | .11 | −.00 | .05 | .14 | .13 | −.03 |
| Price | .09 | .15 | .12 | −.00 | .10 | .20 | −.08 | .12 | .20 |
| Protein source | .02 | .01 | .01 | .05 | −.05 | .15 | −.12 | .05 | .04 |
| Multiple $R^b$ | .75 | .82 | .84 | .64 | .82 | .78 | .74 | .82 | .78 |
| Multiple $R^2$ | .56 | .68 | .71 | .41 | .68 | .61 | .54 | .67 | .60 |
| Standard error | 1.18 | 1.08 | 1.00 | 1.37 | 1.15 | 1.10 | 1.12 | 1.12 | 1.13 |
| Sample size | 512 | 467 | 598 | 189 | 296 | 449 | 98 | 175 | 352 |

[a] T refers to Telephone Interviews.

[b] All the multiple R's are significant at .01 level.

b.  Interestingly, the multiple correlation coefficient between affect and evaluative beliefs tends to increase with time; it is higher in later telephone interviews than the first. Probably, learning of the beliefs about the brands over time causes this correlation to improve.

c.  Only a few of the seven evaluative beliefs consistently come out as the important predictors. These include taste, price, and substitute for meal. Taste is by far the most significant evaluative belief, which individually explains more variance than all other beliefs combined. Except in the case of C-Telephone 1, nutrition and protein are the least important predictors. This is somewhat surprising in view of the fact that a good deal of the promotional effort of all three brands was directed to the nutritional appeals of the products.

d.  Although taste is consistently the most dominant belief across all brands and telephone interviews, there are changes in relative importance of other beliefs from one telephone interview to the next. Furthermore, most of the changes are found in the two new brands. For example, both filling and substitute for meal, which were important in the first telephone interview, decline sharply in the last interview, and vice versa is true of price and snack. These changes are very probably due to the change in promotional and advertising appeals.

In summary, we can conclude that evaluative beliefs are significantly related to affect.

## IV. BEHAVIORAL INTENTION AND EVALUATIVE BELIEFS

Some researchers have suggested that affect and behavioral intention measure the same thing.[10] However, as we discussed before, behavioral intention, instead of being an equivalent of affect, is at best a function of affect. Furthermore, two other factors (social and anticipated situation) are also hypothesized as determinants of behavioral intention. We should accordingly find that evaluative beliefs have less predictive power in explaining variance of behavioral intention than in that of affect.

Table 5.2 summarizes results of nine multiple regressions (3 brands X 3 interviews) in which intention to buy was the criterion variable and the seven evaluative beliefs were the predictor variables.

### Table 5.2

### Prediction of Behavioral Intention by Evaluative Beliefs

| Beta weights | A | | | B | | | C | | |
|---|---|---|---|---|---|---|---|---|---|
| | $T_1^a$ | $T_2$ | $T_3$ | $T_1$ | $T_2$ | $T_3$ | $T_1$ | $T_2$ | $T_3$ |
| Taste | .35 | .33 | .36 | .23 | .25 | .25 | .01 | .27 | .30 |
| Substitute for meal | .12 | .12 | .07 | .16 | .15 | −.00 | .15 | .15 | .11 |
| Nutrition | −.03 | .01 | −.07 | −.16 | .10 | −.01 | .03 | −.13 | −.02 |
| Snack | .05 | .11 | .13 | .14 | .20 | .12 | .01 | .17 | −.03 |
| Filling | .10 | .01 | .09 | .05 | .04 | .05 | .18 | .05 | .09 |
| Price | .19 | .19 | .20 | .19 | .10 | .18 | −.01 | .05 | .16 |
| Protein source | .01 | .04 | .01 | .04 | −.10 | .05 | .02 | .09 | .03 |
| Multiple $R$ | .59 | .60 | .62 | .50 | .54 | .47 | .31$^b$ | .48 | .52 |
| Multiple $R^2$ | .35 | .37 | .38 | .25 | .29 | .22 | .10 | .23 | .28 |
| Standard error | 1.15 | 1.16 | 1.09 | 1.14 | 1.11 | 1.04 | 1.26 | 1.08 | .98 |
| Sample size | 528 | 488 | 621 | 201 | 319 | 471 | 101 | 192 | 367 |

[a] T refers to Telephone Interviews.

[b] Not significant. All other multiple $R$'s are significant at .01 level.

a.  Except for one case (C-Telephone 1), all the regressions are significant at .01 level. The amount of variance in intention predicted by the evaluative beliefs ranges from a low of 10 percent (C-Telephone 1) to a high of 38 percent (A-Telephone 3). Compared to the prediction of affect, however, the range is considerably less.

b.  Only a small number of the evaluative beliefs are important predictors of intention. These include taste, price, snack, and substitute for meal. Furthermore, taste is consistently the most dominant evaluative belief except in the case of C-Telephone 1.

c.  Although the evaluative beliefs tend to explain more variance as time progresses, the increases are not as large as was the case in prediction of affect.

The regression analyses clearly indicate that evaluative beliefs are much better predictors of affect than of behavioral intention. This has to be expected from the conceptual framework described earlier. Furthermore, in view of the fact that evaluative beliefs systematically explain from 1½ times to as much as 5½ times more variance in affect than in intention, any equivalence between affect and intention has to be ruled out. This does not mean that affect and intention are not significantly correlated. Rather it suggests that the correlation is not likely to be perfect or near perfect.

To examine the extent of relationship between affect and intention, product-moment correlations were calculated for each of the three brands at each telephone interview. Table 5.3 summarizes the results. All the correlations are positive as would be expected, but none is perfect. The correlations range from .254 to .631 and all are significant at the .01 level.

Table 5.3

Correlations between Affect and Intention

Telephone Interview

| Brand | 1 | | 2 | | 3 | |
|-------|-------------|--------|-------------|--------|-------------|--------|
|       | Correlation | Sample | Correlation | Sample | Correlation | Sample |
| A     | .610        | 665    | .599        | 607    | .631        | 633    |
| B     | .488        | 256    | .554        | 390    | .480        | 475    |
| C     | .254        | 110    | .481        | 229    | .504        | 374    |

It is interesting also to note that whenever the predictive power of evaluative beliefs is quite disparate between affect and intention, the correlation between affect and intention is low, and vice versa. Take, for example, brand C-Telephone 1. The variance explained in affect is 54 percent (Table 5.1) but it is only 10 percent in the case of intention (Table 5.2). This is the largest disparate case in the data, and matches exactly with the lowest correlation between affect and intention (Table 5.3). A rank order correlation of .70 was obtained between the ranking of correlations in Table 5.3 and the ranking of differences in predictive power of evaluative beliefs related to affect and intention.

Yet another way to support the proposition that affect and intention are significantly related but are not the same is to examine the relative contribution of each of the evaluative beliefs in prediction of affect and intention. The evaluative beliefs were rank ordered, based on their total contribution in all nine situations in predicting both affect and intention. The rank-order correlation was found to be .90, which is significant at least at .01 level.


## V. MEASUREMENT OF ATTITUDE FROM EVALUATIVE BELIEFS

It is clear from the evidence presented in the last two sections that evaluative beliefs are central to the prediction and explanation of both affect and behavioral intention. Also, it is possible to consider evaluative beliefs as the fundamental concept that determines subsequent behavior, for behavioral intention as a determinant of behavior is itself determined by evaluative beliefs. All of this suggests that attitude be defined and measured from evaluative beliefs about an object.

If we think of evaluative beliefs as representing an $n$-dimensional space, then a person's evaluation of an object on the set of $n$ evaluative beliefs can be considered a point in this space. This point represents that individual's attitude toward the object, and the centroid of several points (sample) is a reflection of aggregate attitude toward the object.

This would, however, be true if the evaluative beliefs were uncorrelated because they would then form an orthogonal space, which can be mathematically analyzed by the principles of Euclidean geometry. However, seldom are the evaluative beliefs orthogonal (uncorrelated) to one another. It is, therefore, necessary that a set of $n$ evaluative beliefs be reduced to $r$ orthogonal dimensions by making linear combinations of truly independent evaluative beliefs. A procedure is developed and fully described in Howard and Sheth, Chapter 6.[13] Here we will only briefly summarize it.

The data related to evaluation of a brand by a sample of respondents on a set of evaluative beliefs can be summarized in a matrix $X$, whose rows are the $n$ evaluative beliefs and whose columns are the $N$ respondents. Then element $X_{ji}$ represents individual $i$'s evaluation on the $j$th belief. The dimensionality of this matrix can be obtained by the use of the Eckart-Young theorem in which as much of the total information in $X$ is summarized in as few dimensions as possible.[7]

Any rectangular matrix $X$ ($n < N$) can be resolved into its basic structure. Thus

$$X = U\Gamma W \tag{4}$$

where

> $X$ is the data matrix containing buyer $i$'s evaluation of a brand on $j$th belief.
>
> $U$ is an $n \times n$ orthogonal matrix of vectors; by definition $U' = U^{-1}$ and $UU' = I$.
>
> $\Gamma$ is an $n \times N$ diagonal matrix of roots containing positive values in the first $n$ diagonal cells and zeroes elsewhere; and
>
> $W$ is an $N \times N$ orthogonal matrix of vectors; by definition $W' = W^{-1}$ and $WW' = I$.

Resolving the data matrix $X$ into the product of three matrices as defined above enables us to construct an approximate matrix, $\widehat{X}_r$ of rank $r$, whose dimensionality is much less than the original matrix. This approximation is of the least squares type and hence $\widehat{X}_r$ summarizes as much of the original information as possible. It is constructed by taking the first $r$ elements of each of the three basic matrices. Thus

$$\widehat{X}_r = U_r \Gamma_r W_r \tag{5}$$

where $U_r$ is the $n \times r$ section of $U$, $\Gamma_r$ is the $r \times r$ section of $\Gamma$, and $W_r$ is the $r \times N$ section of $W$.

Mathematically, the elements in $U_r$ represent projections of points corresponding to the row elements of $X$ on the unit-length vectors. Since the rows are a set of evaluative beliefs, the $U_r$ matrix represents *aggregate* (centroid) evaluative beliefs about the brand. Similarly, $W_r$ represents projections of points corresponding to the column variables of $X$ on the same unit-length vectors. Since the column summarizes a person's evaluation of the brand on all of the beliefs, the $W_r$ matrix represents *individual* scores. Every individual then has $r$ scores, each representing his score on a dimension. These scores are called the *attitude scores*.

It will be noted that attitude scores can be unidimensional or multidimensional depending upon the dimensionality of the data matrix $X$. In other words, $r$ ranges from one to the number of evaluative beliefs. If all the beliefs are completely uncorrelated, then a multidimensional $(r = n)$ attitude measurement will result.

The resolution of the data matrix $X$ into its basic structure is easily accomplished by getting a square matrix from $X$ and then finding its characteristic roots and vectors. If we post-multiply $X$ with its transpose $X'$, we obtain a cross-product matrix, $P = XX'$. The elements $P_{ji}$ contain the sums of squares in the diagonal and sums of cross products in the off-diagonal cells. These sums are anchored to raw scores as opposed to deviation or standard scores. If the original raw data matrix $X$ were at first transformed to a matrix $Y$ of deviation scores $(Y_{ji} = X_{ji} - \overline{X_j})$, the post-multiplication of $Y$ with its transpose $Y'$ would result in the well known variance-covariance matrix. On the other hand, if the original raw data matrix were transformed into a matrix $S$ of standard scores $(S_{ji} = Y_{ji}/\sigma_j)$, and post-multiplied by its transpose, the resultant matrix would be the correlation matrix. Since $P = XX'$, we can state that

$$P = (U\Gamma W)(W'\Gamma U') = U\Gamma^2 U' \qquad (6)$$

Then

$$W = \Gamma^{-1}U'X \qquad (7)$$

The matrix $U$ contains the characteristic vectors of $X$, and $\Gamma^2$ contains the corresponding characteristic roots. The characteristic roots are ordered so that $\lambda_1^2 > \lambda_2^2 > \ldots > \lambda_n^2$. Their sum equals the trace of matrix $P$ and therefore, the total variance present in the data matrix $X$. By choosing the first $r$ roots that summarize a large percentage of total variance (say 85 to 90 percent) and the corresponding vectors, we can construct the $\hat{X}_r$ matrix.

Following the above procedures and standardizing the value to remove bias resulting from varying sample sizes,[25] the aggregate and individual attitude scores were created for brands A, B, and C for every telephone interview. Surprisingly, in every case only one dimension was found to be present since it summarized at least 90 percent of total variance in every case. Furthermore, none of the second, third, etc., dimensions summarized more than 5 percent of variance and hence they were considered insignificant.

The finding of only one dimension may appear to support the suggestion by several researchers[18,10] that attitude is a unidimensional concept. But this inference is not fully accurate because all the brands and the evaluative beliefs they are rated upon are very similar. In general, we should expect more than one dimension; but because one attribute (taste) was so dominant in determining affect and intention, only one dimension was found in this study.

Table 5.4 summarizes the standardized aggregate attitude scores of brands A, B, and C. The aggregate values of each evaluative belief show only a small change from the first telephone interview to the third. However, most of the changes are found to be regarding the new brands. This is to be expected since they were so newly introduced in the market that consumers could not have strong positive feelings about them, and there was heavy promotional effort for them between the first and third telephone interviews.

### Table 5.4

### Aggregate Attitude Scores of Three Brands[a]

| Evaluative Belief | A | | | B | | | C | | |
|---|---|---|---|---|---|---|---|---|---|
| | $T_1^b$ | $T_2$ | $T_3$ | $T_1$ | $T_2$ | $T_3$ | $T_1$ | $T_2$ | $T_3$ |
| Taste | 5.8 | 5.8 | 5.6 | 5.2 | 5.5 | 5.6 | 5.1 | 5.3 | 5.0 |
| Substitute for meal | 5.1 | 5.0 | 5.0 | 4.9 | 4.9 | 4.8 | 4.7 | 4.8 | 4.3 |
| Nutrition | 6.0 | 6.0 | 6.0 | 5.6 | 6.0 | 5.8 | 5.5 | 5.8 | 5.4 |
| Snack | 5.8 | 5.9 | 5.8 | 5.6 | 5.7 | 5.6 | 5.2 | 5.6 | 5.3 |
| Filling | 5.6 | 5.6 | 5.4 | 5.2 | 5.5 | 5.4 | 5.1 | 5.3 | 4.8 |
| Price | 5.3 | 5.3 | 5.1 | 5.2 | 5.3 | 5.0 | 5.3 | 5.0 | 4.5 |
| Protein source | 6.1 | 6.1 | 6.0 | 5.7 | 6.1 | 5.8 | 5.5 | 5.8 | 5.5 |
| Sample | 628 | 581 | 954 | 246 | 373 | 479 | 113 | 231 | 374 |
| Aggregate affect (7-point scale) | 5.48 | 5.48 | 5.25 | 4.98 | 4.87 | 5.02 | 4.79 | 4.69 | 4.84 |
| Aggregate intention (5-point scale) | 3.29 | 3.18 | 3.20 | 3.04 | 2.68 | 2.59 | 2.71 | 2.48 | 2.54 |

[a]The aggregate scores are standardized to remove bias due to varying sample sizes. They approximate very closely the average values of each of the evaluative beliefs.

[b]T refers to Telephone Interviews.

Although at the aggregate level changes in attitude scores are much smaller, the individual consumer's attitude scores undergo strong changes over time. Also, they are quite different for the three brands. Table 5.5 reproduces attitude scores of some of the individuals to show this wide variation.

Since individual attitude scores summarize (in one dimension in the present case) the information related to evaluative beliefs about the brand, it is logical to assume that a high degree of correlation exists between attitude scores and affect, and attitude scores and intention. This would be particularly true in this study because earlier we found a good relationship

## Table 5.5

### Some Examples of Standardized Individual Attitude Scores

| Consumer | A | | | C | | |
|---|---|---|---|---|---|---|
| | $T_1^a$ | $T_2$ | $T_3$ | $T_1$ | $T_2$ | $T_3$ |
| 171 | 1.20 | N/A$^b$ | .82 | 1.08 | 1.13 | 1.12 |
| 350 | .67 | .89 | 1.49 | N/A | .84 | .78 |
| 517 | .96 | .90 | 1.10 | .88 | .89 | .96 |
| 839 | 1.18 | N/A | .70 | N/A | 1.15 | 1.24 |
| 909 | .94 | .93 | .95 | .98 | .89 | .93 |

$^a$T refers to Telephone Interviews.

$^b$N/A= not available.

between evaluative beliefs on the one hand, and affect and intention on the other hand.

Table 5.6 summarizes product-moment correlations between attitude scores, and affect and intention. They range from a low value of .295 (C-Telephone 1; attitude with intention) to a high value of .745 (A-Telephone 3; attitude with affect). It is interesting to note that the variations of correlations across brands and time periods are identical to the variations in multiple $R$'s between evaluative beliefs, and affect and intention. In fact, but

## Table 5.6

### Relationship between Attitude Scores, Affect, and Intention

| Correlation of attitude with: | A | | | B | | | C | | |
|---|---|---|---|---|---|---|---|---|---|
| | $T_1^a$ | $T_2$ | $T_3$ | $T_1$ | $T_2$ | $T_3$ | $T_1$ | $T_2$ | $T_3$ |
| Affect | .649 | .717 | .745 | .568 | .706 | .703 | .695 | .695 | .674 |
| Intention | .534 | .559 | .562 | .454 | .489 | .429 | .295 | .423 | .490 |
| Multiple correlation of evaluative beliefs with: | | | | | | | | | |
| Affect | .75 | .82 | .84 | .64 | .82 | .78 | .74 | .82 | .78 |
| Intention | .59 | .60 | .62 | .50 | .54 | .47 | .31 | .48 | .52 |

$^a$T refers to Telephone Interviews.

for a constant difference within a brand, the two values are very similar to each other. This should be expected, however, in view of the fact that an attitude score of a buyer is nothing more than a weighted linear combination of his seven evaluative beliefs about the brand.

## VI. RELATIONSHIP OF AFFECT AND ATTITUDE WITH BEHAVIOR

In this section, the final linkage is attempted between affect and behavior and attitude and behavior. Behavior is defined in terms of a consumer's buying of a brand of the product as reported in biweekly diaries.

Prediction of behavior from affect or attitude is a difficult task. First, numerous unanticipated situational factors intervene between a person's predisposition toward an object and his overt behavior with respect to it. Furthermore, confronted with the reality of behaving and the inherent greater commitment to subsequent consequences, the individual tends to hesitate or postpone behavior. Second, and perhaps more important, is the *interdependent* relationship between beliefs (and therefore affect and intention) and behavior, as was pointed out in the earlier section. This interdependence creates problems in establishing one-way causality between affect or attitude and behavior.

It would appear that without prior expectations of the consequences it is improbable that a person would manifest goal-directed behavior toward an object or entity. These expectations may be built over time, or they may be developed just prior to behavior. It is even possible that in the process of examining and sensing the object or entity, the expectations are developed. But expectancy is antecedent to goal-directed, purposeful behavior.

Prior to first-time goal-directed behavior the individual is likely to learn expectations from informational sources. These can be symbolic sources such as mass media, direct mail, or friends and relatives in which either pictorial or linguistic representations of the object are the main avenues of information. Or they can be significative sources such as store display, store shelves, showrooms, free sample, etc., in which the physical attributes of the object directly provide information.

However, once the goal-directed behavior is manifested, the individual experiences the consequences of his behavior. He uses this experience as a source of learning in which he revises his total beliefs, including evaluative beliefs, about the object. It should be pointed out that this revision of beliefs is a function of (1) the need to achieve cognitive consistency with behavior and (2) the positive or negative consequences actually experienced from behavior. The former has been the major theme of all the cognitive consistency theorists including the balance, dissonance, and congruency schools of thought.[1,10] On the other hand, the latter is a direct derivative of reinforcement learning.

This interdependent relationship can be stated as follows:

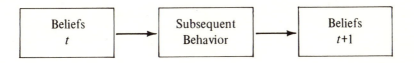

It will be seen that one way to reduce an interdependent relationship to an independent-dependent relationship is by the use of longitudinal analysis in which beliefs and behavior are *a priori* known to be manifested at different time periods.

The present study had the unique opportunity to establish time-related dependencies between attitude and behavior. Since the study was longitudinal it was possible to establish antecedent and subsequent behaviors as determinants and consequences of attitude, respectively. Furthermore, with respect to the new brands (B and C), attitude measures preceded purchase behavior because the brands were not introduced in the market at the time of initial attitude data collection.

In the case of each of the three brands, therefore, the following time-related linkages were established between affect and attitude with behavior:

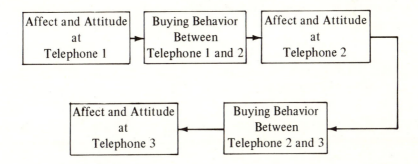

Operationally, buying behavior was defined as the number of purchases of a brand between telephone interviews. Since this time interval was relatively short (one month to two months), there were very few respondents who bought more than three times. Hence the following four discrete categories were used: (1) no purchase, (2) one purchase, (3) two purchases, and (4) more than two purchases.

On the attitude side, three types of variables were used for comparative purposes. First was the *summated* evaluative beliefs, as suggested by Fishbein.[9] Second was the seven-point affect scale. Third was the attitude score derived from evaluative beliefs as described in the previous section.

A bivariate regression analysis was performed for each brand at each of the linkages. Furthermore, there are three distinct regressions to include affect, summated beliefs, and attitude scores. Hence, a total of 36 (3 brands X 4 linkages X 3 measures of attitude) regressions were undertaken. The results are summarized in Table 5.7. The findings are:

a.  The relationship between attitudes and behavior is very low across all three measures of attitudes.

b.  In general, summated beliefs are least related to behavior, affect next, and attitude scores most. This may suggest that in the process of summing evaluative beliefs, an artifact (average) is probably created which suppresses a true relationship.

c.  The time-related dependencies operate both ways, albeit with low predictions. This implies that there is, in fact, a true *interdependent* relationship between attitudes (beliefs) and behavior.

The findings are disappointing in view of the fact that evaluative beliefs were very good predictors of affect and intention. However, there are several structural aspects that are important to look at. First, all the correlations are positive. This means that the linkage proposed in the conceptual framework is probably valid. Second, there is a clear and consistent finding that attitudes and behavior are interdependent, again validating that part of the conceptual framework. Third, while the prediction of behavior from attitudes remains about the same for the well-known brand across two telephone interviews, it increases sharply in the case of both of the new brands. This would be a plausible finding in terms of learning theory.

Finally, the findings clearly suggest the important role that situational factors play. There is evidence from other analyses of this study that there were two major unanticipated situational factors present in the data. The first was the introduction of C in the market and the consequent competitive promotional efforts that consumers felt from two new brands with somewhat

---

$P$ = Purchase (number of times a brand was bought)
$A$ = Attitudes (measured in three ways: summated evaluation beliefs, affect, and attitude scores)
$T_1$ = First Telephone Interview
$T_2$ = Second Telephone Interview
$T_3$ = Third Telephone Interview

# Table 5.7

## Relationship between Attitudes and Behavior

| Relationship with Buying Behavior | A | | | B | | | C | | |
|---|---|---|---|---|---|---|---|---|---|
| | Summated Beliefs | Affect | Attitude Score | Summated Beliefs | Affect | Attitude Score | Summated Beliefs | Affect | Attitude Score |
| $P_{T_1-T_2} = f(A_{T_1})$ | | | | | | | | | |
| Correlation coefficient ($r$) | .22 | .24 | .23 | .03 | .04 | .09 | 00 | .04 | .31 |
| % variance explained ($r^2$) | 5.0 | 6.0 | 5.3 | <1 | <1 | <1 | 00 | <1 | 9.5 |
| Sample | 656 | 349 | 581 | 263 | 206 | 246 | 122 | 114 | 113 |
| $A_{T_2} = f(P_{T_1-T_2})$ | | | | | | | | | |
| Correlation coefficient ($r$) | .23 | .27 | .24 | .12 | .10 | .14 | .20 | .19 | .26 |
| % variance explained ($r^2$) | 5.5 | 7.1 | 5.8 | 1.5 | 1.0 | 2.0 | 4.0 | 3.5 | 6.8 |
| Sample | 602 | 349 | 581 | 394 | 391 | 372 | 256 | 231 | 231 |
| $P_{T_2-T_3} = f(A_{T_2})$ | | | | | | | | | |
| Correlation coefficient ($r$) | .23 | .26 | .21 | .16 | .14 | .19 | .19 | .16 | .27 |
| % variance explained ($r^2$) | 5.3 | 6.5 | 4.4 | 2.7 | 2.0 | 3.6 | 3.6 | 2.4 | 7.1 |
| Sample | 602 | 349 | 581 | 394 | 391 | 372 | 256 | 231 | 231 |
| $A_{T_3} = f(P_{T_2-T_3})$ | | | | | | | | | |
| Correlation coefficient ($r$) | .21 | .25 | .20 | .14 | .17 | .17 | .14 | .20 | .20 |
| % variance explained ($r^2$) | 4.3 | 6.1 | 4.0 | 1.9 | 2.9 | 2.9 | 2.0 | 3.9 | 4.0 |
| Sample | 641 | 349 | 628 | 401 | 478 | 479 | 406 | 377 | 374 |

different appeals. Second, at times the new products were not available in the store when the housewife went to buy them. She either did not buy or bought a competing brand instead.

All of this indicates that what is found to be a very high correlation between behavioral intention and behavior in the laboratory type experimental studies[6,9] may be due to two factors, both of which are likely to be nonexistent in naturalistic situations. They are (1) contiguity of expressing behavioral intention and actual behavior and (2) lack of situational variations from one individual to the other and from one time period to the other because these are controlled in the experiment.

Despite this, the relationship between attitudes and behavior is felt to be too small. Some other explanation must exist for this low relationship. It would appear that part of the problem is anchored to the operational definition of behavior. What was predicted is not buying vs. not-buying, but buying a brand so many times within a given time period. At the same time, the intervals chosen were small enough (in relation to the purchase cycle of this product) to allow only a few purchases. In fact, a large number of consumers did not buy even once, particularly in the case of the two new brands. There are at least three indications that this seems to be a plausible cause of low relationship between attitudes and behavior.

First, the relationship between attitudes and behavior is consistently greater for the well-known brand where purchase frequency was higher and many more consumers bought the product at least once as compared to the new brands.

Second, Day[4] utilized the same data with respect to the well-known brand (A), but used the relative frequency measure of purchase *over* the five-month period. He could predict behavior from initial attitudes (his measure was affect) at a substantially higher level than what is found here.

Third, the respondents were classified as buyers vs. nonbuyers depending upon whether they bought a brand at least once between two telephone interviews. In Table 5.8, their average attitude scores are presented. It is clear that attitude scores of the buyers are consistently larger than those of the nonbuyers. Similar results between users and nonusers were found by Pellemans[19] with respect to affect and attitude scores.

## SUMMARY AND CONCLUSIONS

In this study, an attempt was made to integrate conceptual propositions related to beliefs, affect, behavioral intention, and behavior. Based on the linkages proposed, an empirical investigation in naturalistic conditions was undertaken. The data came from a study conducted at Columbia University

## Table 5.8

### Average Attitude Scores of Buyers and Nonbuyers

| Buying Behavior Between: | Telephone 1 | | | Telephone 2 | | | Telephone 3 | | |
|---|---|---|---|---|---|---|---|---|---|
| | A | B | C | A | B | C | A | B | C |
| *Mail and telephone 1* | | | | | | | | | |
| Nonbuyer | .632 | N/A | N/A | .602 | N/A | N/A | .668 | N/A | N/A |
| Buyer | .926 | | | .879 | | | .873 | | |
| *Telephone 1 and 2* | | | | | | | | | |
| Nonbuyer | .659 | .258 | .125 | .616 | .393 | .244 | .672 | .512 | .406 |
| Buyer | .910 | .340 | .228 | .892 | .747 | .830 | .814 | .790 | .860 |
| *Telephone 2 and 3* | | | | | | | | | |
| Nonbuyer | .660 | .250 | .116 | .604 | .397 | .244 | .653 | .502 | .381 |
| Buyer | .795 | .501 | .295 | .850 | .664 | .508 | .823 | .890 | .800 |

[a]Buyer is a respondent who bought the brand at least once during the time interval specified, and nonbuyers are all others.

based on the Howard-Sheth theory of buyer behavior. On this logitudinal study of 954 housewives, measures of evaluative beliefs, affect, behavioral intention, and behavior were derived with respect to three brands of a convenience food product at three different times.

The results clearly suggested that evaluative beliefs are very good predictors of affect and behavioral intention. However, their prediction of behavior, although generally better than that provided by affect, is substantially low. Some explanations were provided for this low prediction in terms of presence of situational factors (new brand introduction and lack of availability) and problems in the operational measurement of buying behavior. In general, the study provided good support for the conceptual framework that relates beliefs, affect, behavioral intention, and behavior.

**References**

1. Abelson, R. P., et al., eds., *Theories of Cognitive Consistency: A Source Book* (Chicago: Rand McNally, 1968).
2. Allport, G. W., "Attitudes," in C. Murchison, ed., *A Handbook of Social Psychology* (Worcester, Mass.: Clark University Press, 1935), pp. 798–844.
3. Cohen, A. R., *Attitude Change and Social Influence* (New York: Basic Books, 1964).
4. Day, G. S., "Buyer Attitudes and Brand Choice Behavior" (Doctoral Dissertation, Columbia University, 1967).
5. Dulany, D. E., "The Separable Effects of the Information and Affect Conveyed by a Reinforcer," paper presented at the annual meeting of the Psychonomic Society, October 1964.
6. Dulany, D. E., "Awareness, Rules, and Propositional Control: A Confrontation with S-R Behavior Theory," in T. R. Dixon and D. L. Horton, eds., *Verbal Behavior and General Behavior Theory* (Englewood Cliffs: Prentice-Hall, 1968), pp. 340–387.
7. Eckart, C., and G. Young, "The Approximation of One Matrix by Another of Lower Rank," *Psychometrika* 1 (September 1936): 211–218.
8. Festinger, L., "Behavioral Support for Opinion Change," *Public Opinion Quarterly* 28 (1964): 404–417.
9. Fishbein, M., ed., *Readings in Attitude Theory and Measurement* (New York: John Wiley & Sons, Inc., 1967), pp. 389–400, 477–492.
10. Fishbein, M., "The Relationship Between Beliefs, Attitudes, and Behavior," in S. Feldman, ed., *Cognitive Consistency, Motivational Antecedents and Behavioral Consequences* (New York: Academic Press, 1966), pp. 200–223.
11. Fishbein, M., and B. H. Raven, "The AB Scales: An Operational Definition of Belief and Attitude," *Human Relations* 15 (1962): 35–44.
12. Hovland, C. I., "Reconciling Conflicting Results Derived from Experimental and Survey Studies of Attitude Change," *American Psychologist* 14 (January 1959): 8–17.
13. Howard, J. A., and J. N. Sheth, *The Theory of Buyer Behavior* (New York: John Wiley & Sons, Inc., 1969).
14. Insko, C. A., *Theories of Attitude Change* (New York: Appleton-Century-Crofts, 1967).
15. McGuire, W. J., "The Nature of Attitudes and Attitude Change," in G. Lindzey and E. Aronson, eds., *Handbook of Social Psychology* (Reading, Mass.: Addison-Wesley, 1968).
16. McGuire, W. J., "Attitudes and Opinions," *Annual Review of Psychology* 17 (1963): 475–514.
17. Myers, J. G., *Consumer Image and Attitude* (Berkeley: Institute of Business and Economic Research, University of California, 1968).
18. Osgood, C. E., and P. H. Tannenbaum, "The Principle of Congruity in the Prediction of Attitude Change," *Psychological Review* 62 (1955): 42–55.

19. Pellemans, P. A., "Investigations on Attitude and Purchase Intention toward the Brand" (Doctoral Dissertation, Columbia University, 1970).
20. Rokeach, M., *Beliefs, Attitudes and Values: A Theory of Organization and Change* (San Francisco: Jossey-Bass, Inc., 1968).
21. Rosenberg, M. J., "Cognitive Structure and Attitudinal Affect," *Journal of Abnormal and Social Psychology* 53 (November 1956): 367–372.
22. Sheth, J. N., "Are There Differences in Post-Decision Dissonance Reduction Between Housewives and Students?" *Journal of Marketing Research* 7 (May 1970): 243–245.
23. Sheth, J. N., "Problems in Summing Beliefs Prior to Correlating with Affect" (Unpublished paper).
24. Sheth, J. N., "Using Factor Analysis to Estimate Parameters," *Journal of the American Statistical Association* 64 (September 1969): 808–822.
25. Sheth, J. N., "Attitude as a Function of Evaluative Beliefs," paper presented at the AMA Consumer Behavior Workshop, August 22-23, 1969.

# 6. Investigations on Attitude and Purchase Intention toward the Brand

Paul A. Pellemans

## 1. BASIC CONCEPTS

We are basically interested in two variables: attitude toward the brand and purchase intention toward the same brand. Both concepts should be considered within the framework of the Howard-Sheth Theory of Buyer Behavior.

*Attitude,* a verbal expression of the respondent's evaluation of a brand or service, indicates in which direction, positive or negative, the prospective buyer will tend to respond to the brand's message.

*Intention* integrates attitudes toward the brand and constraints—high price, lack of brand availability, social influence, time pressure, etc.—that may prevent the prospective buyer from fulfilling a purchase plan of a brand toward which he eventually expresses a favorable attitude. Since it indicates the strength of his expectation to buy a unit of the brand within a specified time period, intention is a summary measure of the buyer's purchase plan.

Attitude and intention evaluate the brand's cognitive and conative behavioral dimensions. If attitude and purchase intention were measured at the exact time of purchase, we suspect that they would be rated very high and thus be closely related. At other times, however, attitude toward an object is often expected to be divergent from intention toward the same object. Indeed, factors such as high price, lack of availability, social and time pressures may decrease the level of intention even though attitude toward the object is very favorable.

This does not mean attitudes are not related to behavioral intentions. We may reasonably formulate the hypothesis that our intentions are functions of given attitudes: the more favorably inclined an individual is toward a given stimulus, the more likely he is to behave positively toward it.

Examining the role of reinforcement, Doob[1] pointed out that our behavioral intentions as well as behavioral actions can be either positively or negatively reinforced. If there were always a positive reinforcement, then there would always be a clear relationship between attitude and intention. But there is often negative reinforcement due to the constraints contained in our intention measure.

How is the relationship between attitude and intention viewed in the literature? Ferber and Wales[2] proceeded to the study of individual cases rather than aggregate data, and Fishbein[3] was able to get a good estimate of attitude by looking at the whole of an individual's behavioral intentions, whatever the existing relationship between attitude and a single behavioral intention. The correlation coefficient between an attitude and the sum of behavioral intentions was 0.60.

Howard and Sheth[4] state that intention connects the buyer's attitude toward a brand with the purchase of that brand. Intention is a modification of the buyer's attitude in that it integrates attitude and constraints, such as high price, brand unavailability, social and time pressures, into a single measure. The level of activity of these constraints accounts for differentiation between attitude and intention.

From what precedes, we hypothesize that attitude and intention are related, but that the strength of the relationship depends on past reinforcement and level of activity of the constraints contained in intention.

## 2. INTRODUCING THE EXPERIMENT

*Attitude* is measured with a single, seven-point, bipolar general-liking semantic-differential scale that reflects the respondent's verbal evaluation of a brand's potential to satisfy his motives relevant to the purchase of this product class. One pole of the scale read, "In general I like it (the brand)," while the other pole read, "In general, I don't like it."

We believe that this measure is abstracted implicitly from the many feelings, statements, and actions that an individual makes with respect to a given brand. It is the resultant of the individual's own experience that may have been fed by information communicated by personal and impersonal means.

One measure of *intention to buy* was used in the experiment. Respondents were asked how likely they were to buy the brand in the next month, and they were requested to answer the question on an ordinal nominative scale: definitely will, probably will, not sure one way or another, probably will not, and definitely will not.

Although it is not certain that there is the same distance between *definitely will* and *probably will*, or between *probably will* and *not sure*, etc., equal interval values from 1 to 5 were assigned to his nominative scale for the computation of the results. The scale is clearly ordinal, and we accepted the assigned values for the analysis of the data.

We will investigate the respondents' attitudes and purchase intentions toward *three brands of the same product class*: a mature brand A and two new brands B and C.

Hypotheses about the influence of classificatory variables that will subcategorize our sample will be formulated. We are basically interested in the recognition of the influence that these classificatory variables exercise on subgroups of the various respondents' attitudes and purchase intentions toward the three brands.

For each subgroup of respondents as a whole, we will have an absolute level of attitude and an absolute level of purchase intention, obtained by averaging the respondent's attitudes and intentions for that subgroup. The range of attitudes across categories of the classificatory variables is compared to the corresponding range of intentions. Adjusting the scales to make them comparable, we determine where the impact of the classificatory variable is the stronger, on attitude or on intention. A slight correction is introduced to take into account the asymmetry of distributions of both attitudes and intentions. We also calculated the correlation coefficients between attitude and intention for the total sample.

## 3. RESULTS

### A. Attitude Change Versus Intention Change

There is general agreement that attitude precedes intention in the behavioral process. It is not our purpose to argue whether attitude is the cause or effect of intention; indeed, both could be the effect of some other, unknown causal variable. We would like, however, to get some fresh insight as to whether or not attitude changes before intention does.

According to the Howard-Sheth theory of buyer behavior, intention is a summary variable that integrates attitude and constraints such as high price, unavailability of the brand, time and social pressures. It thus implies that attitude is built before intention, since the latter contains the former.

We arbitrarily determine high or low levels of attitude and intention. For the attitude scale, the three highest values are high while the four last ones are considered low. We considered the two highest values of the five-point ordinal scale as representing a high purchase intention; the next three values were considered low. In fact, what we adopt as high or low is secondary since we are primarily interested in how the distributions of the respondents' attitudes and intentions vary on the time scale according to the established borderlines.

We analyzed the data in that respect by taking the distribution of the respondents' attitudes and intentions toward each brand at pairs of points in time. We postulated that when an attitude or intention develops or matures, it should first be low and then eventually increase; decline will follow. Attitude and intention are not assumed to mature simultaneously: a lag is very likely. Our findings demonstrate that, for all categories, attitude changes tend to precede intention changes.

If we withdraw that postulate and just consider which one, attitude or intention, changes while the other remains constant at two subsequent points in time without regard to which one increases first, we recognize that intention tends to be more volatile than attitude. This is normal, since intention is a summary measure that groups attitude and such constraints as high price, brand unavailability, social and time pressures, which may change quite often with time while attitude tends to remain steadier.

If we look, however, at the share of the respondents who did not change, we find that about 60 percent of the respondents kept a similar intensity attitude-intention relationship toward brand A. The score is somewhat better than 40 percent for new brands B and C. This is again logical, since respondents do not yet know much about the new brands and have not yet built any consistent pattern toward the latter.


## B. Intervening Variables

Intervening variables are "input" and "output" variables. The classification refers to the terminology used in the Howard-Sheth theory of buyer behavior. In the analysis of our data, we select only a few of the input variables mentioned in the theory—advertising recall, word of mouth, and brand unavailability. The output variables studied—usership and elapsed time since last purchase—are not found as such in the theory.

*Advertising Recall.* Advertising recall is an "input" variable. Respondents were asked whether they had seen within the last week or two any advertisement for the brand.

Hypothesis: Respondents who recall some brand advertising will tend to express a more favorable attitude and purchase intention toward the brand.

The hypothesis is based on the assumption that advertising, if recalled, will tend to call the prospective buyer's attention to the positive aspects of the brand and reduce the effects of doubts or negative feelings toward the brand.

Findings:

1.  Advertising recalled is positively associated with the absolute level of attitude and the absolute level of purchase intention. The pattern is supported by the findings for both mature and new brands. They thus support our hypothesis.

2.  Advertising recalled influences purchase intention more than attitude toward any brand.

3.  New brands B and C tend to be more influenced by advertising recalled than mature brand A in terms of ranges of attitude and purchase intention across categories.

*Word-of-Mouth Activity.* Word of mouth is an input variable. Respondents were asked whether they talked with anyone within the last week or two about the brand. If so, they were further requested to state whether comments were favorable, unfavorable or mixed.

Hypothesis: Favorableness of comments will be directly related to the level of attitude and purchase intention. If the "favorable comments" subgroup is the most numerous, the general group "talked" will exhibit a more favorable attitude and purchase intention toward the brand than the "not talked" group.

It is believed, indeed, that the favorableness of the comments will be remembered only if they have been integrated in the level of attitude and thus in the purchase intention.

Findings:

1.  The majority of the respondents did not talk about the brand; but when they did talk about it, two-thirds to three-fourths of them tended to have favorable comments about the brand.

2.  Discussing the brand increases attitude and purchase intention toward any brand.

3.  Levels of attitude and purchase intention are directly related to the level of favorable comments.

4.  Discussing the brand and favorableness of comments influences purchase intention more than attitude.

5.  Word-of-mouth has a greater influence on new brands than on the mature brand.

*Lack of Availability of the Brand.* Lack of availability of the brand, an input variable, is one of the constraints integrated in our intention measure. Respondents were asked whether, say in the past month, they tried to buy the brand and found it unavailable.

Hypothesis: Lack of availability of the brand is likely to increase the respondents' attitude and purchase intention toward the brand.

Difficulties in finding the brand may be interpreted as a sign of the brand's success; the buyer will thus feel somewhat deprived of something he may like and will look forward to the purchase of that brand. Consequently, attitude and intention toward that brand will be augmented.

Findings:

1.  Not finding the brand upgrades attitude and purchase intention toward all three brands. Findings thus support our hypothesis.
2.  Lack of availability of the brand tends to influence purchase intention more than attitude toward the brand.
3.  Lack of availability of the brand tends to have a stronger impact on new brands B and C than on mature brand A.
4.  The distribution of mature brand A was better than that of new brands B and C.

*Usership.* Usership is an output variable. It refers to whether the respondent used the brand previously. Respondents who were aware of the brand's existence were requested to state whether they were users of the brand.

Hypothesis: Current users of the brand will manifest a more favorable attitude and purchase intention than nonusers.

We expect, indeed, that users have built some buying habit toward the brand; there is some reinforcement effect that will protect attitude and intention from competing stimuli.

Findings:

1.  Current users exhibit a more favorable attitude and purchase intention toward the brand than nonusers. Results thus support our hypothesis.
2.  Usership influences purchase intention more than attitude.
3.  Usership exerts a stronger impact on mature brand A than on new brands B and C.

*Elapsed Time since Last Purchase.* Elapsed time since last purchase is classified among the output variables. It is not mentioned as such in the Howard-Sheth theory. If respondents were users of the brand, interviewers were instructed to ask them when they last bought the brand—more than 2 months, 1–2 months, 2 weeks–1 month, less than 2 weeks.

Hypothesis: Levels of attitude and purchase intention are inversely related to the elapsed time since last purchase.

Attitude and intention, indeed, are the closest to the maximum when they are measured at the closest point of time to actual purchase.

Findings:

1.  Levels of attitude and purchase intention toward mature brand A are inversely related to the elapsed time since last purchase of the same brand.

2.  Purchase intention toward new brand B and attitude toward new brand C *tend* also to be inversely related to the elapsed time since last purchase.

3.  Elapsed time since last purchase tends to influence purchase intention more than attitude.

4.  In terms of regularity of pattern expected by the hypothesis, elapsed time since last purchase exerts a greater influence on mature brand A than on new brands B and C.

5.  The number of respondents in each category also tends to be inversely related to elapsed time since last purchase.

## C. Endogenous and Exogenous Variables

For endogenous and exogenous variable terminology, refer to the Howard-Sheth theory of buyer behavior. We select only a few of the Howard-Sheth theory variables. Among the endogenous variables: evoked set, confidence in choice of brand, and satisfaction. Among the exogenous variables: housewife's education and importance of purchase.

*Evoked Set.* Evoked set is an endogenous variable. It refers to the brands that become alternatives to the buyer's choice decision in order to satisfy a specific need. To determine whether the brand belongs to the buyer's evoked set, respondents were asked whether they would consider buying the brand.

Hypothesis: Respondents will tend to have a more favorable attitude and purchase intention toward a brand that belongs to their evoked set.

It is very unlikely, indeed, that a respondent would consider buying a brand toward which he does not express a favorable attitude and purchase intention.

Findings:

1.  Attitude and purchase intention toward the brand are more favorable when the brand belongs to the respondent's evoked set. Results thus support our hypothesis.

2.  The impact of evoked set is stronger on purchase intention than on attitude.

3.  New brands B and C seem to be influenced by evoked set more than mature brand A.

*Confidence in Choice of Brand.* Confidence is an endogenous variable. The term refers to the extent to which the individual trusts his ability to judge the brand. The concept "confidence," as defined here, applies to the individual brand and not to "product class." To determine the respondent's confidence in ability to judge the brand, respondents were asked whether, with respect to the brand, they were extremely confident, very confident, somewhat confident, only slightly confident, or not confident at all.

Hypothesis: The more confidence people have in their ability to judge the brand, the more favorable their attitude and purchase intention will be toward the brand.

Howard and Sheth[4] postulate that confidence and intention are directly related. We also know that intention is a modification of attitude-integrating constraints. Consequently, attitude, intention, and confidence are related.

Findings:

1.  Level of confidence is directly related to the levels of attitude and purchase intention toward any brand, mature or new.

2.  The impact of confidence is the strongest on purchase intention toward mature brand A. For new brands B and C, it is at one time attitude, another time intention that is most influenced by confidence.

3.  The more successful a brand is (this is the case of mature brand A when compared to new brands B and C), the more people tend to be confident in their ability to judge the brand.

4.  The impact of confidence is stronger on mature brand A than on new brands B and C.

*Satisfaction.* Satisfaction is an endogenous variable. It is defined as the buyer's cognitive state of being adequately or inadequately rewarded in a buying situation for the sacrifice he has undergone.[4] Brand users were asked whether their satisfaction with the brand was extreme, quite, slight, or none.

Hypothesis: The higher the satisfaction with the brand, the more favorable the attitude and purchase intention toward the brand.

Reinforcement of past experience, indeed, will upgrade the level of attitude and purchase intention toward the brand.

Findings:

1.  Level of satisfaction is directly related to level of attitude and purchase intention.

2.  Satisfaction exerts a stronger influence on attitude than on intention.

3.  Satisfaction exercises a stronger impact on mature brand A than on new brands B and C.

4.   It was found that more people were extremely satisfied with mature brand A when it is compared to new brands B and C. In fact, it appears that the buyer bothers to inform himself only about the brand he likes.

*Housewife's Education.* Housewife's education is an exogenous variable. Respondents were asked what was the last grade completed in school.

Hypothesis: Attitude and intention will be inversely related to the respondent's education level.

Educated people, indeed, will tend to be more demanding as a result of their education and likely higher incomes. They will thus be more severe toward the brand.

Findings:

1.   Attitude toward mature brand A and new brand C is inversely related to the respondent's education level.
2.   Purchase intention tends to be inversely related to the respondent's education level. The statement is supported by the findings for all brands.
3.   Education level tends to influence attitude more than intention.
4.   Level of education has a stronger impact on mature brand A than on new brands B and C.

*Importance of Purchase.* Importance of purchase is an exogenous variable. Howard and Sheth[4] include in importance of purchase the criteria by which the buyer ranks a range of product classes in terms of his motive; it is a measure that indicates how much effort will be spent to get information. Respondents were asked to state whether their interest in differences among brands of product class ABC is extreme, much, somewhat, only slight, or none.

Hypothesis: Level of interest in differences among brands is directly related to levels of attitude and purchase intention toward the brand.

Indeed, interest reflects the respondent's sensitivity to information about the brand. According to the Howard-Sheth theory, information feeds brand comprehension, which in turn affects attitude, which affects intention.

Findings:

1.   Attitude and purchase intention toward the brand are directly related to the level of importance of purchase.
2.   Importance of purchase tends to influence purchase intention more than attitude.

3.    Importance of purchase influences mature brand A more than new brands B and C.

4.    The smaller the interest in differences among brands, the more respondents with lower values of attitude and intention.

## D.  Diagnosis of the Brands

To examine the performance of brands A, B, and C, the writer looked at several indices that are not reproduced in the present paper. Figures and more detailed information should be referred to the original work.[7] We reproduce here the average attitude and purchase intention and the correlation coefficients between both variables for the total sample (Table 6.1).

Brand A shows a stable pattern over time for any results considered. The results achieved by brand A are consistently better than those of new brands B and C. Brand A has definitely reached its level of maturity.

Attitudes toward brand B show an upward pattern over time; the rate of increase is very low between T2 and T3 when compared to T1 and T2. Purchase intention toward this brand declines slowly over time. Inhibitors that are summarized in the single measure of intention, and that might be identified graphically (in some way) as the distance between attitude and intention, increase their activity over time.

Brand C shows a U curve pattern with no significant improvement over time for the results considered. Inhibitors also become more active over time.

For any point in time, on an interbrand basis, i.e., mature brand A versus new brands B and C, the range of purchase intentions is wider than the range of attitudes. Purchase intention is on the positive side of the intention scale for brand A and on the negative side for new brands B and C. Attitude is on the positive side of the attitude scale for all brands. The "distance" between attitude and intention is the smallest for brand A and the greatest for brand B.

At the absolute level, attitude is consistently higher than purchase intention. This was also found for all the results dealing with the classificatory variables.

The correlation between attitude and intention toward mature brand A is consistently higher than the correlation between attitude and intention toward new brands B and C.

In addition several indices other than attitudes toward specific brand attributes[7] show that, at T3, new brands B and C seem to have reached a plateau at an absolute level significantly inferior to that of mature brand A. In addition, in terms of satisfaction of consumers' needs, new brands B and C do not seem to have succeeded in building an image differentiated from brand A.

## Table 6.1

### Correlation Coefficients between Attitude and Purchase Intention toward the Brand Average Attitude and Purchase Intention

|  | Mature Brand A | | | | New Brand B | | | New Brand C | | |
|---|---|---|---|---|---|---|---|---|---|---|
|  | MQ | T1 | T2 | T3 | T1 | T2 | T3 | T1 | T2 | T3 |
| Correlation (r) | 0.659 | 0.610 | 0.599 | 0.631 | 0.483 | 0.554 | 0.480 | 0.254 | 0.481 | 0.504 |
| Attitude | 4.78 | 5.31 | 5.25 | 5.22 | 4.94 | 4.77 | 5.00 | 4.76 | 4.60 | 4.80 |
| Intention | 3.33 | 3.20 | 3.08 | 3.18 | 2.97 | 2.61 | 2.56 | 2.65 | 2.41 | 2.52 |
| Sample Size | 701 | 665 | 607 | 633 | 256 | 390 | 475 | 110 | 229 | 374 |

MQ = Mail Questionnaire
$T_1$, $T_2$, $T_3$ refer to Telephone Interviews at different points in time.

## 4. CONCLUDING COMMENTS

### A. Overview

The findings are summarized in Table 6.2, dealing with the impact of the classificatory variables on attitude and purchase intention toward mature brand A and new brands B and C.

Table 6.2

Impact of Classificatory Variables on Attitude and
Intention toward the Brand

| Classificatory Variables | Stronger Impact On | | | |
|---|---|---|---|---|
| | Attitude | Intention | Brand A | Brand B, C |
| *Endogenous* | | + | | |
| Evoked set | | | | + |
| Confidence | | + | + | |
| Satisfaction | + | | | |
| *Exogenous* | | | | |
| Education | + | | + | |
| Importance of purchase | | + | + | |
| *Input* | | | | |
| Advertising | | + | | + |
| Word-of-mouth | | + | | + |
| Lack of availability | | + | | + |
| *Output* | | | | |
| Elapsed time since last purchase | | + | + | |
| Usership | | + | + | |

Findings may be summarized as follows:

1.  The classificatory variables simultaneously influence attitude and purchase intention.

2.  The magnitude of that influence is not identical for both attitude and intention.

3.  The magnitude of influence of these classificatory variables is not identical for mature brand A and new brands B and C.

4.  Correlation between attitude and intention toward the brand confirms other results.[3,4]

## B. Implications for Marketing and Future Research

We see two main implications in the area of marketing strategy. One is the use of inhibitors as detectors of a brand's success or failure, the other is the use of confidence and importance of purchase as a basis for segmenting the market.

Findings have demonstrated that new brands B and C have not succeeded in being admitted into the respondents' favorable purchase intentions. Over time, inhibitors affecting purchase intention toward new brands B and C increase in intensity. At T3, when compared to T2, we assessed that inhibitors affecting mature brand A were declining in intensity.

We realize that to draw valid conclusions our data should be matched against actual purchase behavior. We believe, however, that the examination of the inhibitors' intensity for all brands that compose the product class or the buyer's evoked set would be worthy of investigation as an element that greatly explains sales performance. *Inhibitors' intensity and sales performance are expected to be inversely related.*

It was shown that confidence, purchase intention, and attitude are associated. We also recognized that the more successful a brand is, the more confident people are about it. It is our belief that people who are not confident or are only somewhat confident are likely to be rather inconsistent in terms of actualizing their purchase intention. Respondents who are extremely confident in their brand choice are certainly more reliable. Segmenting the market on the basis of confidence in brand choice could certainly improve the forecasting ability of purchase intention (see Chapter 7).

What we just cited about confidence is also valid for importance of purchase as a criterion of segmentation. People who are extremely interested in differences among brands are likely to be more consistent in their intention-actual purchase behavior.

We thus propose that the forecasting ability of purchase intention is directly related to the level of confidence in brand choice and the level of importance of purchase to the buyer.

In terms of implications for future research, next to the examination of the other variables of the Howard-Sheth theory, and research in order to improve the attitude and intention scales, we feel that some other variables should be investigated:

1. For instance, the possibility of using a buyer's deliberateness measure as a basis of market segmentation that would improve the forecasting ability of buyer's intention or inhibitors. The possibility of operationalizing these dimensions should certainly be examined first.

2. Kollat and Willett[5] indicate that the intention typology could consist of major stages of planning. Either the customer knows product and

brand, or product only, or product class only; or he may only recognize the need for the product, or not even that.

3.   The Lavidge-Steiner model[6] points to an increasing probability of purchase as the consumer moves through the following stages: awareness, knowledge, liking, preference, and conviction. A segmentation of the respondents on that basis and a study of the extent to which these factors affect the level of attitude, of intention, and of actual purchase behavior are worthy of investigation.

There are certainly many topics related to ours that should be reviewed and examined to improve the forecasting ability of purchase intention measures. Inquiries about purchase intentions intercept the purchase process at a rather late stage. We should not rely on intention alone as a measuring tool of prospective purchase behavior since attitude provides more information on the consumer's reaction to the brand, but intention will better predict purchase.

Our study has shown that the black box of the buyer may not be so black after all. To be realistic, conclusions of any empirical investigation should be accepted within a framework of probability of stability or of change of factors affecting the experiment over time. In simpler words, the time dimension should never be evaded.

**References**

1. Doob, Leonard, "The Behavior of Attitudes," *Psychological Review* LIV (1947): 135–156.
2. Ferber, Robert, and Hugh W. Wales, *Motivation and Market Behavior* (Homewood, Illinois: Richard D. Irwin, 1958).
3. Fishbein, Martin, "The Relationship between Beliefs, Attitudes and Behavior," in S. Feldman, ed., *Cognitive Consistency, Motivational Antecedents and Behavioral Consequents* (New York: Academic Press, 1966), pp. 199–223.
4. Howard, John A., and Jagdish N. Sheth, *The Theory of Buyer Behavior* (New York: John Wiley & Sons, Inc., 1969).
5. Kollat, David T., and Ronald P. Willett, "Customer Impulse Purchasing Behavior," *Journal of Marketing Research* IV (February 1967): 21–31.
6. Lavidge, Robert J., and Gary A. Steiner, "A Model for Predictive Measurements of Advertising Effectiveness," *Journal of Marketing* XXV (October 1961): 59–62.
7. Pellemans, Paul A., "Investigations on Attitude and Purchase Intention toward the Brand" (Doctoral Dissertation, Graduate School of Business, Columbia University, 1970).

# 7.   Attitude Stability, Changeability, and Predictive Ability

George S. Day

Attitude researchers and theorists have long recognized that the polarity of an attitude toward an object provides only partial information about the strength of motives relevant to behavior toward that object.[8] Two additional motive properties that are often considered are *involvement* with the attitude object and *confidence* in the attitude judgment. The key feature of those two motive properties is that they jointly determine the stability of the observed attitude. As the Sherifs[10] have found in their studies of attitude change, it is this component of the attitude structure that largely determines the ease with which an attitude can be changed.*

With the exception of the Howard-Sheth theory of buyer behavior,[6] which treats confidence as a central construct, the marketing literature has devoted little attention to these variables. The consequent lack of empirical data has made it difficult to appraise their importance. The purpose of this paper is to remedy this lack within the context of the data from the Buyer Behavior Research Project. The emphasis will be on the effect of attitude stability on the rate of change of brand attitudes and the predictive value of these attitudes.

## THE NATURE OF ATTITUDE STABILITY

Although involvement and confidence are closely associated, they do have different characteristics and implications, so we will look at them separately.

*Stability is closely related to cognitive complexity, "the richness of the ideational content or the number of ideas the person has about the subject."[9]

130

## Involvement

This describes the general level of interest in the object, or the centrality of the object to the respondent's ego. The specific roles that involvement plays have been well summarized by Engel, Kollat, and Blackwell: (1) Attitudes are easier to change when the existing mass of stored information is small. (2) Attitudes having centrality are the most resistant to change: "This is a function of the extent to which the object is intimately related to the self-concept, important values or motives." (3) "Attitudes that are highly interconnected with others resist change. Human beings strive, of course, to retain balance in an attitude system, and change in one generally leads to change in another."[3]

Studies of involvement in the marketing context have focused on differences between products.* From such studies** Bogart has developed some basic propositions about product interest:

1.   An expensive item is more likely to arouse the consumer's emotional involvement. . . .

2.   A product about which the consumer feels deeply is most likely to arouse an active, purposeful search for information when he is in the market.

3.   A product category in which the customer perceives brands as being very different creates a more purposeful selective interest in advertising.

4.   Most products . . . arouse comparatively little involvement. They are likely to be inexpensive and they demand rather effortless or routine decision making.[1]

The difficulty with applying this concept of involvement to brand attitudes is that high product interest will not necessarily lead to a strong interest in the differences between brands. This is likely to be the case when the buyer is interested in the benefits that can be delivered by the product, but doesn't perceive that there are significant differences between brands. Of course, lack of interest in the product class will usually result in a lack of interest in the differences between brands. Nonetheless, whenever we are talking about brand attitudes the relevant information is always the most specific, so measures of brand interest are always preferred.

---

*See, for example, Howard and Sheth, which equates involvement with importance of purchase as "the saliency of one product class with respect to another."
**In one of these studies interest was a function of: (1) the degree to which the consumer found the product pleasant, or pleasant to use; (2) the degree of interest in reading and hearing about new developments in the product field; and (3) willingness to talk about the product.

**Confidence**

The degree of confidence depends on the amount of uncertainty about the correctness of the brand judgment, or ambiguity as to the meaning of the attitude object. Both these factors depend, in turn, on the amount of information the buyer has about the brand. A lack of information may result either because the buyer is seeking information but can't obtain enough with a reasonable search cost or because the buyer is not interested in obtaining information.

The latter reason suggests that there is likely to be a significant relationship between interest in the difference between brands and confidence in brand judgments. This relationship is described in Table 7.1, using data from the mail questionnaire. For each of four products, the respondents were asked, "How interested are you in differences among brands?" and "How confident are you in your ability to judge between different brands of these products?" Products D and E are reasonably similar (in terms of use opportunities, product characteristics, and so forth) to the product class of primary interest during the market test. The other two products, aspirin and detergents, were included because they were known to be high interest products, and had average prices similar to those of products D and E.

The results strongly support the hypothesis of a relationship between confidence and interest. The measure of association, Goodman-Kruskal Gamma, which was chosen because it has a proportional reduction of variance interpretation, ranged from 0.41 for aspirin to 0.67 for product D. Examination of the off-diagonal entries reveals no clear-cut pattern. That is, there is no tendency for high confidence to be associated with low interest or vice versa. In view of the strength of the relationship between interest and confidence, the question is whether one of these measures alone is a satisfactory proxy for attitude stability. In the next section we describe a model that provides a partial criterion for the choice of one measure over the other.

## A MODEL OF THE ATTITUDE-BEHAVIOR RELATIONSHIP

During the development of this model,[2] it was argued that any model that attempts to understand how attitudes predict subsequent brand-choice decisions must consider simultaneously (i) the inhibiting and facilitating effects of the environment, and (ii) that the extent of these effects depends on the stability as well as the polarity of the attitude. First we will describe a general model with the above characteristics, and then test it with data for one brand of an established and stable convenience food product that was not a substitute for the brand that was being market tested.

Table 7.1

Relationship of Confidence and Interest

1. *Brand D*

Confidence in Brand Judgments

|  |  | Extremely or very | Somewhat | Slightly or not at all | Total |
|---|---|---|---|---|---|
| Interest in differences between brands | Extremely or very | 138 | 68 | 20 | 226 |
|  | Somewhat | 52 | 95 | 49 | 196 |
|  | Slightly or not at all | 57 | 67 | 391 | 515 |
|  | Total | 247 | 230 | 460 | 927 |

2. *Brand E*

|  |  |  |  |  |  |
|---|---|---|---|---|---|
| Interest in differences between brands | Extremely or very | 158 | 80 | 25 | 263 |
|  | Somewhat | 64 | 105 | 51 | 220 |
|  | Slightly or not at all | 53 | 77 | 301 | 432 |
|  | Total | 275 | 262 | 377 | 915 |

3. *Aspirin*

|  |  |  |  |  |  |
|---|---|---|---|---|---|
| Interest in differences between brands | Extremely or very | 280 | 101 | 22 | 403 |
|  | Somewhat | 51 | 102 | 34 | 187 |
|  | Slightly or not at all | 108 | 75 | 153 | 336 |
|  | Total | 439 | 278 | 209 | 926 |

4. *Detergent*

|  |  |  |  |  |  |
|---|---|---|---|---|---|
| Interest in differences between brands | Extremely or very | 432 | 170 | 31 | 633 |
|  | Somewhat | 53 | 109 | 31 | 193 |
|  | Slightly or not at all | 25 | 31 | 59 | 115 |
|  | Total | 510 | 310 | 121 | 941 |

## The Nature of the Model

The *inputs* to the model are assumed to be an interval scale measure of a brand attitude at one point in time and an estimate of the probability of purchasing the brand during a subsequent period of time (this probability is conditional on purchase of the product class). In this model we will treat brand attitudes as unidimensional measures of affect (or evaluation), on the assumption that there is congruency between this affect component, the cognitive (knowledge) component, and the conative (intentions) component of the attitude. When there is congruency, of course, the additional components do not add information that will improve predictions. This assumption has been supported in many circumstances,[4] but will be tested in this situation. The interval scale assumption is more difficult to support. However, the available evidence on the semantic differential scale[7] indicates that this assumption is tenable within acceptable error limits.

For convenience we will describe the model in functional form, assuming that the relationship of attitude to subsequent behavior is linear. However, any monotonically changing function would serve just as well.

$$P\{K|P\}_i = a - \beta A_i + u_i \qquad i = 1, \ldots, n \qquad (1)$$

where:

$P\{K|P\}_i = $ the estimated probability of person $i$ buying brand K, given the purchase of product P, in the fixed time period considered.

$A_i = $ the *initial* attitude of person $i$ toward brand K (scaled so that a very favorable attitude has a low score).

$\beta = f$(inhibiting and facilitating effects of the environ- (2) ment, when estimated over all $n$ buyers of the product).

$u_i = f$(stability of attitude, buying style, nature of the (3) environment encountered and random error).

The environment referred to in Equation (2) includes the relative attraction of competing brands, the preferences of family and friends, changes in advertising and promotion, price changes, out-of-stocks, and so forth. These influences will tend to *inhibit* the behavior of buyers who were initially very favorable toward the brand. The main reason is that these buyers are unable to increase their probability of purchase (because of the ceiling effect), and may well reduce it. Thus, for the set of buyers with extremely favorable attitudes, the *average* observed effect is a reduced probability of choice. The same argument holds for the *facilitating* effect of the environment on the behavior of buyers who were initially neutral or unfavorable toward the brand. Thus there is some chance a person will buy a brand she doesn't like, if the deal is very attractive or her favorite brand is out of stock.* The slope parameter, $\beta$, measures the extent of the influence of the environment. A small value of $\beta$ implies that behavior is largely determined by conditions at or near the time of purchase, and that prior knowledge of buyer's brand attitude contributes very little information.

Equation (3) provides a specific recognition that buyers with the same initial evaluation may respond differently to similar environmental influences (deals, price changes, promotions, displays, out-of-stocks, and so forth) encountered during the time period being studied. In part, the differences in response will depend on the stability of the initial attitude. As discussed above, stable attitudes are more difficult to change and thus will be less influenced by the environment they encounter. There is the further possibility that the person's "buying style" will have much the same effect. Here we are thinking of various characteristics of buyers, such as perceived impulsiveness, innovativeness, and economy consciousness, that have been recently developed to explain facets of buying behavior. Such measures fit logically into this model since they also provide information about differences in responses to similar environmental influences. Finally, Equation (3) also accounts for differences in the environmental influences encountered. For example, not all buyers will encounter the same proportion of out-of-stocks.

### Estimating the Predictive Relationship

In this particular case, the attitude scale was a seven-point semantic differential scale with opposite poles reading "In general I like it" and "In general I don't like it" (scaled so a favorable attitude had a low score).

The *linear* least-squares regression equation for the relationship was:

$$P\{K|P\}_i = 71.6 - 9.8A_i + u_i \qquad (4)$$

$$(1.16)$$

$r^2 = 0.242$ and $F(1,218) = 71.3$, significant $p < .001$.

These results were not significantly altered with a logarithmic transform of the predictor variable, or with higher-order polynomial regression equations.

---

*This "damping" effect of the environment will also lead to attitude change. In particular, extreme values will move toward the mean attitude value.

The relative flatness of the slope of the relationship, coupled with the modest proportion of response variability absorbed, suggests that environmental influences have a considerable impact on brand-choice decisions in this product class. The next question is whether this is equally true for all segments.

### Defining Segments of Homogeneous Response

The segment dimensions were chosen from the two largest Beta coefficients in a multiple regression equation with the residual of Equation (4) as dependent variable, and the variables in Table 7.2 as independent

Table 7.2

Independent Variable Descriptions

A. *Determinants of the stability of the attitude.*

   1. Interest in the differences among brands in the product class.
   2. Confidence in judgments about brands in the product class.

B. *Determinants of "buying style."*

   3. Perceived impulsiveness in buying.
   4. Economy consciousness.
   5. Perceived time pressure.

C. *Demand, price, and store response variables.*

   6. Total number of units purchased.
   7. Average price paid per unit.
   8. Range from highest to lowest price paid.
   9. Dealing dummy variable (0 = no purchases on deal).
  10. Store activity dummy variable (0 = all purchases of product made in one store).

D. *Exposure to information.*

  11. Number of visitors to house.
  12. Number of invitations to visit friends.
  13. Television viewing (hours per week by respondent).

E. *Socioeconomic and demographic variables.*

  14. Size of city.
  15. Size of household.
  16. Age of housewife.
  17. Presence of children.
  18. Education of housewife.
  19. Occupation of head of household.
  20. Household income.
  21. Hours housewife employed.

variables. The subscripts in Equation (5) correspond to the order of the independent variables in Table 7.2. The coefficients are in Beta form.

$$u_i = 2.62 + 0.166X_{20} + 0.165X_2 + 0.161X_{10} + 0.155X_7 + 0.110X_{11} \quad (5)$$

$$+ 0.105X_{14}$$

$$R^2 = 0.153 \text{ and } F(21,190) = 1.60, \text{ significant } p < .05.$$

According to this result the two variables that account for the largest amount of variability in response to environmental influences are household income ($X_{20}$) and confidence in judgments about the brands in the product class ($X_2$). These two variables are combined to define six segment groups. The coefficient for interest in difference between products ($X_1$) was not significant.

**Differences in Segment Response Characteristics**

Several interesting patterns emerge when the attitude-subsequent behavior relationship is estimated separately for each segment group. The results are summarized in Table 7.3. If we look at the extreme groups, which are 1 (high confidence—high income) and 5 (low confidence—high income), the differences in the *slopes* ($\beta$ of 14.4 versus 4.7) and in the *dispersion* ($R^2$ of .540 versus .041) are startling.

The income variable plays an interesting role as an *intensifier* of the differences between groups. This can be seen from a separate analysis, when confidence alone was used as the basis for classifying the sample into segment groups. Then the spread in $R^2$ between the high and low confidence groups was 0.454 to 0.125, which means the dispersion differs by a factor of 13.2 when income is included and only 3.6 when it is not included. In either case consideration of attitude stability is crucial to an understanding of the predictive value of brand attitudes. Fortunately it appears feasible to use the measure of confidence as the proxy for attitude stability, thus avoiding the complexity of a two-dimensional variable.

**Choice of Evaluative Versus Intentions Components**

So far we have used the evaluative component of attitudes as the basis for study, on the assumption that it is congruent with purchase intentions. Yet intentions are often regarded as more useful than evaluations, particularly for the purpose of predicting behavior, because (a) "intentions combine a

## Table 7.3

### Comparison of Segment Groups

| Group | Size of Group | Means of Classification | | $R^2$ (Adjusted) | Coefficients | Mean Values | |
| --- | --- | --- | --- | --- | --- | --- | --- |
| | | Confidence in judgments | Income | | | Attitude $(A_i)$ | Behavior $P\{K|P\}_i$ |
| 1 | 25 | High | High | .540[a] | $P\{K|P\}_i = 83.0 - 14.4A_i$ (2.8) | 2.52 | .611 |
| 2 | 28 | High | Low | .415[a] | $P\{K|P\}_i = 70.9 - 11.8A_i$ (2.7) | 2.60 | .518 |
| 3 | 56 | Medium | High | .225[a] | $P\{K|P\}_i = 71.6 - 11.0A_i$ (2.8) | 3.27 | .467 |
| 4 | 47 | Medium | Low | .192[a] | $P\{K|P\}_i = 71.0 - 8.1A_i$ (2.5) | 2.46 | .591 |
| 5 | 29 | Low | High | .041 | $P\{K|P\}_i = 51.9 - 4.7A_i$ (4.4) | 3.55 | .399 |
| 6 | 35 | Low | Low | .245[a] | $P\{K|P\}_i = 77.0 - 8.8A_i$ (2.7) | 3.45 | .553 |
| Total Sample | 220 | — | — | .242 | $P\{K|P\}_i = 71.6 - 9.8A_i$ (1.16) | 3.00 | .519 |

[a]Significant $P < .005$.

consumer's regard for the item with an assessment of its purchase probability,"[11] and (b) following a related argument, intentions measures are thought to be more closely related to confidence, and thus to contain more information.[5] Both these assertions can be empirically examined here. The findings are, of course, not projectible beyond this product class, but will provide preliminary guidance.

The question of predictive ability was tested by introducing a five-point intentions measure into a multiple regression equation with purchase probability as the dependent variable, after attitudes had already been used. The effect was to increase the $R^2$ from .242 to .251. The partial correlation coefficient for the intentions measure was not significant, indicating that most of the information relevant to predicting behavior was contained in the attitude measure.

The related question, of the relationship of confidence to attitude and intentions, requires the use of data from product D, which is in the class into which the new brand (B) was introduced. Attitudes, intentions, and confidence data were obtained for new brand B, and an established brand A of the same product, during all three telephone interviews. Figure 7.1 compares these two brands, during the first and third interviews, in terms of the proportion of respondents in each response category who said they were "extremely" or "very" confident of their ability to judge each brand.

Two features of the data in Figure 7.1 are noteworthy. First is that attitudes (as evaluations) and intentions differ primarily in the shape of their relationship with confidence. The relationship with attitudes is distinctly nonmonotonic, with the neutral region of the scale having the smallest proportion of high confidence respondents. The relationship with intentions is monotonic from "definitely will buy" (in the next month) to "definitely will not buy," but the shape and rate of descent of the slope is very similar to the slope from an extremely positive to a neutral attitude.* Overall it appears that both measures contain approximately the same amount of information about confidence. The second finding of interest is the building of confidence between the first and third interviews. The effect is most pronounced for the

---

*Despite the nonmonotonic relationship of confidence and attitude, the association between those two variables is fairly close to that between intentions and confidence (in these results the entire confidence scale was used).

| Brand (Interview) | Relationship with Confidence (Goodman-Kruskal Gamma) | |
| --- | --- | --- |
| | Attitude (evaluation) | Intentions |
| Brand B (T$_1$) | .78 | .89 |
| Brand B (T$_3$) | .62 | .78 |
| Brand A (T$_1$) | .40 | .66 |
| Brand A (T$_3$) | .61 | .78 |

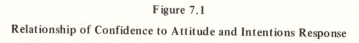

Figure 7.1

Relationship of Confidence to Attitude and Intentions Response

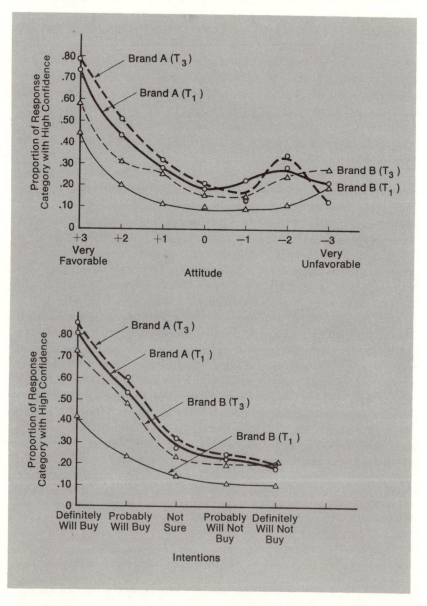

"probably will buy" intention category for both brands, as perhaps this somewhat ambivalent category is most influenced by panel membership and usage experience or information exposure.

## ATTITUDE STABILITY AND ATTITUDE CHANGE

An important inference from the model of the attitude-behavior relationship is that high confidence in brand judgment is associated with attitudes that are more difficult to change, and thus are less influenced by changes in the environment. Evidence has already been presented on the extent of the influence of the environment on groups of buyers with varying degrees of attitude stability. Now we turn to the effect of attitude stability on the amount of attitude change.

The results are based on the amount of change in attitude toward brands B and A (the new and established brands, respectively) between the second ($T_2$) and third ($T_3$) telephone interviews. For each brand taken separately, the sample was first split into high, medium, and low confidence groups* according to the response in the second telephone interview ($T_2$). Then, for each of the three groups, a turnover table was formed by cross-tabulating the attitude response at $T_2$ with the attitude response at $T_3$. In order to facilitate comparisons between turnover tables in Table 7.4, all data were standardized by dividing each cell value by the row sum. These results can be interpreted as transition probabilities.

A consistent consequence of a decrease in confidence in judgments of both brands is a decline in the proportion of respondents who remained in the favorable category** between $T_2$ and $T_3$. For brand B, for example, the probability of a person with high confidence remaining in the positive category is 120 percent greater than the probability when confidence is low. This is completely consistent with our hypothesis about the relationship of attitude change and confidence. It is surprising that this is the only diagonal entry that demonstrates this predicted pattern of change. In fact the level of confidence has *no* impact on the amount of change in the "neutral/unfavorable" or "aware only" categories for the new brand (B), while there is *less* change in the "neutral/unfavorable" category for the established brand (A) as confidence decreases. These contrary results are primarily an artifact of the

---

*These three categories were derived from a five-point scale: extremely and very confident = high; somewhat confident = medium; and slightly or not at all confident = low.

**The favorable category includes the two most favorable responses on a seven-point semantic differential scale. The remaining five responses were combined into a "neutral/unfavorable" category. A further category included those who were aware of the brand but did not have an attitude.

## Table 7.4

### The Effect of Attitude Stability on Amount of Attitude Change

#### Brand B (New)

| At T₂ | | Favorable | Neutral/ Unfavorable | Aware | Not Aware | n |
|---|---|---|---|---|---|---|
| (A) | Total Sample: | | | | | |
| | Favorable | .59 | .22 | .13 | .06 | 173 |
| | Neutral/unfavorable | .20 | .60 | .12 | .08 | 164 |
| | Aware (without attitude) | .27 | .36 | .25 | .12 | 151 |
| | Not aware | .12 | .24 | .18 | .46 | 152 |
| | | | | | | 640 |
| (B) | High Confidence | | | | | |
| | Favorable | .72 | .17 | .08 | .03 | 85 |
| | Neutral/unfavorable | .27 | .60 | .07 | .06 | 30 |
| | Aware | .30 | .45 | .24 | .05 | 20 |
| | | | | | | 135 |
| (C) | Medium Confidence | | | | | |
| | Favorable | .55 | .25 | .14 | .06 | 56 |
| | Neutral/unfavorable | .13 | .57 | .16 | .14 | 42 |
| | Aware | .40 | .20 | .24 | .16 | 25 |
| | | | | | | 123 |
| (D) | Low Confidence | | | | | |
| | Favorable | .34 | .34 | .22 | .10 | 32 |
| | Neutral/unfavorable | .20 | .61 | .12 | .07 | 92 |
| | Aware | .24 | .40 | .26 | .10 | 93 |
| | | | | | | 217 |

At T₃

## Table 7.4 (Cont.)

*Brand A* (Established)

| At T$_2$ | | Favorable | At T$_3$ Neutral/ Unfavorable | Aware | n |
|---|---|---|---|---|---|
| (A) | Total Sample | | | | |
| | Favorable | .78 | .16 | .06 | 313 |
| | Neutral/unfavorable | .24 | .65 | .11 | 208 |
| | Aware (without attitude) | .16 | .52 | .32 | 113 |
| | Not aware | * | * | * | 6 |
| | | | | | 640 |
| (B) | High Confidence | | | | |
| | Favorable | .85 | .12 | .03 | 223 |
| | Neutral/unfavorable | .40 | .52 | .08 | 52 |
| | Aware | .26 | .52 | .22 | 19 |
| | | | | | 294 |
| (C) | Medium Confidence | | | | |
| | Favorable | .62 | .27 | .11 | 56 |
| | Neutral/unfavorable | .32 | .56 | .12 | 62 |
| | Aware | .13 | .45 | .42 | 22 |
| | | | | | 140 |
| (D) | Low Confidence | | | | |
| | Favorable | .48 | .29 | .23 | 35 |
| | Neutral/unfavorable | .10 | .76 | .14 | 93 |
| | Aware | .14 | .55 | .31 | 62 |
| | | | | | 190 |

Attitude change during period T$_2$ to T$_3$; stability based on level of confidence at T$_2$. Data are normalized.

large number of scale positions that were combined to make up the "neutral/unfavorable" category. A respondent could move anywhere within the five scale positions without recording a change. As a result a great deal of actual change has been masked from view.

A second deficiency of this analysis of the relationship of confidence and attitude change is that it does not explicitly account for a concurrent change in confidence. In fact, as Table 7.5 shows, confidence is as likely to change as attitude. This is particularly true for the new brand (B) between $T_2$ and $T_3$, when the pool of respondents who had heard of the brand or had tried it was still growing. At the same time, many respondents who first heard of or tried

**Table 7.5**

**Change in Confidence ($T_2$ to $T_3$)**

*Brand B*

| | | | Confidence $T_3$ | | | |
|---|---|---|---|---|---|---|
| | | High | Medium | Low | Not aware | *n* |
| Confidence $T_2$ | High | .52 | .24 | .18 | .06 | 135 |
| | Medium | .25 | .36 | .27 | .11 | 123 |
| | Low | .11 | .24 | .53 | .12 | 217 |
| | Not aware | .14 | .15 | .25 | .46 | 165 |
| | | | | | | 640 |

*Brand A*

| | | High | Medium | Low | Not aware | |
|---|---|---|---|---|---|---|
| Confidence $T_2$ | High | .76 | .16 | .07 | .01 | 294 |
| | Medium | .30 | .44 | .22 | .04 | 139 |
| | Low | .13 | .26 | .57 | .04 | 190 |
| | Not aware | .12 | .18 | .70 | . 0 | 17 |
| | | | | | | 640 |

Cell values are standardized.

the brand before $T_2$ probably heard nothing subsequently to reinforce or even maintain their previous level of confidence. This is an important consideration in the analysis of attitude change, because a loss of confidence may well lead to a less favorable attitude, and vice versa. Thus the data on attitude change in Table 7.5 represent both a change in attitude and a change in confidence.

## SUMMARY AND CONCLUSIONS

This paper has focused on the nature and effects of attitude stability, which is a component of motive strength only partially measured by attitude polarity. Although stability represents the joint effect of interest in the difference between brands and confidence in brand judgments, it is feasible to use confidence alone. To some extent, confidence is related to both attitude intensity and the likelihood of purchase, but the strength of the relationship indicates that the measure does provide different information about the structure of attitudes.

Two effects of different levels of confidence were identified. The first was the association of high confidence (which implies stable attitudes) with attitudes that are more difficult to change. Consequently, the more stable attitudes are less influenced by the environment and thus are much better predictors of subsequent purchase behavior. This is the most important finding reported here, for it shows that a good deal of the unimpressive performance of brand attitudes is traceable to one or two market segments with unstable attitudes. Within these segments interbrand differences are virtually meaningless and each brand choice is largely based on the environmental situation at the time of purchase.

## References

1. Bogart, Leo, *Strategy in Advertising* (New York: Harcourt, Brace and World, 1967).
2. Day, George S., *Buyer Attitudes and Brand Choice Behavior* (New York: Free Press, 1970).
3. Engel, James F., David T. Kollat, and Roger D. Blackwell, *Consumer Behavior* (New York: Holt, Rinehart and Winston, 1968).
4. Fishbein, Martin, "The Relationship between Beliefs, Attitudes and Behavior," in S. Feldman, ed., *Cognitive Consistency, Motivational Antecedents and Behavioral Consequences* (New York: Academic Press, 1966).
5. Howard, John A., "Confidence as a Validated Construct" (unpublished paper, Graduate School of Business, Columbia University, 1968).
6. Howard, John A., and Jagdish N. Sheth, *The Theory of Buyer Behavior* (New York: John Wiley & Sons, Inc., 1969).
7. Osgood, Charles E., G. J. Suci, and P. H. Tannenbaum, *The Measurement of Meaning* (Urbana: University of Illinois Press, 1957).
8. Peak, Helen, "Attitude and Motivation," in M. R. Jones, ed., *Nebraska Symposium on Motivation* (Lincoln: University of Nebraska Press, 1955), pp. 149–188.
9. Scott, W. A., "Attitude Measurement," in G. Lindzey and E. Aronson, *Handbook of Social Psychology* (Reading, Mass.: Addison-Wesley, 1968).
10. Sherif, Carolyn W., Muzafer Sherif, and Roger Nebergall, *Attitude and Attitude Change: The Social Judgment-Involvement Approach* (Philadelphia: Saunders, 1965).
11. Wells, William D., "Measuring Readiness to Buy," *Harvard Business Review* 39 (July-August 1961): 81–87.

# III

## System Stability

# 8. Simulation of Buyer Behavior

## Michael Perry

### INTRODUCTION

The purpose of the present work was to construct a computer simulation model that would be capable of predicting the consumer's choice among several brands of the same product class. The fundamental factors and processes of the model are derived from the Howard-Sheth theory of buyer behavior.[5] However, the model indicated only some of the variables and the functional relations that have to be measured for predicting consumer behavior.

In order to determine the usefulness of the model, some means of validation was needed. The data of the test market study were used for this purpose, and the validation was done by comparing the outcomes of the simulation model to the findings from the purchase diaries and telephone interviews.

To make the validation meaningful, all the data used as input to the model were gathered *before* the introduction of the new brand, namely, the data that were included in the mail questionnaire.

The data collected by the diaries and telephone interviews that were conducted *after* the introduction of the new brand were used merely for validation purposes, and were not integrated in the model's processes.

There were two reasons for that approach. First, if the same data had been used both for input and for validation, the results would not have been reliable. Second, the ultimate goal of building the model was to furnish a tool for predicting *future* consumer behavior on the basis of past behavior. In the present case particularly, the purpose of building the model was to replace the traditional market test and to predict the purchases of the new brand, even without introducing it in the market.

The validation of the model was done by using a specific case and a specific set of data. Thus, conclusions about the validity of the model can be drawn about that specific case and the model that replicates it. However, since the computer model is a particular case of a more general and basic model, the performance of the former throws some light on the latter.

## THE SIMULATION MODEL

Five major premises lie at the core of the Fundamental Structure of the Model Simulation:

1)    At any given point in time a consumer has particular motivations and attitudes, indicating his orientation and preference toward any product or brand in the market. This includes "indifference" or "null" attitude, the latter meaning that he never heard of the product.

2)    The attitude may or may not be important for the consumer's behavior, depending on his self-confidence in his ability to judge the product or the brands.

3)    The consumer's motivation, attitude, and self-confidence may change as a result of receiving information about the product or the relevant brands.

4)    Motivation, attitude, and self-confidence are the major determinants of the consumer's intention to buy, and thus a change in them is most likely to cause a change in his intention.

5)    The consumer's intention to buy will lead him to a purchase, unless there are some constraints on his intention, such as price and availability.

On the basis of these premises the components and determinants of the consumer's behavior are established. They may be divided into two major groups—those referring to and describing the consumer, and those referring to and describing the consumer's environment.

The main classes of the consumer's components are his personality traits, his behavioral habits (shopping, reading magazines, watching TV, etc.), and his disposition toward the product. The elements of his disposition are the motives, attitude, self-confidence, and intention-to-buy. Disposition is an intermediate variable for predicting the purchase behavior.

The consumer's environment can be considered, for the purpose of this model, as a collection of sources of information that affect his attitude, and consequently, his purchase. The major classes are personal communication (conversations with friends, family members, etc.), impersonal communication (messages from TV, magazines, billboards, and similar media), in-store cues (product display, package), and the product itself.

Since this is a computer model, it may be useful to describe its framework in terms of a computer program. Every computer program consists of three parts: input, process, and output. The input is all the data provided to the computer from external sources. The process is the changing of the input by the computer according to a predetermined set of rules and instructions. The output is the outcome of the process, provided by the computer. The three parts of the present model are shown in Figure 8.1. The input is the consumer's personality traits and the sources of information available to him. The process is the flow of information to the consumer and his decision making. The output is the purchasing behavior.

Figure 8.1

The Model's Elements

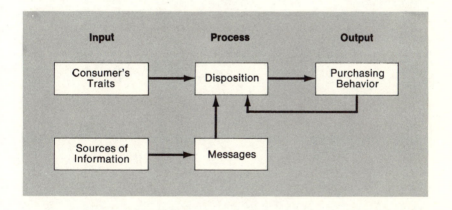

Once the components of the model are established, the functional relations among them are required in order to make the model operational. The basic process of the model is the flow of information in the form of messages from the different sources to the consumer. This process is portrayed in Figure 8.2.

Obviously, the consumer is not exposed to every message in the market. The degree of exposure depends mainly on the message's timing and location and the consumer's behavior habits, e.g., watching TV or reading magazines. Even when exposed to a message, the consumer does not necessarily perceive all its content. His perception depends mainly on the subject (product or brand), the source of the message, and his attitude toward the subject. A message may change the consumer's attitude either in a negative or in a

Figure 8.2
The Model's Fundamental Process: Flow of Information

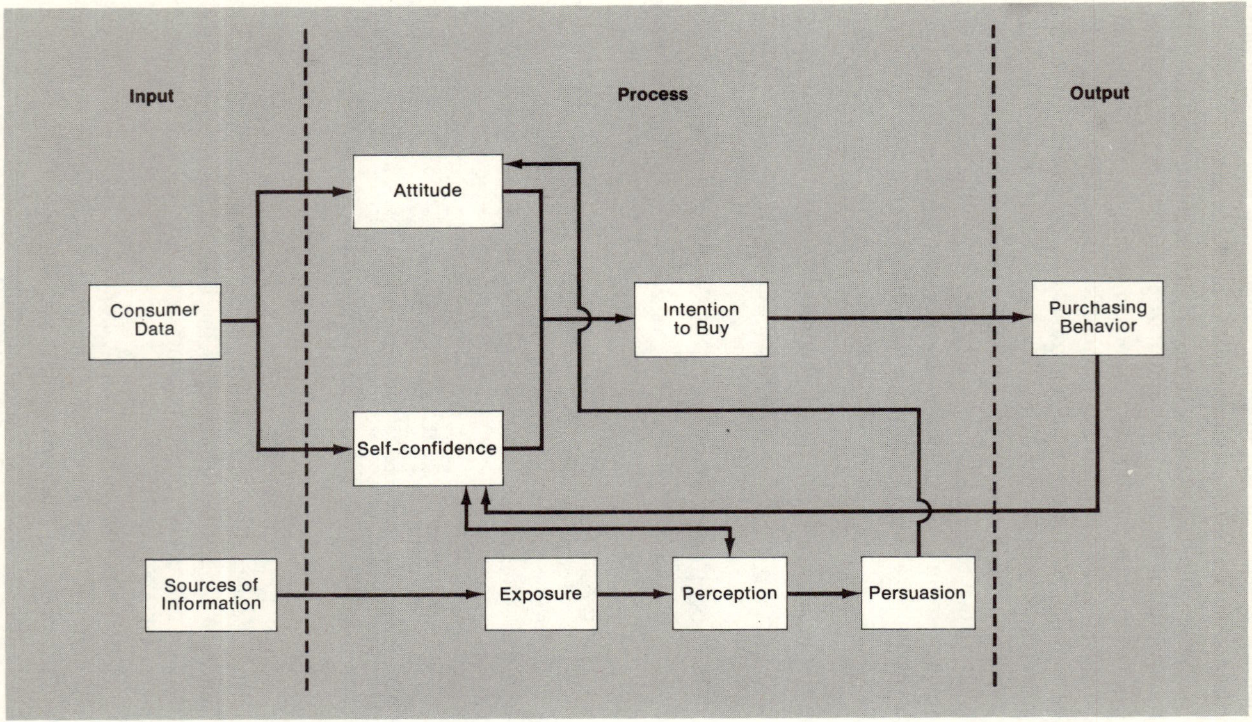

positive direction, depending on his previous attitude, the content of the message, and its power of persuasion. It may also change the consumer's self-confidence in judging the product, since accumulating additional information may increase his abilities to make a decision. These changes affect the consumer's intention to buy, and consequently, his behavior.

The final step of the sequence of changes is the decision to purchase (or not to purchase) a specific brand. The execution of this decision provides a feedback to the consumer, and serves as another source of information for the next purchase.

This step concludes the process of the model and achieves the goal of predicting the consumer's behavior.

A flow chart of the fundamental processes of the present simulation model is presented in Figure 8.3. The program starts by reading input data on the characteristics and disposition of the first consumer. These data are available from the mail questionnaire. On the basis of the disposition, the program computes the intention-to-buy for each brand. Then the program reads the data on sources of information. These data are predetermined, according to the promotion strategies of the relevant marketing management, or according to a random process.

After the input data is read, the consumer starts to accumulate information. The program examines each message available—as it was inserted in the input data—and answers the following questions: Is the message perceived? Is the message persuasive? How does it fit the direction of the previous disposition? If the message was not perceived, the program skips to the next message. If it was perceived, the program counts it, and answers the next question.

When all the messages available to the first consumer have been examined, the program computes the new disposition: the specific self-confidence, the attitude, and the intention-to-buy. From the last variable, the program derives the final decision: does the consumer buy or not buy the product, and which brand does he buy?

The entire period of the simulated test market was divided into ten two-week periods. Each such period is represented in the simulation model by a cycle. In other words, when the consumer goes through one complete process of accumulating information and making a purchase decision, it is assumed that two weeks have "passed." For another period of two weeks, he has to go through the process again.

After the first consumer completes his first cycle and makes his first purchase decision, the program starts reading input data for the second consumer. The program goes through the same process, until this second consumer also completes the first cycle and makes his decision. He is followed by all the other consumers. At the end of the first cycle and each

## Figure 8.3

## Flow Chart of Computer Model

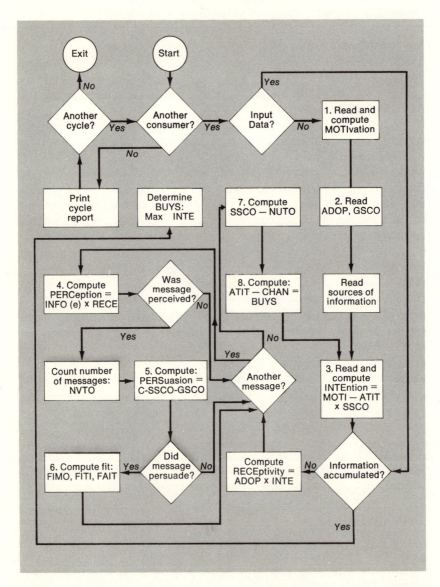

consecutive cycle of the final consumer, the program prints a report on the outcome of the cycle. This report includes the distributions of attitude, specific self-confidence, intention-to-buy, and the number of messages perceived. In addition, it includes the number of simulated consumers who bought each brand. These variables will serve as criteria for evaluation of the model.

## VALIDATION

### Internal Analysis

It might be useful to distinguish the following types of analyses, which were conducted to validate the present model: (a) Internal analysis; (b) Prediction analysis; (c) Sensitivity analysis. Each of these examined different criteria of validation.

Internal analysis examined the face validity, the dynamic validity, the static validity, and the internal validity.[4] The major question that this analysis attempted to answer was: Does the model, as it stands by itself and without any comparison to the real world, "make sense"? Internal analysis is done by running the simulation model many times on the computer. In each run, different parameters and variables are changed, usually one or two at a time. The outcome of each run is observed, and new changes are made until satisfactory results are obtained. The final outcome of the internal analysis is presented in Tables 8.1 and 8.2. Each "cycle" represents approximately two weeks in the "real world." The numbers in the body of the table are the means and the standard deviations of the variables in each cycle. Due to the large number of consumers, it was not possible to do the internal analysis on an individual basis.

What constitutes "satisfactory" results of the internal analysis depends on the criterion of validation. For face validity it is sufficient if "things seem right" to satisfy the investigator. This criterion is good for quick impression and intuitive evaluation. It appears that the results in Tables 8.1 and 8.2 do "seem right." The prediction of the number of consumers who will purchase the brand is derived proportionally from the value of the Intention-to-Buy. In turn, the latter is proportional to the functional relations of the Specific Self-Confidence and the Attitude. All these findings do not indicate yet that the relations postulated are "true" and reflect reality. All they indicate is that the internal logic of the model and the outcome of this logic "make sense."

For dynamic validity, the "viability" of the model has to be examined. It appears from the results that the model is viable. The appropriate variables change over time and the prediction is changed accordingly. The model definitely shows dynamic behavior similar to that in reality. At the same

## Table 8.1

### Final Output of Internal Analysis, Mean Values of Variables
### (Number of Consumers = 500)

| Variables | | | | | Cycle | | | | | |
|---|---|---|---|---|---|---|---|---|---|---|
| Old Brand | 1 | 2 | 3 | 4 | 5 | 6 | 7 | 8 | 9 | 10 |
| SSCO | 1.762 | 1.590 | 1.430 | 1.378 | 1.380 | 1.382 | 1.383 | 1.386 | 1.389 | 1.408 |
| ATIT | 1.142 | 1.274 | 1.430 | 1.526 | 1.646 | 1.706 | 1.778 | 1.826 | 1.862 | 1.898 |
| INTE | 5.222 | 6.246 | 7.186 | 8.150 | 8.766 | 9.550 | 10.046 | 10.662 | 11.266 | 12.032 |
| NUAD | 0.202 | 0.266 | 0.246 | 0.306 | 0.326 | 0.388 | 0.410 | 0.450 | 0.438 | 0.492 |
| NUCO | 0.114 | 0.110 | 0.132 | 0.162 | 0.182 | 0.182 | 0.184 | 0.228 | 0.230 | 0.292 |
| Buys | 50 | 53 | 58 | 60 | 55 | 50 | 52 | 56 | 58 | 63 |
| New Brand | | | | | | | | | | |
| SSCO | 1.432 | 0.868 | 0.312 | −0.232 | −0.780 | −1.392 | −1.936 | −2.496 | −3.148 | −3.784 |
| ATIT | 0.092 | 0.196 | 0.314 | 0.400 | 0.492 | 0.590 | 0.676 | 0.754 | 0.796 | 0.846 |
| INTE | 2.408 | 2.600 | 2.702 | 2.672 | 2.552 | 2.352 | 2.072 | 1.172 | 1.240 | 0.680 |
| NUAD | 0.174 | 0.196 | 0.178 | 0.186 | 0.174 | 0.166 | 0.188 | 0.206 | 0.156 | 0.154 |
| NUCO | 0.068 | 0.066 | 0.064 | 0.082 | 0.106 | 0.064 | 0.096 | 0.072 | 0.072 | 0.084 |
| Buys | 7 | 13 | 23 | 15 | 12 | 18 | 9 | 8 | 7 | 6 |

SSCO = Specific self-confidence in judging the brand
ATIT = Attitude toward the brand
INTE = Intention to buy the brand
NUAD = Number of ads perceived about the brand
NUCO = Number of conversations about the brand
Buys = Number of consumers that will buy the brand according to the model's prediction

## Table 8.2

### Final Output of Internal Analysis: Standard Deviations of Variables
### (Number of Consumers = 500)

Cycle

| Variables | 1 | 2 | 3 | 4 | 5 | 6 | 7 | 8 | 9 | 10 |
|---|---|---|---|---|---|---|---|---|---|---|
| **Old Brands** | | | | | | | | | | |
| SSCO | 1.805 | 1.952 | 1.973 | 1.985 | 1.997 | 2.003 | 2.015 | 2.024 | 2.151 | 2.203 |
| ATIT | 1.924 | 0.535 | 2.137 | 2.218 | 2.262 | 2.291 | 2.284 | 2.288 | 2.301 | 2.310 |
| INTE | 2.508 | 2.612 | 2.638 | 2.549 | 2.627 | 2.659 | 2.713 | 2.765 | 2.812 | 2.854 |
| NUAD | 0.234 | 0.235 | 2.291 | 0.279 | 0.203 | 0.270 | 0.294 | 0.261 | 0.173 | 0.281 |
| NUCO | 0.180 | 0.176 | 0.227 | 0.281 | 0.310 | 0.252 | 0.242 | 0.196 | 0.185 | 0.202 |
| Buys | 1.083 | 0.953 | 1.152 | 1.321 | 1.005 | 0.994 | 1.251 | 0.953 | 1.111 | 1.231 |
| **New Brand** | | | | | | | | | | |
| SSCO | 0.823 | 1.242 | 1.621 | 1.941 | 2.227 | 2.327 | 2.458 | 2.682 | 2.732 | 2.798 |
| ATIT | 0.289 | 0.401 | 0.501 | 0.562 | 0.630 | 0.691 | 0.750 | 0.793 | 0.798 | 0.823 |
| INTE | 1.279 | 1.498 | 1.761 | 1.943 | 2.211 | 2.317 | 2.432 | 2.463 | 2.521 | 2.583 |
| NUAD | 0.114 | 0.144 | 0.192 | 0.109 | 0.141 | 0.103 | 0.125 | 0.155 | 0.133 | 0.177 |
| NUCO | 0.059 | 0.063 | 0.060 | 0.038 | 0.067 | 0.082 | 0.032 | 0.094 | 0.027 | 0.030 |
| Buys | 1.010 | 1.133 | 0.985 | 1.224 | 1.015 | 0.991 | 1.001 | 1.215 | 1.137 | 1.102 |

time, the dynamic process does not lead to a very rapid increase or to large fluctuations in any of the variables. The change is gradual and slow, thus indicating the stability or the static validity of the model.

The reliability of the model is tested by running the simulation more than once with the same parameters and the same initial values. The outcomes of all the runs are compared, and, if the differences between the runs are not significant, the model is considered to be "reliable." In the present case, a Student $t$ test was conducted on outcomes of two similar runs, and no $t$ value was significant at the .01 level.

The conclusion from the internal analysis is that the present model, as judged by its own output, is consistent and reliable. This is the first thing to determine, since without it there is no sense in pursuing the simulation any further. However, this is only a necessary, but not a sufficient, condition for the model to be a true representation of reality, and to also be operative and useful.

## Prediction Analysis

The most important criterion of the usefulness, and to some degree the truthfulness, of a simulation model is its predictive ability; that is, how well does the model predict reality? For the purpose of prediction analysis, the simulation has to run with some input for several periods of time, and the outcomes of these runs have to be compared with the real corresponding events.

In the present study, the simulation ran for ten cycles, each representing about two weeks. At the end of each cycle, it was "predicted" how many consumers would buy Brand A (the old brand) and how many would buy Brand B (the new brand). These predictions were compared with data from purchase diaries obtained from the consumers who participated in the Columbia panel.

Two general problems of prediction analysis should be raised. First, on what level of generality should the prediction be made? Should the model predict the behavior of each individual consumer, or is it sufficient to predict the total number of purchases for the entire simulation? Second, in what sequence should the predicted events and the actual events be compared? In the present case, for example, the model may predict the consumers' behavior very well, but not in the right sequence, i.e., the model may predict that one of the consumers will make a purchase during the second cycle (the third and fourth weeks), while actually he made the purchase in the fifth week (during the third cycle), and thus the analysis will show a "wrong" prediction. This difficulty is hard to solve, and it will have to be taken into consideration.

The comparison between the predictions of the model and the actual purchasing behavior is given in Table 8.3. In the first row for each brand the

**Table 8.3**

**Predicted and Actual Purchasing Behavior**
**(Number of Consumers = 500)**

Cycle

| | 1 | 2 | 3 | 4 | 5 | 6 | 7 | 8 | 9 | 10 | Sum |
|---|---|---|---|---|---|---|---|---|---|---|---|
| **Old Brand** | | | | | | | | | | | |
| Total predicted | 50 | 53 | 58 | 60 | 55 | 50 | 52 | 56 | 58 | 63 | 555 |
| Total bought | 85 | 79 | 69 | 71 | 25 | 50 | 30 | 54 | 42 | 45 | 550 |
| Predicted and actually bought | 15[b] | 12[a] | 13[a] | 9 | 13[b] | 12[b] | 7[b] | 10[a] | 11[b] | 13[b] | |
| Prediction expected by chance | 8.5 | 8.3 | 8.0 | 8.5 | 6.0 | 5.0 | 3.0 | 6.0 | 5.0 | 5.6 | |
| **New Brand** | | | | | | | | | | | |
| Total predicted | 7 | 13 | 23 | 15 | 12 | 18 | 9 | 8 | 7 | 6 | 118 |
| Total bought | 4 | 10 | 24 | 12 | 11 | 18 | 8 | 9 | 11 | 11 | 118 |
| Predicted and actually bought | 0 | 1 | 1 | 2 | 0 | 1 | 0 | 0 | 0 | 1 | |

[a] _t_ test: significant at the level .05

[b] _t_ test: significant at the level .01

number of consumers who will buy this brand, according to the simulation model, is given. The second row is the number of consumers who actually bought the brand in the two-week period corresponding to the computer cycle. The third row is the number of consumers who were predicted to buy and who also actually bought. Thus, the difference between the numbers in row 1 and row 3 designates those who were predicted to buy, but actually did not buy. On the other hand, the difference between the numbers in row 2 and row 3 designates those who actually bought, but were not predicted to buy.

If the criterion of validation is based on aggregate data, i.e., how many purchases will actually be made of each brand as compared to the prediction, then the predictive ability is very good. The simulation model has predicted (on the basis of 500 consumers) that during the entire period there will be 555 purchases of the old brand and 118 of the new brand. In terms of market share, this prediction means that the old brand will have 82.5 percent of the market and the new brand will have 17.5 percent. Actually, the old brand had 82.4 percent and the new brand had 17.6 percent. The difference between the prediction and reality is 0.1 percent.

Previous models (e.g., Amstutz's model)[1] have measured predictive ability on the basis of aggregate data. By this criterion, the performance of the present model is very impressive indeed. However, one of the modifications and the advantages of the present model is its capability of comparing predicted and actual behavior on an individual level. It is clear that the more specific and precise the event predicted, the less the probability of a successful prediction. On the other hand, much more information will be obtained from a comparison of specific events.

Clearly, the key to testing the predictive ability on the individual level is the number of those who actually bought and were also predicted to buy, presented in rows 3 and 7 of Table 8.3. The two questions that ought to be answered are: first, is this number significantly better than a prediction based on chance alone? Second, what is the degree of predictive ability as represented by this number?

One way of performing the significance test is to construct the following contingency table for each cycle:

|                 |       | Predicted Behavior |          |          |
|-----------------|-------|-------------------|----------|----------|
|                 |       | Buy               | Not      | Total    |
| Actual Behavior | Buy   | $C_{11}$          | $C_{12}$ | $C_{1.}$ |
|                 | Not   | $C_{21}$          | $C_{22}$ | $C_{2.}$ |
|                 | Total | $C_{.1}$          | $C_{.2}$ | $N$      |

The cells $C_{11}$ and $C_{22}$ of the table represent correct predictions, and the cells $C_{12}$ and $C_{21}$ represent wrong predictions. Since the distribution of the wrong predictions is of no interest, the test should concentrate on the upper-left and lower-right cells only. A chi-square test would therefore not be exactly appropriate.[6] Rather a Student $t$ test of proportions would be more appropriate.

Usually this test is designed to evaluate the significance of the total number of correct predictions. However, in the present case, this would not be appropriate either. A modified test was used first, and only then was the more common test performed. The reason is that the major interest lies with those who were predicted to buy and actually bought, and the significance of this prediction is the most important. The modified test concentrated on this group alone.

This test is based *only* on the correct predictions for those who actually bought and were also predicted to buy. For the purpose of the test, the proportion of these correct predictions (namely, Buy-Buy) that can be expected by chance will be computed. Then the proportion of the correct predictions produced by the model will be computed, and the significance of the difference between them will be found by using the $t$ test for proportions. The value of $t$ is given by:

$$t = \frac{P(\text{P}) - P(A)}{\sqrt{P(A)\,(1 - P(A))/N}}$$

where

$P(\text{P})$ = proportion of consumers who were predicted to buy and actually bought

$P(A)$ = proportion of correct predictions that can be expected by chance alone

$N$ = total number of consumers in the sample.

The value of $P(A)$ is computed by multiplying the proportion of all consumers who were predicted to buy by the proportion of all consumers who actually bought. These relations are given by:

$$P(A) = \left(\frac{C_{.1}}{N}\right) \times \left(\frac{C_{1.}}{N}\right)$$

where $C_{.1}$ and $C_{1.}$ are the marginals of the first row and the first column of the contingency table.

The level of significance of the $t$ test described above is given in Table 8.4. Evidently, most of the predictions for the old brand are significant, while those for the new brand are not. This means that the simulation model is able to identify a significant number of those individual consumers who will actually buy the old brand, beyond a random guessing. It is not able, however, to identify the individual consumers who will buy the new brand.

A significance test that will consider all correct predictions is a $t$ test based on what is known as "the matching problem." In this test, the total number of correct predictions is compared to the total number of predictions expected by random guessing, and the significance of the difference is measured by using the standard deviation of the expected predictions.

In mathematical notations, the $t$ value is

$$t = \frac{P - M}{S}$$

where

$P = C_{11} + C_{22}$, the total number of correct predictions produced by the model

$M = L/N$, the mean of the distribution of predictions expected by chance

$L = \Sigma C_{.i} C_{1.}$ and $N$ = sample size

$S = (L^2 - NL (C_{.1} + C_{1.}) + N^2 L)/[N^2 (N - 1)]$, the standard deviation of the chance distribution.

The results of this test are given in Table 8.4, and they are very similar to the previous test.

The next question to answer is, "How good is the prediction?" What is the degree of the predictive power of the model? The most appropriate measures of this predictive power are the measures of Proportional-Error-Reduction.[2,7] Since the data are nominal (i.e., categories), it is possible to use the measures proposed by Goodman and Kruskal,[3] Lambda, or Tau for cross-classification. The Lambda measure is based on optimal prediction, as determined by the largest category of the criterion variable (in the present case, the actual behavior). Since the majority of consumers did not buy the product, the optimal prediction will be to predict every consumer as a nonbuyer. This will always produce the minimum number of wrong predictions. However, from the marketing management point of view, it will be useless, because its goal is to identify those who *will* buy the product, and not just state that the majority *will not* buy the product. Thus, the more

## Table 8.4

### Significance of Predictive Ability
### (Number of Consumers = 500)

| | | | | | Cycle | | | | | |
|---|---|---|---|---|---|---|---|---|---|---|
| | 1 | 2 | 3 | 4 | 5 | 6 | 7 | 8 | 9 | 10 |
| Old Brand | | | | | | | | | | |
| Predicted and actually bought | 15 | 12 | 13 | 9 | 13 | 12 | 7 | 10 | 11 | 13 |
| Predicted and did not buy | 380 | 380 | 386 | 378 | 433 | 412 | 425 | 400 | 411 | 405 |
| Total correct predictions | 395[b] | 392 | 399[a] | 387 | 446[b] | 424[b] | 432[b] | 410[a] | 422[b] | 418[b] |
| Correct predictions expected by chance | 382 | 384 | 389 | 386 | 425 | 410 | 424 | 402 | 400 | 403 |

[a] $t$ test: significant at the level .05
[b] $t$ test: significant at the level .01

163

appropriate measure in the present case is Tau, which is based on proportional prediction. This kind of prediction takes into consideration both those who bought and those who did not buy.

The value of Tau was measured for all predictions of the old brand, and found to be in the range of 0 to .05. The interpretation of the larger value is that the simulation model has reduced the number of wrong predictions by 5 percent as compared to the number obtained with random guessing. This value is not very impressive, and from a statistical point of view, it is not significant. However, it will be demonstrated in the next section that the value of the model for practical use is beyond this seemingly small improvement.


**Sensitivity Analysis**

The prediction validity of the model indicates only the final performance, but it does not say anything about the causes and the determinants of this performance. A model may predict well, but for the wrong reasons or as a result of compensating errors. Thus, an analysis of the hypotheses, the variables, and the parameters of the model is needed.

As part of the market survey, which the simulation model attempts to replicate, three telephone interviews were conducted. The first interview was conducted during the period represented by the second cycle in the computer; the second interview was during the fifth cycle; and the third interview during the tenth cycle. In each interview, the consumers were asked, among other things, the following questions: What is your specific Self-confidence, Attitude, and Intention-to-Buy toward each of the two brands? Did you see an ad lately or did you discuss with other people any of the brands? The answers were scaled similarly to the answers in the mail questionnaire at the beginning of the survey. The means and the standard deviations for these variables are given in Table 8.5. It can be seen from the table that in general the trend of the variables related to the old brand is increasing, and the trend of the new brand is decreasing. The standard deviations indicate low dispersion around the mean.

For purposes of comparison, the corresponding means and standard deviations produced by the model are also presented in Table 8.5. Since there are only three points in each time series, a regression analysis will be meaningless, and only a qualitative evaluation can be made. It can be seen that the trends of the variables produced by the model and those indicated by the telephone interviews are very similar except for the attitude measure of the new brand. Even the absolute numbers are very close to each other.

## Table 8.5

### Comparison of Variables' Means

| Variable | Source | Cycle (period) | | | | | |
|---|---|---|---|---|---|---|---|
| | | 2 | | 5 | | 10 | |
| | | Mean | S.D. | Mean | S.D. | Mean | S.D. |
| SSCO | Model | 1.590 | 1.952 | 1.380 | 1.997 | 1.408 | 2.203 |
| | Tel. interview | 1.818 | 2.357 | 1.856 | 2.355 | 1.924 | 2.102 |
| ATIT | Model | 1.274 | 0.535 | 1.646 | 2.262 | 1.898 | 2.310 |
| | Tel. interview | 1.086 | 2.751 | 1.108 | 2.836 | 1.240 | 2.806 |
| INTE | Model | 6.246 | 2.612 | 8.766 | 2.627 | 12.032 | 2.854 |
| | Tel. interview | 1.846 | 2.602 | 1.760 | 2.650 | 2.102 | 2.480 |
| NUAD | Model | 0.266 | 0.235 | 0.326 | 0.203 | 0.492 | 0.281 |
| | Tel. interview | 0.334 | 0.222 | 0.344 | 0.226 | 0.436 | 0.246 |
| NUCO | Model | 0.110 | 0.176 | 0.182 | 0.310 | 0.292 | 0.202 |
| | Tel. interview | 0.186 | 0.151 | 0.168 | 0.196 | 0.328 | 0.220 |
| New Brand | | | | | | | |
| SSCO | Model | 0.868 | 1.242 | -0.780 | 2.227 | -3.784 | 2.798 |
| | Tel. interview | 1.164 | 1.789 | 2.400 | 2.588 | 0.536 | 1.041 |
| ATIT | Model | 0.196 | 0.401 | 0.492 | 0.630 | 0.846 | 0.823 |
| | Tel. interview | 0.644 | 1.933 | -0.018 | 0.054 | 0.308 | 1.133 |
| INTE | Model | 2.600 | 1.498 | 2.552 | 2.211 | 0.680 | 2.583 |
| | Tel. interview | 1.024 | 1.483 | 1.006 | 1.734 | 0.876 | 1.821 |
| NUAD | Model | 0.196 | 0.144 | 0.174 | 0.141 | 0.154 | 0.177 |
| | Tel. interview | 0.226 | 0.175 | 0.254 | 0.189 | 0.178 | 0.146 |
| NUCO | Model | 0.066 | 0.063 | 0.106 | 0.067 | 0.084 | 0.030 |
| | Tel. interview | 0.058 | 0.055 | 0.124 | 0.109 | 0.062 | 0.058 |

## EVALUATION

The first and most important criterion for evaluating the model is its performance in predicting the consumer's behavior. The predictions are made at two levels: aggregate and individual. Although the more important for the present model is the individual prediction, the aggregate performance contributes to the face validity of the model, and should therefore be looked at too.

The aggregate prediction consisted of two elements: (1) the sum of the purchases made in all ten cycles; and (2) the number of purchases made in each cycle separately. In both cases the number of "purchases" was predicted under the assumption that only one purchase would be made in each cycle. However, with the product concerned this assumption was reasonable, and very few consumers actually purchased more than once in a period of two weeks.

The sum of purchases of both brands was very close to the actual sum. The difference between the predicted and actual number was .01 percent. When the aggregate prediction was made on a cycle basis, the correlation between the model's output and the actual behavior was not as impressive.

The prediction of behavior on the individual level consisted of identifying consumers who did buy or did not buy in each cycle. The results were significantly better than random guessing with respect to the old brand, while they were not significant with respect to the new brand.

The foregoing analysis of performance raises a few questions. (1) Why was the prediction of the sum of purchases better than the prediction of aggregate purchases at each cycle? (2) Why was the aggregate prediction better than the individual prediction? (3) Why was the prediction for the old brand better than the prediction for the new brand? (4) What does the prediction performance indicate about the validity of the entire model? The answers to the first three questions will increase the understanding of the model's outcome and will help to answer the fourth question.

It has already been said that the more specific the level and the event of the prediction the lower is the likelihood of being correct. Thus, when the matching between the simulation and the real world is done on a cyclic basis, it is harder to get good results than when the matching is on a basis of the sum for all cycles. In the latter case, there are compensations between the differences in the specific cycles. Another explanation for the better performance of the total sum might be that although the functional relations between the variables were correct, the specific parameters were wrong. For example, the model could have assigned too much or too little persuasive power to the messages of information in each cycle, and therefore caused a shift of the purchasing decision from one cycle to another. Yet, this did not change the total number of purchases.

The same applies to the differences between aggregate and individual predictions. In fact, in the individual level there was double matching: one between buyers and one between cycles. If the matching had been separated, two predictions would have been made, one of "buyers" and "nonbuyers," regardless of the time cycles, and the other of the number of purchases at each cycle, regardless of the individual who made this purchase.

The double matching probably made it more difficult to predict correctly. The nonsignificant predictions of the new brand can be explained either by the fact that the number of buyers of this brand was too small to indicate any meaningful results or that with respect to this brand there was a unique process (such as learning) in operation, and the model did not account for it.

What does the prediction performance indicate about the validity of the model itself? The predictions are definitely not of such quality as to support the postulates of the model beyond doubt. (In fact, even if there had been a perfect prediction, it still does not prove that the hypotheses of the model are true, since there might be compensating errors.) However, the predictions are significantly better than random guessing in two cases (the total aggregate buying and the individual buying of the new brand), which indicates that there is some merit in the model. This makes it worthwhile to pursue the investigation further.

The major premises of the model are formulated as follows:

(a)   At any time, a consumer has particular motives and attitudes indicating his orientation and preference toward any product or brand in the market. This includes "indifference" or "null" attitude, meaning that he has never heard of the product.

(b)   The attitude may or may not be important for the consumer's behavior, depending on his confidence in his ability to judge the product of the brands.

(c)   The consumer's motives, attitude, and self-confidence may change as a result of receiving information about the product or relevant brands.

(d)   Motives, attitude, and self-confidence are the major determinants of the consumer's intention to buy, and thus a change in them is most likely to cause a change in this intention.

(e)   The consumer's positive intention to buy will lead him to a purchase, unless there are some constraints on his intention, such as price and availability.

In addition to these premises it was postulated that the functional relations between the disposition's elements are of the form:

MOTIVES + ATTITUDE × SELF-CONFIDENCE = INTENTION-TO-BUY

The foregoing postulates constitute a fairly simple model. First, there are only a few important variables. Second, the functional relations between them are assumed to be linear and equally weighted. Third, changes in the level of the variables are due to the single cause of accumulating additional information. Many of the variables and relations that are part of more comprehensive and general models of buyer behavior[5] have been omitted.

The validation of the model's postulates has been done by comparing the values of the simulation's variables to their counterpart in the real world. Unfortunately, there were only three points in time when data on these variables were collected, and with this small number of points, no meaningful statistical regression can be done. Thus the comparison between the model outcome and the real world was done by judgmental evaluation.

Again, nothing actually has been proved by the distributions of the prediction variables, but it can be said that they are stable and do not exhibit great fluctuations. When they are changed gradually (not drastically) in any direction, their dispersion is not large, and their magnitude resembles the magnitude of their counterparts in the real world. However, all this does not mean that the hypotheses of the model are correct. It does mean that they are sufficient to give face validity to the model and to justify further analyses and attempts to improve it.

References

1. Amstutz, Arnold E., *Computer Simulation of Competitive Market Response* (Cambridge, Mass.: The M.I.T. Press, 1967).
2. Costner, H. L., "Criteria for Measures of Association," *American Sociological Review* 30 (June 1965): 341—353.
3. Goodman, L. A., and W. H. Kruskal, "Measures of Association for Cross-Classification," *American Statistical Association Journal* 54 (March 1958): 732—764.
4. Hermann, C., "Validation Problems in Games and Simulations with Special Reference to Models of International Politics," *Behavioral Science* 12 (May 1967): 216—231.
5. Howard, John A., and Jagdish N. Sheth, *The Theory of Buyer Behavior* (New York: John Wiley & Sons, 1969).
6. Lubin, A., "Linear and Nonlinear Discriminating Functions," *British Journal of Psychological Statistics* 3 (1950): 90—104.
7. Perry, Michael, "Measures of Association in Business Research," Paper presented at the ORSA/TIMS Annual Meeting in San Francisco, 1968.

# 9. Information Sensitivity and Brand Choice

## Terrence V. O'Brien

### 1. INTRODUCTION

Descriptions of consumer decision-making often include the notion of a collection of separate stages of thinking linked together over time. The potential buyer supposedly passes through these several stages in a specified order as he approaches an ultimate brand choice decision.

Lavidge and Steiner[39] offered the most fundamental statement of this view, defining the sequence of stages as cognitive, affective, and conative. While no direct verification has been attempted, Palda,[47] from piecemeal, indirect research, showed the lack of evidence to support the model, which he called the hierarchy of effects. Others have rejected the model, but still on the basis of indirect evidence. For example, Robertson concludes:

> The cognitive stage is the realm of information and ideas while the affective stage is the realm of attitudes and feelings. The evidence from this study suggests, however, that these are not distinct stages in the purchase sequence. Information and ideas seem to be immediately processed by the individual in line with his value systems and positive or negative feelings emerge. Separating this process into two distinct stages appears misleading.
>
> Since information is not perceived and processed by the individual in a neutral manner, advertising designed to encourage cognitive learning before affective learning does not seem appropriate.*

*The quote is from Robertson's[53] (p. 52) discussion of Touch-Tone telephone adoption in Deerfield, Illinois. Measurements were made at only one point in time, allowing no more than speculation about a possible sequence. Even so, the speculation is at times

A direct investigation of the sequence of stages of consumer decision-making necessarily involves longitudinal data and methodology that accounts for time priorities among the measured variables. Such a methodology is used for this research and is defined in the next section.

A further requirement for examining decision processes over time is inclusion of feedbacks that may occur throughout the system. The simple hierarchy of effects is nondynamic, a one-way street. One of several classes of feedback is analyzed here, the information-sensitizing effects of cognitive activity. Other types of feedback also deserve investigation in future research.

Information is input to the hierarchy at its first level, the cognitive stage. Information sensitivity is an output of the activity within the stages of the hierarchy that regulates the rate and quality of subsequent information input.

The objectives of this research, then, are twofold: to demonstrate the accuracy of viewing and the feasibility of measuring consumer decisions as a series of activities over time, and to demonstrate the sensitizing effects (selective exposure, attention, and memory) that result from the consumer's involvement in the brand choice process.

## 2. METHODOLOGY

### 2.1 Hypotheses

Ten variables were selected to represent the (a) input, (b) cognitive, (c) affective, and (d) conative stages. The variables were (a) ADS, TV, WOM stimulus exposure, and favorableness of WOM; (b) awareness, knowledge, and confidence; (c) attitude; and (d) intention and purchase. All but purchase were measured on the three telephone interviews, while the diary provided purchase information for each respondent.

Stimulus exposure refers to commercial or noncommercial input of information about a brand. Measurement was by two approaches: (1) width of exposure, the number of different types of sources for ADS (advertisements) and WOM (word of mouth) contact; and (2) depth or rate of exposure, the number of commercial contacts for the TV (television) variable.

---

faulty. For example, his finding (p. 49) that ". . . awareness and knowledge [—the two cognitive measures—] of the product did not distinguish the innovator and non-innovator groups. . ." is the basis for rejecting the sequence theory. However, non-adopters are as likely as adopters to have investigated the innovation but come to a decision *not* to purchase. That is, one of the last stages of a sequence model is a purchase decision, intention, or plan, which may be positive or negative. The prior stages are viewed as necessary for that decision but not individually sufficient for predicting its outcome. Prediction of a single stage from another one far removed from it in the system is impossible because of the effects of stages between them.

Hypothesis 1:   A positive, monotonic relationship is proposed for all stimulus exposure variables with awareness.

Word of mouth stimulus exposure is logically prior to reported favorableness of WOM, but an *a priori* prediction of positive or negative association is not possible since favorableness itself cannot be predicted.

Awareness is conscious memory of the existence of the brand. It is ordinarily measured with unaided recall as a high level and aided recall (recognition) as a low level.

Hypothesis 2:   Awareness is logically prerequisite to most other states and is positively associated with subsequent knowledge, confidence, and purchase.

This last relationship represents an unintended or impulse purchase. The measuring instrument records memory of the brand and a subsequent purchase act, but no intervening shifts in affective or conative states.

Knowledge of the narrow product class (in which all brands are physically identical) measures comprehension of stimulus (brand) characteristics. Its relations with attitude and stimulus exposure are the same as those for confidence, since both knowledge and confidence are expected to be measuring the same thing, the respondent's perceived extent of stimulus structure.

Confidence to evaluate a specific brand is a self-expressed measure of stimulus structure or clarity.

Hypothesis 3:   Confidence and knowledge are expected, over time, at first to stimulate and then to inhibit stimulus exposure and attitude.

Boredom cycle or collative theories underlie these predictions. Low levels of confidence and knowledge are expected to yield little motivation for active information seeking or selective attention. The brand is not conceived of as something useful, and the potential consumer is not personally involved with it.[35,36] High levels of confidence and knowledge are equivalent to complete clarity of the brand, full definition, and therefore boredom, loss of interest, and information tuneout.[17] But at moderate levels of confidence and knowledge, the consumer is learning about the brand and gathers or accepts data about it. The brand is judged as something potentially useful, and a more final judgment is sought.

Confidence and knowledge are also expected to influence attitude in the same nonmonotonic fashion. Low confidence and knowledge are equivalent to low familiarity, to low or no evaluation of the stimulus, and therefore low affect regarding attitude. The consumer does not see the brand as beneficial and will not tend to classify it as favorable. High confidence and knowledge are equivalent to overfamiliarity, lack of ambiguity about the stimulus, more realism than at any other time about stimulus benefits, and therefore low affect. Medium levels of confidence and knowledge correlate with current interest in the brand, a current judgment process of the brand, and a distortion toward higher benefits than will ultimately occur. There is highest affect at this time.*

Attitude is an evaluative relationship of preference or desire for a brand.

> Hypothesis 4:   A positive and prior association is expected for attitude with intention.

This is based on marketers' traditional attitude-leads-intention postulate.

Intention to purchase a brand is the extent of commitment to a future action; it is self-prediction of anticipated behavior or, more simply, plans.

> Hypothesis 5:   Intention is expected to be predictive of actual purchase.

## 2.2 The Tau Beta Correlation Coefficient

An ordinal correlation measure was desired, consistent with scale properties of the data, and Kendall's tau beta was found to be appropriate.[30] It measures the relative dominance of positive or negative linear association between two variables, is nearly identical to the Pearson $r$ in its interpretation, and is defined as

> [(the number of times that a randomly selected pair of respondents is observed to vary together in a positive direction for their responses to both variables) − (the number of times that the pair varies together in a negative direction)] ÷ [the total number of pairs, with tied pairs—those on the main diagonal—disregarded].

That is, where $C$ and $R$ are corrections for ties

$$\tau = (P - N)/[(\tfrac{1}{2}n(n - 1) - C)(\tfrac{1}{2}n(n - 1) - R]^{\frac{1}{2}}$$

---

*The same pattern of confidence, knowledge, and attitude is expected to hold whether or not purchase is ultimately made. In either case, confidence and knowledge will increase and never decline over time, while attitude will increase and then decrease in favorability. For purchasers the attitude cycle will be longer to include time for the purchase action and for the high expectation and affect that motivate purchase. For nonpurchasers the attitude will simply decline sooner.

where

$P$ = number of positive pairs

$N$ = number of negative pairs

$n$ = number of table entries, the grand total

$C = \tfrac{1}{2}c_1 (c_1 - 1) + \tfrac{1}{2}c_2 (c_2 - 1) + \ldots + \tfrac{1}{2}c_i(c_i - 1)$

$R = \tfrac{1}{2}r_1 (r_1 - 1) + \tfrac{1}{2}r_2 (r_2 - 1) + \ldots + \tfrac{1}{2}r_j(r_j - 1)$

$i$ = number of columns

$j$ = number of rows

$c_i$ = number of entries in column $i$

$r_j$ = number of entries in row $j$.

Kendall[31] (pp. 38–39) shows the sampling distribution for tau beta with large $n$ to be approximately normal with standard deviation

$$\sigma = [2(2n + 5) \,/\, 9n(n - 1)]^{\tfrac{1}{2}}$$

Therefore, $\tau/\sigma$ is standard normal with zero mean and unit variance, and its significance can be assessed. Similarly, for any two tau beta scores, their sum or difference is also standard normal, such that

$$Z = (\tau_1 \pm \tau_2) \,/\, (\sigma_{\tau_1} + \sigma_{\tau_2})$$

For three variables $x$, $y$, and $z$, Kendall[32] (pp. 117–122) defines a first order partial correlation coefficient in exactly the same form as for partial product moment correlation:

$$\tau xy.z = (\tau xy - \tau yz \;\tau xz) \,/\, [(1 - \tau y^2 z)(1 - \tau x^2 z)]^{\tfrac{1}{2}}$$

Unfortunately, the distribution of partial tau beta is undefined, so its variance and statistical significance cannot be computed.

Moran[44] derives a coefficient of multiple determination, $^T R^2 z.yx$, and a significance test for it that is analogous to that for ordinary multiple correlation. Specifically,

$$^T R^2 z.yx = (\tau y^2 z + \tau x^2 z - 2\,\tau xy \;\tau yz \;\tau xz) \,/\, (1 - \tau y^2 z)$$

To test the significance, we compute

$$F = [(n - p)\,(^T R^2 z.yx)] \,/\, [(p - 1)(1 - {}^T R^2 z.yx)]$$

which has an $F$ distribution under the null hypothesis with degrees of freedom

$$(p-1)/(n-p)$$

where

  $p$ = number of variables
  $n$ = sample size.

### 2.3 The Cross-Lagged Correlation Approach

This approach uses the difference in abilities of one variable to predict another over time to assign causal priority to one variable or the other. The approach has been presented, intuitively justified, and illustrated.[49,50] It has been substantiated mathematically by comparing known causal structures among variables with computed correlations and partial correlations.[51]

The general procedure to establish causal priority is to compare cross-lagged correlations for pairs of variables throughout our hypothesized information sensitivity and sequence-of-states network.

For a pair of variables $x$ and $y$ measured at times 1, 2, and 3, six cross-lagged correlations are possible: $x1y2$, $x2y3$, $x1y3$, $y1x2$, $y2x3$, and $y1x3$. Three comparisons are made, called cross-lagged differences: $x1y2 - y1x2$; $x2y3 - y2x3$; and $x1y3 - y1x3$. If an original correlation $x1y2$ is statistically significant and its difference $x1y2 - y1x2$ is also significant, then $x$ is said to have causal priority over $y$ for given timelag 1 to 2.

Partial correlations are computed to assess the effects of simultaneous association between variables and the effects of serial (or auto-) correlation of each variable (with itself) over time. Thus, prior levels of dependent variables are accounted for, as well as subsequent levels of predictor variables. If the original cross-lagged correlations are not appreciably affected, then the original conclusion regarding causal priority remains unchanged. However, if the original cross-lagged correlation is greatly reduced (that is, in an absolute sense, toward zero), then the causal priority conclusion is rejected. For example, if $x1y2 = 0.55$, but $x1y2.x2$ (read, the correlation of $x1$ with $y2$, given $x2$) = 0.06, then (1) the serial effect of $x1x2$ is strong; or (2) the simultaneous effect $x2y2$ is strong; or (3) both (1) and (2); and (4) in any of the three cases we reject an interpretation of causal priority over time.

Multiple correlations are also computed, such as $y3.x1x2$ (read, the correlation of $x1$ and $x2$ with $y3$), to measure the strength of cumulative prediction with each variable as before.

Paired-variable causal-priority conclusions are then placed in a network and the mediation of other variables is examined. For example, if $x$ causes $y$

and $z$, and $y$ causes $z$, then the mediation of $x$ to $y$ to $z$ is examined by partial correlations. If the $xz$ correlation drops to zero when $y$ is accounted for, then the $xz$ link is rejected. If the $xz$ correlation is unaffected by $y$, the link remains.

## 3. FINDINGS

Table 9.1 summarizes the findings of the cross-lagged correlation analysis, which are discussed in the sections below. The main flow of effects over time is shown in Figure 9.1 and feedback effects in Figure 9.2.

**Figure 9.1**

**The Main Flow of Effects over Time**

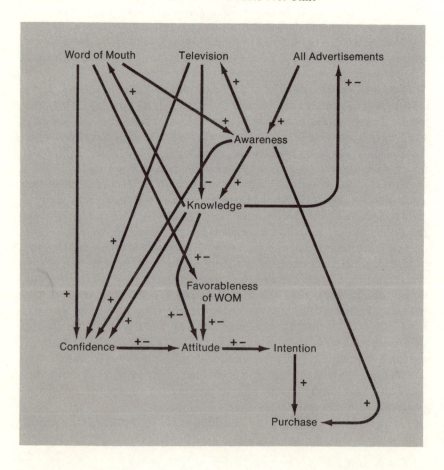

Figure 9.2

Feedback Effects

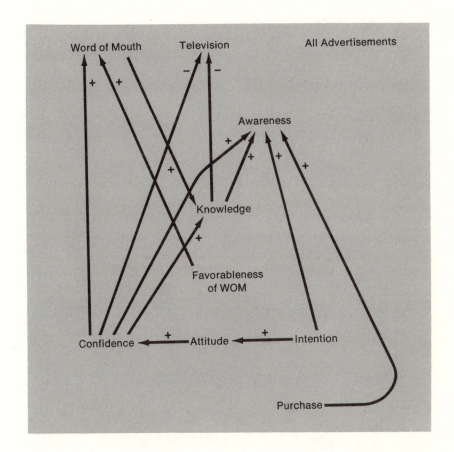

Criteria for the effects shown in Figure 9.1 are as follows: (1) There is at least one statistically significant cross-lagged or multiple correlation. (2) There is evidence of either (a) consistent causal direction, such as the majority of cross-lagged differences or of partial differences in the indicated direction, or (b) significant causal direction, such as at least one statistically significant cross-lagged or multiple correlation difference. (3) There is no mediation through another main effect.* Most of the effects, though, were

---

*For example, awareness to intention was found (by partial correlations for time-interposed variables) to be mediated by knowledge, confidence, and attitude. However, awareness to purchase was found not to be mediated by any other variables in the system.

## Table 9.1
### Summary of Findings

| Variables: predictor. criterion. | Cross-lagged Correlation No. computed | Cross-lagged Correlation Approximate coefficient | Cross-lagged Correlation No. statistically significant | Cross-lagged Difference No. computed | Cross-lagged Difference No. in indicated direction | Cross-lagged Difference No. statistically significant | Partial Correlation No. computed | Partial Correlation Approximate coefficient | Partial Difference No. computed | Partial Difference No. in indicated direction | Multiple Correlation No. computed | Multiple Correlation Approximate coefficient | Multiple Correlation No. statistically significant | Multiple Difference No. computed | Multiple Difference No. in indicated direction | Multiple Difference No. statistically significant |
|---|---|---|---|---|---|---|---|---|---|---|---|---|---|---|---|---|
| | 2 | 3 | 4 | 5 | 6 | 7 | 8 | 9 | 10 | 11 | 12 | 13 | 14 | 15 | 16 | 17 |
| 1. ADS Awareness | 5 | 0.1 | 2 | 5 | 3 | 0 | 8 | 0.1 | 8 | 5 | 1 | 0.1 | 0 | 1 | 1 | 0 |
| 2. ADS Knowledge | 5 | 0.0 | 0 | 5 | 1 | 0 | 8 | 0.0 | 8 | 1 | 1 | 0.1 | 0 | 1 | 0 | 0 |
| 3. ADS Confidence | 5 | 0.0 | 0 | 5 | 4 | 0 | 8 | 0.0 | 8 | 7 | 1 | 0.0 | 0 | 1 | 1 | 0 |
| 4. TV Awareness | 5 | 0.0 | 0 | 5 | 1 | 0 | 8 | 0.0 | 8 | 2 | 1 | -.1 | 0 | 1 | 0 | 0 |
| 5. TV Knowledge | 5 | -.1 | 2 | 5 | 3 | 0 | 8 | -.1 | 8 | 5 | 1 | -.1 | 0 | 1 | 0 | 0 |
| 6. TV Confidence | 5 | 0.1 | 1 | 5 | 3 | 1 | 8 | 0.1 | 8 | 4 | 1 | 0.1 | 0 | 1 | 0 | 0 |
| 7. WOM Favorable | 5 | ±.1 | 3 | 7 | 5 | 0 | 12 | ±.1 | 12 | 7 | 1 | -.2 | 0 | 1 | 1 | 0 |
| 8. WOM Awareness | 5 | 0.2 | 5 | 5 | 5 | 1 | 8 | 0.2 | 8 | 6 | 1 | 0.2 | 1 | 1 | 1 | 1 |
| 9. WOM Knowledge | 5 | 0.1 | 5 | 5 | 2 | 0 | 8 | 0.1 | 8 | 4 | 1 | 0.2 | 1 | 1 | 1 | 0 |

Table 9.1 (Cont.)

| Variables: predictor. criterion. | Cross-lagged | | | | | | Partial | | | | Multiple | | | | | |
| | No. computed | Approximate correlation coefficient | No. statistically significant | No. computed | No. in indicated direction | No. statistically significant | No. computed | Approximate correlation coefficient | No. computed | No. in indicated direction | No. computed | Approximate correlation coefficient | No. statistically significant | No. computed | No. in indicated direction | No. statistically significant |
| | | | | Difference | Difference | Difference | | | Difference | Difference | | | | Difference | Difference | Difference |
| 1 | 2 | 3 | 4 | 5 | 6 | 7 | 8 | 9 | 10 | 11 | 12 | 13 | 14 | 15 | 16 | 17 |
| 10. WOM Confidence | 5 | 0.2 | 5 | 5 | 5 | 0 | 8 | 0.2 | 8 | 7 | 1 | 0.3 | 1 | 1 | 1 | 1 |
| 11. Favorable WOM | 5 | 0.1 | 2 | 7 | 2 | 0 | 12 | 0.1 | 12 | 5 | 1 | 0.2 | 0 | 1 | 0 | 0 |
| 12. Favorable Attitude | 5 | ±.4 | 5 | 5 | 4 | 4 | 8 | ±.2 | 8 | 7 | 1 | -.3 | 1 | 1 | 1 | 0 |
| 13. Awareness ADS | 3 | 0.0 | 0 | 5 | 2 | 0 | 8 | 0.0 | 8 | 3 | 1 | 0.0 | 0 | 1 | 0 | 0 |
| 14. Awareness TV | 3 | 0.1 | 1 | 5 | 4 | 0 | 8 | 0.1 | 8 | 6 | 1 | 0.1 | 0 | 1 | 1 | 0 |
| 15. Awareness WOM | 3 | C.1 | 3 | 5 | 0 | 0 | 8 | 0.1 | 8 | 2 | 1 | 0.2 | 1 | 1 | 1 | 0 |
| 16. Awareness Knowledge | 3 | 0.2 | 3 | 3 | 2 | 0 | 6 | 0.1 | 6 | 4 | 1 | 0.2 | 1 | 1 | 1 | 1 |
| 17. Awareness Confidence | 3 | 0.2 | 3 | 3 | 3 | 0 | 6 | 0.2 | 6 | 6 | 1 | 0.3 | 1 | 1 | 1 | 1 |
| 18. Awareness Attitude | 3 | ±.2 | 3 | 3 | 3 | 2 | 6 | ±.1 | 6 | 6 | 1 | -.2 | 1 | 1 | 1 | 1 |

Table 9.1 (Cont.)

| | Cross-lagged | | | | | | Partial | | | | Multiple | | | | | |
| | | Correlation | | Difference | | | | Correlation | Difference | | | Correlation | | Difference | | |
| Variables: predictor. criterion. | No. computed | Approximate coefficient | No. statistically significant | No. computed | No. in indicated direction | No. statistically significant | No. computed | Approximate coefficient | No. computed | No. in indicated direction | No. computed | Approximate coefficient | No. statistically significant | No. computed | No. in indicated direction | No. statistically significant |
| 1 | 2 | 3 | 4 | 5 | 6 | 7 | 8 | 9 | 10 | 11 | 12 | 13 | 14 | 15 | 16 | 17 |
| 19. Awareness Interest | 3 | 0.2 | 3 | 3 | 3 | 0 | 6 | 0.1 | 6 | 3 | 1 | 0.2 | 1 | 1 | 1 | 0 |
| 20. Awareness Purchase | 3 | 0.1 | 2 | 3 | 1 | 1 | 3 | 0.1 | 3 | 2 | 1 | 0.2 | 1 | 0 | 0 | 0 |
| 21. Knowledge ADS | 3 | $\pm.1$ | 1 | 5 | 4 | 0 | 8 | $\pm.1$ | 8 | 7 | 1 | $-.1$ | 0 | 1 | 0 | 0 |
| 22. Knowledge TV | 3 | $-.1$ | 1 | 5 | 2 | 0 | 8 | $-.1$ | 8 | 3 | 1 | $-.1$ | 0 | 1 | 1 | 0 |
| 23. Knowledge WOM | 3 | 0.1 | 3 | 5 | 3 | 0 | 8 | 0.1 | 8 | 4 | 1 | 0.2 | 1 | 1 | 0 | 0 |
| 24. Knowledge Awareness | 3 | 0.1 | 3 | 3 | 1 | 0 | 6 | 0.1 | 6 | 2 | 1 | 0.2 | 1 | 1 | 0 | 0 |
| 25. Knowledge Confidence | 3 | 0.2 | 3 | 3 | 3 | 1 | 6 | 0.2 | 6 | 6 | 1 | 0.3 | 1 | 1 | 1 | 1 |
| 26. Knowledge Attitude | 3 | $\pm.2$ | 3 | 3 | 2 | 1 | 6 | $\pm.1$ | 6 | 5 | 1 | $-.2$ | 1 | 1 | 1 | 0 |
| 27. Confidence ADS | 3 | 0.0 | 0 | 5 | 1 | 0 | 8 | 0.0 | 8 | 1 | 1 | 0.0 | 0 | 1 | 0 | 0 |

Table 9.1 (Cont.)

| Variables: predictor. criterion. | Cross-lagged | | | | | | Partial | | | | Multiple | | | | | |
| | Correlation | | | Difference | | | Correlation | | Difference | | Correlation | | | Difference | | |
| | No. computed | Approximate correlation coefficient | No. statistically significant | No. computed | No. in indicated direction | No. statistically significant | No. computed | Approximate correlation coefficient | No. computed | No. in indicated direction | No. computed | Approximate correlation coefficient | No. statistically significant | No. computed | No. in indicated direction | No. statistically significant |
| 1 | 2 | 3 | 4 | 5 | 6 | 7 | 8 | 9 | 10 | 11 | 12 | 13 | 14 | 15 | 16 | 17 |
| 28. Confidence TV | 3 | -.1 | 1 | 5 | 2 | 0 | 8 | -.1 | 8 | 4 | 1 | -.1 | 0 | 1 | 1 | 0 |
| 29. Confidence WOM | 3 | 0.2 | 3 | 5 | 0 | 0 | 8 | 0.1 | 8 | 1 | 1 | 0.2 | 1 | 1 | 0 | 0 |
| 30. Confidence Awareness | 3 | 0.2 | 3 | 3 | 0 | 0 | 8 | 0.1 | 6 | 0 | 1 | 0.2 | 1 | 1 | 0 | 0 |
| 31. Confidence Knowledge | 3 | 0.1 | 3 | 3 | 0 | 0 | 6 | 0.1 | 6 | 0 | 1 | 0.2 | 1 | 1 | 0 | 0 |
| 32. Confidence Attitude | 3 | ±.3 | 3 | 3 | 0 | 0 | 6 | ±.2 | 6 | 1 | 1 | -.4 | 1 | 1 | 0 | 0 |
| 33. Attitude Favorable | 3 | +.3 | 3 | 5 | 1 | 0 | 8 | 0.1 | 8 | 1 | 1 | 0.3 | 1 | 1 | 0 | 0 |
| 34. Attitude Awareness | 3 | 0.1 | 3 | 3 | 0 | 0 | 6 | 0.1 | 6 | 0 | 1 | 0.1 | 0 | 1 | 0 | 0 |
| 35. Attitude Knowledge | 3 | 0.1 | 3 | 3 | 1 | 1 | 6 | 0.1 | 6 | 1 | 1 | 0.2 | 1 | 1 | 0 | 0 |
| 36. Attitude Confidence | 3 | 0.3 | 3 | 3 | 3 | 2 | 6 | 0.2 | 6 | 5 | 1 | 0.4 | 1 | 1 | 1 | 1 |

Table 9.1 (Cont.)

| Variables: predictor. criterion. | Cross-lagged | | | | | | Partial | | | | Multiple | | | | | |
|---|---|---|---|---|---|---|---|---|---|---|---|---|---|---|---|---|
| | Correlation | | | Difference | | | Correlation | | Difference | | Correlation | | | Difference | | |
| | No. computed | Approximate coefficient | No. statistically significant | No. computed | No. in indicated direction | No. statistically significant | No. computed | Approximate coefficient | No. computed | No. in indicated direction | No. computed | Approximate coefficient | No. statistically significant | No. computed | No. in indicated direction | No. statistically significant |
| 1 | 2 | 3 | 4 | 5 | 6 | 7 | 8 | 9 | 10 | 11 | 12 | 13 | 14 | 15 | 16 | 17 |
| 37. Attitude Interest | 3 | 0.4 | 3 | 3 | 0 | 0 | 6 | 0.2 | 6 | 1 | 1 | 0.5 | 1 | 1 | 0 | 0 |
| 38. Attitude Purchase | 3 | 0.1 | 3 | 3 | 3 | 2 | 3 | 0.1 | 3 | 3 | 1 | 0.2 | 1 | 0 | – | – |
| 39. Interest Awareness | 3 | 0.1 | 3 | 3 | 0 | 0 | 6 | 0.1 | 6 | 3 | 1 | 0.2 | 1 | 1 | 0 | 0 |
| 40. Interest Attitude | 3 | ±.4 | 3 | 3 | 3 | 2 | 6 | ±.3 | 6 | 5 | 1 | -.5 | 1 | 1 | 1 | 1 |
| 41. Interest Purchase | 3 | 0.2 | 2 | 3 | 2 | 1 | 3 | 0.1 | 3 | 3 | 1 | 0.3 | 1 | 0 | – | – |
| 42. Purchase Awareness | 3 | 0.1 | 2 | 3 | 2 | 0 | 3 | 0.1 | 3 | 1 | 0 | – | – | 0 | – | – |
| 43. Purchase Attitude | 3 | -.1 | 2 | 3 | 0 | 0 | 3 | -.1 | 3 | 0 | 0 | – | – | 0 | – | – |
| 44. Purchase Interest | 3 | 0.1 | 3 | 3 | 1 | 0 | 3 | 0.1 | 3 | 0 | 0 | – | – | 0 | – | – |

much stronger than the criteria require. In most cases the majority of cross-lagged, partial, and multiple differences were in the indicated direction, most of the cross-lagged and multiple differences were statistically significant, and most of the cross-lagged and multiple correlations were significant.

Criteria for the feedback effects in Figure 9.2 are that they are based on consistent or statistically significant findings from the correlation analysis. In many cases they are the reverse of effects in the main time flow, and a problem therefore arises. We cannot assign short-term causality to such reversal effects (as we have to the main effects) because they are likely to be correlational artifacts of stable causal relationships in the main time flow, and they are in all cases inferior in strength and consistency to the main effects in Figure 9.1.

## 4. INFORMATION INPUTS

### 4.1 ADS Stimulus Exposure

ADS was found to operate positively on awareness, as predicted. ADS is a breadth measure, representing the number of different types of commercial information sources, and we cannot determine whether the breadth itself is responsible for awareness or if the major influence is the rate of exposure. Judging from TV stimulus exposure (which is a rate measure and has no influence on awareness) and from WOM exposure (a breadth measure that influences awareness), the breadth interpretation appears more tenable.

### 4.2 TV Stimulus Exposure

TV was found to operate on confidence, but the strength was low (lagged correlations of about 0.1). This minor effect operated directly—it was not mediated through the main system by awareness or by knowledge—and so is interpreted in the same familiarity sense as is the direct WOM effect on confidence, discussed in the next section.

TV also operated on knowledge, and the relationship was consistently negative. The effect was not mediated by awareness. It appears that high exposure inhibits learning the product characteristics. Then, perhaps familiarity through exposure (the TV positive effect on confidence) is substitutable for knowledge of the product in initiating decision processing. Consumers who act on a rational or technical basis learn about the brand from a variety of sources (the knowledge-early-positive effect on ADS), tune out inundation from particular sources (the knowledge-negative feedback to TV), tune out other sources when they feel they have learned enough (the knowledge-later-negative effect on ADS), and are therefore persons who would have low TV exposure but high knowledge (the TV-negative effect on knowledge). But a second type of consumer may not be oriented to learning technical features of the brand (that is, knowledge), may demonstrate high TV exposure but low knowledge, and act on a familiarity basis. This second type of consumer is confident about his impressions of the brand simply because he has been exposed to the brand—or symbolic representations of it—very frequently (the TV-positive effect on confidence).

### 4.3 WOM Stimulus Exposure

WOM was found to influence awareness, as predicted. It is tautological that awareness must result from one information source or another, but WOM dominance over commercial media is inconsistent with most other research. Arndt[2] (pp. 37–38) summarizes the literature as indicating that WOM influence is heaviest just before the decision—a legitimating or social support concept[28]—while commercial media are influential for early-stage awareness. Our results, though, suggest that WOM is highly influential in establishing and maintaining salience, or front-of-consciousness awareness.

Our awareness is a state concept, not a binary threshold in an adoption process model. Awareness is used here to gauge the prominence of one element of a set, of one brand in a product class, and is equivalent to a brand salience concept.

Several other studies show findings similar to ours. Lampert[37] (p. 33), and Chapter 3 of this book, found significant positive relationships between WOM and awareness, but his measures were at the same points in time. Katz and Lazarsfeld[29] (pp. 175–186) found that personal contacts (WOM) were more important than any single commercial source in influencing purchases of grocery items and housewares.*

A second explanation of our findings of WOM dominance for awareness has to do with the possibly inappropriate comparison of a source breadth measure (WOM) with a source rate measure (TV). But we found that interpersonal source breadth (WOM) is more effective in creating awareness than is commercial breadth (ADS). And we found that TV exposure rate is not at all influential for awareness. The first finding is a consistent comparison, and the second (though not allowing media comparison) suggests some doubt about the frequently high level of importance assigned to commercial media.

---

*But their use of self-report after the purchase itself allows a bias toward higher recall of personal than commercial exposures, and respondent ego enhancement by not reporting himself influenced by commercial sources. This study also suffers from such biases, and particularly from the first type which is difficult to avoid in survey design.

There are probably several other reasons for WOM showing such influence. Information from personal sources is likely to be more vivid, to make a stronger initial impression, and to maintain awareness, because of source credibility[24] (p. 270). On the other hand, if the respondent was the initiator of WOM he is likely to view himself as a purveyor of information and advice—as an expert—and to continue to be attuned to the brand and further facts concerning it.

The finding of a direct effect of WOM on confidence was unexpected; there was no mediation by awareness or by knowledge. It appears that the mere fact of exposure yields familiarity and confidence. The stimulus involved (the brand) need only be identified in the measurement situation as the object to which a response (regarding confidence) is called for. Any finer distinction among levels of awareness has no effect on the reported WOM and confidence relationship. The threshold type of awareness is logically necessary to request additional cognitive information of the respondent, but it was incorrectly hypothesized that knowing something further about the individual's brand salience would allow better prediction of confidence. The hypothesis might hold in a simultaneous sense for the predictors (but was not stated as such), and in fact does hold when any system variable is viewed as a function of a set of prior determining variables. For example, in Figure 9.1 the level of confidence at any time $t$ is a function of the levels of WOM, TV, awareness, and knowledge at some time $t - k$, where $k$ is an undefined causal lag period that could theoretically be the same for each predictor variable.*

Our WOM effects on awareness and confidence are consistent with other current theoretical formulations of behavior. In the Howard and Sheth model,[26] the single mediator between Stimulus Display (an intervening variable; all their variables will be capitalized) and Stimulus Ambiguity is Attention, with Confidence appearing later in the system. (The last three are hypothetical constructs.) But, as conceptualized in this study, confidence is equivalent to respondent-expressed stimulus ambiguity for the brand. Awareness is not part of the Howard and Sheth model, but as defined here it would follow Attention and Perceptual Bias and precede Confidence and Brand Comprehension. Thus, from Howard and Sheth's formulation there should be a direct link between exposure (their Stimulus Display and Attention) and confidence (Stimulus Ambiguity for the brand), which we found to be true.** (And our WOM to awareness finding, along with the

---

*$k$ is undefined, and specifically the variations in $k$ for each predictor, as are the relative weights of the several predictors, because such considerations were outside the scope of this research—which sought to establish simple ordinality (time priority) and so construct a network of effects.
**Howard and Sheth define Stimulus Ambiguity more narrowly than our interpretation of it here. They define Stimulus Ambiguity as referring to symbolic stimuli, not the brand itself; it is "... the lack of clarity of the Stimulus Display in communicating the

stages that follow, is consistent with a main path similar to ours through the Howard and Sheth system.)

Substantiation for the idea that confidence is not wholly determined by awareness (and knowledge), and represents in part a construct of stimulus ambiguity, comes from some recent Berlyne research. He concludes that ". . . Activity ratings and 'interestingness' depend on a balance between arousal value and prospects of reducing arousal promptly by finding ways to organize a pattern." (Berlyne and Peckham,[11] p. 5.) Our *awareness* is similar to Berlyne's *arousal*. Both represent salience of a stimulus. A similarity also exists (although it is negative instead of positive association) for our *confidence* relative to *prospects for reducing arousal*. At high confidence there are low prospects for reducing arousal. The stimulus is well organized in the mind of the respondent; he sees a clear pattern. At low confidence there are high prospects for reducing arousal. The stimulus is not patterned; it is poorly organized. The point is that these awareness-like and confidence-like variables were taken to be somewhat independently determined psychological states, as we also found.

A small effect of WOM was found on favorableness of WOM, but it was at first positive and then negative over time. Then, in early phases of consumer decision processes, the broader the range of information contacts the more favorable is the content recalled to be, and the smaller the range the less favorable. It is likely that unfavorable information discourages further search. Over time, a widening range of contacts includes more with negative information, and the recent negative nature is best remembered and perhaps taken to be the most accurate evaluation of the stimulus.

A small effect was found to operate by WOM on knowledge, verifying that the individual learns something from WOM. But since awareness does not mediate, the individual retains such learning beyond the time of its acquisition, when there is presumably high salience or awareness of the brand.

## 5. SENSITIVITY TO INFORMATION

### 5.1 Feedback to ADS

A predicted feedback effect from cognitive states to stimulus exposure was observed. Knowledge is associated positively and then negatively over time with ADS, but the effect is barely significant. The nature of the

---

descriptive and evaluative aspects of the brand and product class. . ." (1969, preliminary manuscript, Chapter 5, page 11). We have departed from their definition somewhat because it is felt that our confidence variable is measuring elements of their Stimulus Ambiguity and Confidence variables.

relationship indicates an eventual tuneout of information sources as individual learning progresses.

## 5.2 Feedback to TV

Negative effects of confidence and knowledge were observed back onto TV stimulus exposures. The effects are different from those hypothesized. It was expected that the relationships would be nonmonotonic, that low and high levels of confidence and knowledge, occurring early and late in the individual's information processing, would yield low stimulus exposure (low because of disinterest and possibly fear and avoidance, high because of boredom), and that moderate levels of the two would produce maximum exposure. Our monotonic relationships, however, show no ambiguity—fear—avoidance process, but a simple willingness to be exposed to and presumably learn about something new. Once it is learned (high knowledge) and the individual himself assesses his learning as adequate (high confidence), then further exposures are tuned out.

The fictional example below (Figure 9.3) is based on our findings but not actually proved by them. It indicates the continued plausibility of a nonmonotonic relationship of cognition-regulating information input.

Taking a hypothetical two-stage process of TV and confidence effects on each other over time, with the assumption that TV as an input initiates the process, then the result is a nonmonotonic relationship, as shown in graph 3, by combining the results from graphs 1 and 2.

The relationship is also nonmonotonic if we examine aggregate results for each variable individually over time. The distributions of respondents on confidence shows that confidence rises over time (mean values of 2.93, 3.07, and 3.14 on a 1 to 5 scale for time periods 1, 2, and 3), as shown in graph 4. But TV tends to rise and then fall (mean values of 2.89, 2.95, and 2.86 on a 1 to 4 scale), as shown in graph 5. Then combining the two results shows that TV will rise and then fall when plotted against increasing confidence and time, as shown in graph 6, the same result as that obtained in graph 3.

Direct approaches of plotting confidence and knowledge against the three exposure measures at subsequent times, however, failed to show such a curvilinear relationship except for the instance of knowledge and ADS, mentioned previously.

It is possible that our originally expected nonmonotonic relations might hold using other methods or with other product classes. As they stand, though, our findings are consistent with those of the Harvard researchers (see, for example, Arndt[1]). Their findings were a positive relationship between perceived risk (the presumed causal variable) and information seeking, where our confidence and knowledge correspond to negative perceived risk.

Figure 9.3

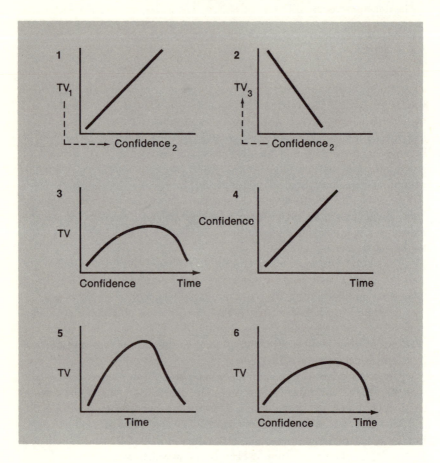

Our TV findings are consistent, too, with those of Berlyne's University of Toronto group, though Berlyne himself has found mixed empirical support for his proposed nonmonotonic relationship between ambiguity and arousal. Some of their laboratory findings are as follows. More irregular (complex and incongruous) figures are chosen over the less irregular for subsequent viewing when the initial exposure is relatively short.[8] Novelty (complexity, incongruity) associates positively with GSR-measured arousal.[12] Figures not previously seen elicit more exploration than familiar ones.[10] Stability, coherence, and clarity of organization associate negatively with arousal.[11] Search associates positively with stimulus and response uncertainty.[55,19] Some of the Berlyne school's results are not consistent with those above (for example, complexity was found to associate negatively with exploratory behavior[11]), but in general the results are consistent.

Feedback effects of confidence and knowledge are accounted for in the Howard and Sheth model[26] through their variables of Stimulus Ambiguity, Confidence, and Arousal Motive, all acting eventually on Overt Search.

## 5.3 Feedback to WOM

Confidence was found to be a good predictor of subsequent WOM activity, with stronger association in shorter lag periods. Awareness was also found to correlate with subsequent WOM, as was knowledge. However, examining all possible interactions of the four variables showed that when confidence mediation is partialled out of the awareness–WOM association, the relationship is substantially weakened. No such mediation was found for the confidence or knowledge feedbacks, so our conclusion is that individuals with high confidence or high knowledge are likely to expand their number of contacts for WOM activity, while awareness operates through confidence for any feedback to WOM.

It appears, then, that the individual is reluctant to initiate WOM unless he knows something about the product and is confident of that knowledge and of his ability to distinguish the subject brand from others. It also appears that the higher the respondent's confidence and knowledge are, the more likely other people are to initiate WOM with the respondent. We cannot verify, though, which direction of initiation–to or by the respondent–is occurring.

A positive but low-strength feedback effect was found for favorableness on WOM. This is consistent with our main time-flow explanation in Section 4.3. The individual responds to favorable information by seeking more information, but unfavorable information inhibits initial sensitivity and start of search, and later curtails search and sensitivity.

## 5.4 Feedback to Awareness

Increasing levels of system states after awareness sensitize the individual to subsequent awareness of the brand, or inhibit awareness if the states become negative. Confidence, knowledge, intention, and purchase were all observed to correlate between 0.1 and 0.2 with subsequent awareness.*

The Howard and Sheth model provides for feedback to their passive state of Attention and to their Overt Search from three of our four variables. They have no feedback from intention.

*Correlations for attitude prior to awareness were also significant, but intention mediated and accounted for the effect. There were no other mediations.

## 5.5 Feedback to Knowledge

A feedback effect from confidence or knowledge was observed over time. This is accounted for in the Howard and Sheth model but not in the direct manner found here. The mediation of perceptual variables (as awareness) that Howard and Sheth suggest was not found. We would expect that, for the individual to increase his knowledge as a function of his state of confidence, there would be perceptual sensitization mediating, not just unconscious (or nonsalient) reprocessing of stored information. Then, we would expect sensitizing to be represented by awareness. But, awareness does not affect the confidence prediction of knowledge when interposed in time between the two.

# 6. THE STAGES OF BRAND CHOICE DECISIONS

Once information is received, the individual processes it in a sequence of stages that basically resembles the hierarchy of effects. That is, cognitive activity precedes affective which precedes conative, with several qualifications discussed below.

## 6.1 Awareness, Knowledge, Confidence, and Purchase

As predicted, awareness was found to be significantly prior to confidence and knowledge. Awareness operates on confidence and knowledge directly and separately, also as expected. However, knowledge was not hypothesized to be prior to confidence.

It was expected that confidence and knowledge would be independently determined by awareness but have only that connection in common. It was expected that an objective measure of completeness of stimulus definition (that is, knowledge) would yield little predictive power in determining subjective assessment of stimulus clarity (that is, confidence), because large individual differences would exist in the amount of information required for confidence.

Results were not as expected; knowledge was found to cause confidence. The results are consistent with predictions of the Howard and Sheth model. Their Brand Comprehension (knowledge) is hypothesized to determine Confidence. Driscoll and Lanzetta[19] found a similar relationship: objective uncertainty (lack of knowledge) determined respondent-expressed subjective uncertainty (lack of confidence).*

*Objective uncertainty was defined much like our knowledge; both were predetermined, finite quantities relating to empirical stimulus (or response situation) characteristics. Subjective uncertainty was also defined similarly to our confidence; both were respondents' statements of their perceived clarity of the stimulus.

The effect of awareness on purchase is consistent with impulse-purchase findings, in that a high percentage of purchases are unplanned (51 percent[34]) and with the Harvard findings[16] of brand loyalty being a positive function of perceived risk. Assuming our product class is low risk and low loyalty (although no actual verification was done), then most of the cognitive and affective information manipulation leading to product class intention formation is bypassed, and the purchase is made directly. There is no extensive deliberation, no mediation by cognitive or affective states or by intention.*

It is also possible that some form of pre-deliberation has occurred. Processing through cognitive and affective stages to form positive intent in response to previous exposure to symbols or to the brand itself may have resulted in latent intent and high awareness, for which corresponding action is cued only by subsequent exposure in a purchase situation. In this case, measurement of system states after the pre-deliberation would find them at neutral or zero levels—at rest.

Generalization might also be the explanation, such that previously formed cognitive and affective relations for a brand name or product-class characteristic generalize to this new product with an old brand name or some old characteristics. Kerby[33] found brand name generalization not to occur with consumer durables, but suggested (p. 317) that

> ... perhaps semantic generalization comes in only when the products involved are relatively unimportant, requiring a minimum of intellectual and emotional effort.

The Howard and Sheth model makes no provision for a low-risk bypass of the system, but it appears that perhaps it should. A significant proportion of consumers may not be concerned with deliberation before action on minor purchases.

### 6.2 Confidence, Attitude, and Intention

The relations among these three variables are more ambiguous than for any others in the system. Attitude met the basic criteria for priority over confidence, as did intention over attitude. But awareness was found to operate through confidence on attitude, attitude through intention on purchase, attitude through intention on awareness, and awareness through attitude on intention. Also, confidence correlations with subsequent attitude and attitude correlations with subsequent intention were about equal in

---

*More precisely, the deliberation is very nearly instantaneous. The nature of deliberation could be found by interviewing immediately after the decision, for example, as the housewife is placing an item in her shopping cart. (See Wells and LoScuito.[59])

strength to attitude predicting confidence and intention predicting attitude, respectively. Taking interactions into account, then, as other variables mediate among these three, our conclusion is that the major causal direction is confidence to attitude to intention.

Pellemans[48] found all three variables highly correlated with each other and found that the presence of high confidence increases the strength of the attitude–intention relationship. Pellemans also found (pp. 74–75, 227–228, and Chapter 6, this book) that attitude precedes intention over time, thus confirming our interpretation.*

### 6.3 Favorableness of WOM and Attitude

The affective content of WOM activity was found to influence attitude. The effect was nonmonotonic; favorableness correlated positively and then negatively with attitude. One of our previous conclusions (see Section 4.3) was that individuals become increasingly accepting of unfavorable WOM comments, and the finding in this section is consistent, as shown in the hypothetical graph, Figure 9.4. Attitude and favorableness of WOM are at first positively related, and both tend to be high. The more sources that are consulted for WOM the more unfavorable the comments are likely to be (situation 1), and the fewer sources the more favorable (situation 2). But, the more extreme is the source regarding favorability, the more the recipient compensates for it and discounts it, so that favorableness of WOM and attitude become negatively related over time. Given our causal chain finding of WOM to favorableness to attitude, and assuming that the typical WOM pattern over time is increase and then decrease,** situation 1 and then 2 will occur in that order through time. Looking at the graph, WOM terminates as negative favorableness is encountered, and attitude rises and falls, as it actually did for respondents.***

---

*The time priority was concluded from 14 of 18 instances where change in attitude preceded change in intention; the other four cases showed an opposite sequence.

**A rise then fall profile was dominant for respondents on WOM and other stimulus exposure variables relative to cognitive variables. For ADS, TV, and WOM, 14%, 21%, and 11% of respondents had rise then fall profiles, respectively. For awareness, confidence, and knowledge, 7%, 10%, and 1% had such profiles. For all six variables the modal profile was no change over time.

***At the first measurement time, 13% of respondents had unfavorable attitudes, 22% neutral, and 65% favorable. At the second measurement it was 20% unfavorable, 15% mixed, and 65% favorable; at the third measurement, 64% unfavorable, 21% mixed, 15% favorable. The distribution of respondents is made up of different subsamples at each time of measurement (i.e., all who responded with other than don't know/no answer), so the figures above do not and cannot show a rise then fall profile. Such conclusion is taken from the simulation results in Section 7.2.

Figure 9.4

| | | Situation 1 Time | | | Situation 2 Time | | |
|---|---|---|---|---|---|---|---|
| | | 1 | 2 | 3 | 1 | 2 | 3 |
| Hi | 5 | | | x | x | | |
| | 4 | | | | | | |
| WOM | 3 | x | | | | x | |
| | 2 | | | | | | |
| Lo | 1 | x | | | | | x |
| Hi | 5 | x | | | | | |
| | 4 | x | | x | x | | x |
| Favorableness | 3 | | | | | x | |
| | 2 | | | | | | |
| Lo | 1 | | | | | | |
| Hi | 5 | | x | x | | | |
| | 4 | x | | | x | | |
| Attitude | 3 | | | | | x | |
| | 2 | | | | | | x |
| Lo | 1 | | | | | | |

## 6.4 Intention and Purchase

Two determinants of purchase were found, awareness (discussed in Section 6.1) and intention. The relationship was strong relative to others in the study, with correlations ranging from 0.1 to 0.3. That intention leads purchase is one of the best established findings in marketing.

## 7. SIMULATION BEYOND THE MEASUREMENT PERIODS

### 7.1 Methodology

The relationships among variables that were established in the correlation analysis are the potential basis for a longer-term view of individual consumer behavior.

Parameters for the simulation consisted of all cross-lagged and serial correlations in the study, such that each variable is defined as a function of itself and other variables over three causal lag periods. The periods 1 to 2, 2 to 3, and 1 to 3 are assigned short, medium, and long effects, respectively. This is consistent with the actual elapsed times, since the length of the period from 2 to 3 was about twice that of 1 to 2. Then, all cross-lagged and serial correlations with a given variable as dependent are summed and percentaged on the sum to yield final weights.

For example, with favorableness of WOM as the dependent variable, WOM stimulus exposure correlates .1537, .0910, and −.1250 for periods 1 to 2, 2 to 3, and 1 to 3, respectively. Attitude correlates .2759, −.2927, and −.3081, and serial (or auto-) favorableness correlates .5709, .2843, and .3214. Then the absolute values of the nine correlations are summed, to 2.3192, each taken as a percentage of the sum, and the signs replaced.* Final weights for short, medium, and long lags for determining favorableness were .07, .04, and −.05 for WOM; .12, −.11, and −.10 for attitude; and .25, .12, and .14 for favorableness itself. Note the high contribution of the one-period prior value of favorableness; most variables showed such stability.

All variables were defined as above, and ADS and TV stimulus exposure were assigned initially high values to represent a television-oriented advertising campaign. In period 1, then, all variables were zero except for ADS and TV, which were 2.0 and 5.0. A run of 30 periods was made. This was expected to be sufficient for the effects of ADS and TV to be felt throughout the system and then die out, with all variables returning to zero.

## 7.2 Results

The simulation is shown in Figure 9.5, where the 30 periods are more than sufficient.** Most variables had stable patterns after the twelfth period or so, and soon approached zero.

---

*The objective here is to represent 100% determination of each variable. Using correlation coefficients as weights is not mathematically correct (more accurate would be the slope of the regression line) but is justifiable in our case, where we have ordinal data and are measuring the relative dependence of one variable on another. We want to know if favorableness is more dependent on attitude one period back, relative to WOM one period ago, relative to favorableness one period ago, relative to attitude two periods ago, etc. Then the correlation coefficients provide a measure of the closeness or strengths of such associations. The coefficients should ideally be adjusted by sample size, but this source of error is small since sample sizes were generally very large.

**Values in Figure 9.4 are scaled for each variable so that profile comparisons can be made. To obtain original values, multiply by factors at the bottom of the table. For example, original or absolute values of favorableness were for period 1, (.001)(0) = 0; period 2, (.001)(0) = 0; period 3, (.001)(0) = 0; period 4, (.001)(1) = .001, the highest point of favorableness; period 5, (.001)(0) = 0; period 6, (.001)(−2) = −.002; period 7, (.001)(−3) = −.003, the lowest point of favorableness; and so forth.

## Figure 9.5

### The System over Time:
### Simulation beyond the Periods of Measurement

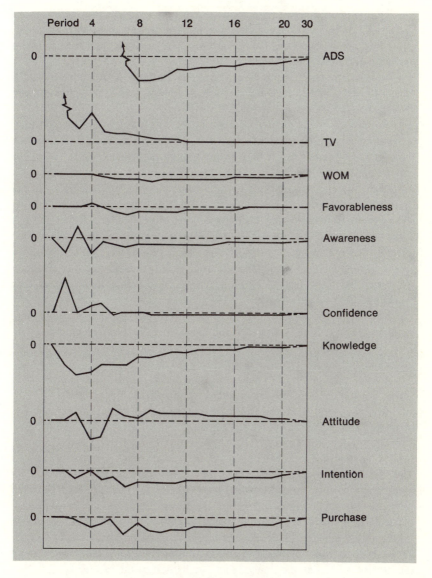

NOTE: To obtain original values, multiply indicated values above (top to bottom) by
0.001, 0.1, 0.01, 0.001, 0.01, 0.01, 0.01, 0.001, 0.001, 0.001.

The most useful aspect of the simulation concerns insight on the motivation for and effects of purchase. We will consider the two peaks of the purchase line as actual purchases. Then, the first purchase is at period 6 and the second at period 8.

What motivates the first purchase? Prior to period 6, four variables are increasing: ADS, knowledge, attitude, and intention. Three are declining: TV, awareness, and confidence. The other two, WOM and favorableness, are also declining, but not substantially.

At the time of first purchase at period 6, intention, attitude, and ADS are all at peaks, and knowledge is still increasing. Confidence is at a low and awareness and TV are still declining.

The process of first purchase appears to be as follows. (1) The consumer is learning about the product class and the brand, as represented by the knowledge increase. (2) He is learning about the brand from a variety of commercial sources, ADS. (3) He is tuning out the inundation of the TV campaign. (4) His expectations of brand benefits are building up toward a decision to purchase, as indicated by attitude and intention. (5) Still, he is not sure, not convinced that his expectations will be realized; his confidence is low. (6) Awareness continues to decline; the effect of the single advertising injection has pretty much worn off. And, of those who were at first receptive to the advertisements, some decided quickly they would not buy, are now less interested, have forgotten the brand, and are pulling down the average awareness level.

What motivates the second purchase? Between periods 6 and 8, two variables are increasing: knowledge and confidence. Three are declining: ADS, TV, and attitude. Three have decreased and then increased: awareness, intention, and favorableness. WOM shows little change.

At the time of second purchase at period 8, confidence is at a peak. Three variables are increasing: awareness, knowledge, and intention. TV is still declining, and attitude and ADS have reached lows. Favorableness is increasing, and WOM still shows little change.

The process of second purchase appears to be as follows. (1) Information tuneout is pervasive after the first purchase, as ADS and TV are quite low. (2) The consumer has mastered the brand now that he has bought it, as confidence is high and knowledge continues to increase. (3) Between purchases his inclination to repurchase declined (as would be expected, particularly immediately after purchase), but then increased again, along with his awareness of it, as he decided to buy a second time; evidence is from the awareness and intention variables. (4) Attitude is becoming more unfavorable relative to its level at the time of first purchase; it could be a rising aspiration level, or that the level of attitude required to motivate a first purchase is higher than at any other time.* A decline, then, is natural afterwards. Consistency and dissonance theories yield wrong predictions here about attitude conforming to behavior, but attitude does increase sharply after the second purchase, as would be expected.

## 8. IMPLICATIONS

### 8.1 Implications for Marketing Management

The activity of variables in the simulation runs down quickly. This is a function of how it was defined, in that arbitrarily high values were assigned to controllable communication factors in the system and the effects left to run their course, but it serves to emphasize the need for continuing injections of communication into the market. There is not sufficient regeneration by consumers (not sufficient initiation of information exposures, not enough search) to maintain high interest and purchases.

Regarding WOM, we can conclude that it is an important determinant of consumer consciousness (awareness) of the brand and that it independently enhances his perceived ability to compare it with other brands.** For the product class studied, at least, WOM is the most important source of consumer information. Then house parties, paid WOM initiators, WOM situations in TV commercials, or similar means, should be effective in producing purchases.

As WOM contacts increase, favorableness of WOM is found to increase. If a period of WOM increase is assumed to be the typical consumer situation, and is the likely objective of marketer-initiated WOM activity, then in marketing strategy some emphasis must be placed on the favorable content of WOM and not simply on an informational use of WOM.

Policy implications of the knowledge-to-confidence effect are simply that at least some prospective customers need denotative facts (knowledge) about the brand to enhance confidence and succeeding states. And growing confidence enhances learning and remembering the brand's features.

*It would be interesting to investigate the hypothesis that attitude is at its historically highest point for a brand at the time just preceding first purchase. Confirmation would suggest that marketers overpromise and/or consumers overanticipate brand benefits, both of which may inhibit repeat purchases. Confirmation would also indicate that behavior-justification effects of attitude (post-decision dissonance) are, while perhaps significant, not nearly so important as motivational effects.

**It is apparent from the lack of activity in the simulation that we have not demonstrated the causes of WOM, but only identified some of the variables that influence it, as discussed in Section 5.3.

One of the major faults of the simple hierarchy of effects is its rigidity. We found bypasses that are not supposed to exist. Policy implications are that for low-risk products all that may be necessary in short-term communication objectives is to establish high awareness, and not to provide information on brand characteristics that in the main system results in learning and affect and intention. Longer-term objectives should include consideration of post-purchase satisfaction through reasonable benefit claims, such that favorable generalization is preserved.

Some of the strongest relations in the system involve attitude. Our findings are consistent with the traditional view that favorable affect is one of the most important marketing objectives. Policy implications are that attitude before purchase indirectly (through intention) influences purchase and largely determines post-purchase evaluation (satisfaction) by the individual. There is something of a self-fulfilling prophecy here in that to the extent the consumer thinks he will enjoy using the brand, he will. Attitude is, therefore, a worthy target for communications, and given that satisfaction causes subsequent purchase (which was not examined here), it should be a continuing target during repeat purchase activity.

In general, further elimination and confirmation of the system of effects should prove to be immensely helpful for marketing policy decisions. A communications reaction system is conceivable, which can be aggregated and segmented and used through time to guide various communication rate and content mixes, much like product life-cycle plotting supposedly guides the broader set of variables that make up the traditional marketing mix.

### 8.2 Implications for Further Research

A more precise and replicable definition of a variable representing the collative (confidence and knowledge) properties is necessary. A promising definition (in progress at J. Walter Thompson) is a count of the number of discriminations required by a stimulus, using eye cameras to establish relations with search activity.

A more complex time-process and theoretical framework is necessary to guide research activity in the early part of the system and especially to integrate diverse findings. Howard and Sheth's perceptual subsystem meets this need, but time hypotheses and more precise predictions of the type of relationships expected, along with empirical substantiation, are now required.

The finer elaborations of collative and search theories need attention by researchers. For example, in consumer behavior research the differential feedback effects on exposure to several different brands in a given product class (and to symbols representing them) have yet to be discovered—that is, the effects of perception and learning of the properties of one brand on perception and learning of properties of other brands in the same product class. Such effects are being investigated by this author in some current research.

The links established here and interpreted in whole as a causal network used differing subsamples. Interpretation of our complete causal system as being representative of the average respondent is therefore not wholly accurate. Future research should, through panel control, make such an interpretation simple and straightforward.

More than the three measurement periods used here should be used in future research to define more precisely the relationships of variables over time.

Other approaches to measuring relationship might be utilized instead of the level-predicts-level approach in this study.

The problem (mentioned in Section 3) of determining the genuineness of feedbacks needs attention before significant progress can be made with a system of effects. A first approach might be as follows. We will measure the true feedback of confidence (C) to WOM (W) by examining the prior effect of the suspected causal variable. That is, our chain is expected to be $W_1 \rightarrow C_2 \rightarrow W_3$. We would compute correlations $C_2 W_3$ and $W_2 C_3$, and first-order partials $C_2 W_3.W_1$ and $W_2 C_3.C_1$. Then, the percentage reduction of $C_2 W_3 - C_2 W_3.W_1$ should be greater than the reduction $W_2 C_3 - W_2 C_3.C_1$.

Finally, lengths of lag periods from one state to another should be investigated to determine true causal delays. No attempt was made in this study to find such true lags, but it appears that they would be less than our shortest lag (four weeks). The evidence is that in most cases the simultaneous correlations were higher than the lagged correlations for a pair of variables, and in many cases the correlations decreased with an increasing length of lag. Then, by varying the interval between measurements for different subsamples on the same pairs of variables from zero (simultaneously) up to, say, several weeks, the maximum correlation will indicate the true causal lag. It is hoped that the maximum correlation would be for other than the simultaneous interval (or, at worst, some bimodal distribution of correlation figures). Different true lags would also be expected to be found for different product classes, such as a home or car purchase versus selection of a soft drink brand in a supermarket.

## 9. SUMMARY

Sequential stages of consumer decisions were investigated, along with selected feedback effects, using cross-lagged correlations. Our sequence of stages basically supports the concept of the hierarchy of effects. Cognitive activity precedes affective activity, which precedes conative intent and behavior. But the true hierarchy of effects is clearly not a rigid process. There are numerous routes a consumer may take through the system, including bypassing supposedly essential stages. Cognitive activity was also shown to affect the rate and quality of subsequent information input to the cognitive stage.

The most important thing demonstrated in this study is the feasibility of viewing consumer decision making as a series of activities over time that are plausibly related to one another. Causal interpretations have been applied, based on our methodological design and its underlying logic, but cause and effect are far less tangible than we would like. The problem, as with most behavioral research, is that one must infer from the empirical findings the operation of psychological processes that cannot be directly observed. It is such processes that frequently interest the researcher, but bridges from psychophysical measurements, self reports, and observed behavior, to mental processes are difficult to construct.

## References

1. Arndt, Johan, "Role of Product-Related Conversations in the Diffusion of a New Product," *Journal of Marketing Research* 4 (August 1967): 291– 295.
2. Arndt, Johan, *Word of Mouth Advertising: A Review of the Literature* (New York: Advertising Research Foundation, 1967).
3. Bauer, Raymond A., and Stephen A. Greyser, *Advertising in America: The Consumer View* (Boston: Division of Research, Graduate School of Business Administration, Harvard University, 1968).
4. Becknell, James C., Jr., Warner R. Wilson, and J. C. Baird, "The Effect of Frequency of Presentation on the Choice of Nonsense Syllables," *Journal of Psychology* 56 (July 1963): 165–170.
5. Benson, Purnell H., "Eliminating Consumer Biases in Survey Data by Balanced Tabulation," *Journal of Marketing Research* 1 (November 1964): 66–71.
6. Berg, Dale H., "An Enquiry into the Effect of Exposure to Advertisements on Subsequent Perception of Similar Advertisements," *Journal of Applied Psychology* 51 (December 1967): 503–508.
7. Berlyne, Daniel E., *Conflict, Arousal and Curiosity* (New York: McGraw-Hill, 1960).
8. Berlyne, Daniel E., "Complexity and Incongruity Variables as Determinants of Exploratory Choice and Evaluative Ratings," *Canadian Journal of Psychology* 17 (September 1963): 274–290.
9. Berlyne, Daniel E., "Motivational Problems Raised by Exploratory and Epistemic Behavior," in Sigmund Koch, ed., *Psychology: A Study of a Science*, Vol. 5 (New York: McGraw-Hill, 1963).
10. Berlyne, Daniel E., and George H. Lawrence, II, "Effects of Complexity and Incongruity Variables on GSR, Investigatory Behavior and Verbally Expressed Preference," *Journal of General Psychology* 71 (July 1964): 21–45.
11. Berlyne, Daniel E., and Sylvia Peckham, "The Semantic Differential and Other Measures of Reaction to Visual Complexity," mimeographed, University of Toronto, 1968.
12. Berlyne, Daniel E., et al., "Novelty, Complexity, Incongruity, Extrinsic Motivation and the GSR," *Journal of Experimental Psychology* 66 (December 1963): 560–567.
13. Boulle, Pierre, *Time Out of Mind* (New York: Vanguard Press, 1966).
14. Broadbent, Donald E., *Perception and Communication* (London: Pergamon Press, 1958).
15. Bucklin, Louis P., and James M. Carman, *The Design of Consumer Research Panels: Conception and Administration of the Berkeley Food Panel* (Berkeley: Institute of Business and Economic Research, University of California, 1967).
16. Cunningham, Scott M., "The Role of Perceived Risk in Product Related Discussion and Brand Commitment," Unpublished DBA thesis, Harvard University, 1965.

17. Danzig, Fred, "Ajax Market Share Improves, but White Knight Turns in His Tin Suit," *Advertising Age* (December 25, 1967): 3, 42.
18. Day, George S., "Buyer Attitudes and Brand Choice Behavior," Unpublished Ph.D. dissertation, Columbia University, 1967.
19. Driscoll, James M., and John T. Lanzetta, "Effects of Two Sources of Uncertainty in Decision-Making," *Psychological Reports* 17 (October 1965): 635–648.
20. Goodman, Leo A., and William H. Kruskal, "Measures of Association for Cross Classifications," *American Statistical Association Journal* 49 (December 1954): 732–764.
21. Hochberg, Julian E., *Perception* (Englewood Cliffs, N.J.: Prentice-Hall, 1964).
22. Hoeffding, Wassily, "A Class of Statistics with Asymptotically Normal Distributions," *The Annals of Mathematical Statistics* 19 (September 1948): 293–325.
23. Hoeffding, Wassily, " 'Optimum' Nonparametric Tests," in Jerzy Neyman, ed., *Proceedings of the 2d. Berkeley Symposium on Mathematical Statistics and Probability* (July 31–August 12, 1950) (Berkeley and Los Angeles: University of California Press, 1951), pp. 83–92.
24. Hovland, Carl I., et al., *Communication and Persuasion: Psychological Studies of Opinion Change* (New Haven: Yale University Press, 1953).
25. Howard, John A., "Confidence as a Validated Construct," Paper presented at the Third Annual Buyer Behavior Conference, Columbia University, New York, May 22–23, 1969.
26. Howard, John A., and Jagdish N. Sheth, *The Theory of Buyer Behavior* (New York: John Wiley and Sons, 1969).
27. James, William, *The Principles of Psychology* (New York: Henry Holt and Co., 1890).
28. Katz, Elihu, "The Two-Step Flow of Communication: An Up-to-Date Report on an Hypothesis," *Public Opinion Quarterly* 21 (Spring, 1957): 61–78.
29. Katz, Elihu, and Paul F. Lazarsfeld, *Personal Influence* (New York: The Free Press of Glencoe, 1955).
30. Kendall, Maurice G., "A New Measure of Rank Correlation," *Biometrika* 30 (June 1938): 81–93.
31. Kendall, Maurice G., *Rank Correlation Methods* (London: Charles Griffin & Co., 1948).
32. Kendall, Maurice G., *Rank Correlation Methods*, 2d. ed. (London: Charles Griffin & Co., 1955).
33. Kerby, Joe Kent, "Semantic Generalization in the Formation of Consumer Attitudes," *Journal of Marketing Research* 4 (August 1967): 314–317.
34. Kollat, David T., and Ronald T. Willett, "Customer Impulse Purchasing Behavior," *Journal of Marketing Research* 4 (February 1967): 21–31.
35. Krugman, Herbert E., "The Measurement of Advertising Involvement," *Public Opinion Quarterly* 30 (Winter, 1966-67): 583–596.

36. Krugman, Herbert E., "Processes Underlying Exposure to Advertising," Paper presented at the seventy-fifth annual convention, American Psychological Association, Washington, D. C., September 5, 1967.

37. Lampert, Shlomo I., "Word of Mouth Activity During the Introduction of a New Food Product," Ph.D. dissertation, preliminary draft, Columbia University, May 1969.

38. Lanzetta, John T., and Vera T. Kanareff, "Information Cost, Amount of Payoff and Level of Aspiration as Determinants of Information Seeking in Decision Making," *Behavioral Science* 7 (October 1962): 459—473.

39. Lavidge, Robert J., and Gary A. Steiner, "A Model for Predictive Measurements of Advertising Effectiveness," *Journal of Marketing* 25 (October 1961): 59—62.

40. Lawrence, Douglas H., "The Nature of a Stimulus: Some Relationships Between Learning and Perception," in Sigmund Koch, ed., *Psychology: A Study of a Science*, Vol. 5 (New York: McGraw-Hill Book Co., 1963).

41. Marketing Science Institute, "Communications Models of the Advertising Process," Research Program Project Description, February 24, 1969.

42. Maslow, Abraham H., "A Theory of Human Motivation," *Psychological Review* 50 (July 1943): 370—396.

43. Menzel, Herbert, and Elihu Katz, "Social Relations and Innovation in the Medical Profession: The Epidemiology of a New Drug," *Public Opinion Quarterly* 19 (Winter, 1955-56): 337—352.

44. Moran, P. A. P., "Partial and Multiple Rank Correlation," *Biometrika* 38 (June 1951): 26—32.

45. Norman, Donald A., *Memory and Attention* (New York: John Wiley and Sons, 1969).

46. O'Brien, Terrence V., "Information Sensitivity and the Sequence of Psychological States in the Brand Choice Process," Unpublished Ph.D. dissertation, Columbia University, 1969.

47. Palda, Kristian S., "The Hypothesis of a Hierarchy of Effects: A Partial Evaluation," *Journal of Marketing Research* 3 (February 1966): 13—24.

48. Pellemans, Paul A., "Investigations on Attitude and Purchase Intention toward the Brand," Ph.D. dissertation, Graduate School of Business, Columbia University, 1970.

49. Pelz, Donald C., "Comments on the Method of Cross-Lagged Correlation," Survey Research Center, xerography, University of Michigan, November 1967.

50. Pelz, Donald C., and Frank M. Andrews, "Detecting Causal Priorities in Panel Study Data," *American Sociological Review* 29 (December 1964): 836—848.

51. Rickard, Stanley E., Jr., "Using Correlations to Test Causal Hypotheses," Ph.D. dissertation, Northwestern University, 1967.

52. Robertson, Thomas S., "A Critical Examination of 'Adoption Process' Models of Consumer Behavior," Paper presented at the Third Annual Buyer Behavior Conference, Columbia University, New York, May 22—23, 1969.

53. Robertson, Thomas S., "Purchase Sequence Responses: Innovators vs. Non-Innovators," *Journal of Advertising Research* 8 (March 1968): 47−52.
54. Sherif, Muzafer, and Carolyn W. Sherif, *An Outline of Social Psychology*, 2d ed. (New York: Harper and Brothers, 1956).
55. Sieber, Joan E., and John T. Lanzetta, "Conflict and Conceptual Structure as Determinants of Decision-Making Behavior," *Journal of Personality* 32 (December 1964): 622−641.
56. Siegel, Sidney, *Nonparametric Statistics* (New York: McGraw-Hill Book Co., 1956).
57. Smirnov, N. V., "Tables for Estimating the Goodness of Fit of Empirical Distributions," *Annals of Mathematical Statistics* 19 (September 1948): 280−281.
58. Weiss, Robert S., *Statistics in Social Research* (New York: John Wiley and Sons, 1968).
59. Wells, William D., and Leonard A. LoScuito, "Direct Observation of Purchasing Behavior," *Journal of Marketing Research* 3 (August 1966): 227−233.
60. Zajonc, Robert B., "The Attitudinal Effects of Mere Exposure," *Technical Report No. 34*, Research Center for Group Dynamics, Institute for Social Research, University of Michigan, September 1965.

# IV

## Full System Analysis

# 10. A Simultaneous-Equation Regression Test of the Howard-Sheth Model

John U. Farley
L. Winston Ring

A general buyer behavior model has many potential uses, as has been shown by the extent that developments related to the Howard-Sheth model[6] shaped the research discussed earlier in this volume. These benefits include sharpened hypotheses about interrelationships among variables important in consumer decision-making processes, help in guiding the proper choice of testing procedures, as well as a framework for orderly discussion of results.

However, a theory is subject to test in its totality as well as to partial applications of the types discussed earlier; this chapter discusses an attempt to construct an overall test of the model. To perform such a test, the model must be structured so that testing is both feasible and appropriate.

## STRUCTURING THE MODEL FOR TESTING

A flow chart of interdependencies among the elements of the theory (Figure 10.1) provides the starting point. (The chart, a preliminary version of the model, which is constantly undergoing modification, is taken as given and self-contained.) First, the variables are divided into two sets—those whose values are determined by interactions within the system (that is, the endogenous variables) and those that are viewed as fixed data read in from

A more complete version of this chapter is contained in Farley and Ring[4] as modified in Farley and Ring.[5]

Figure 10.1

Conceptual Model of Buyer Behavior

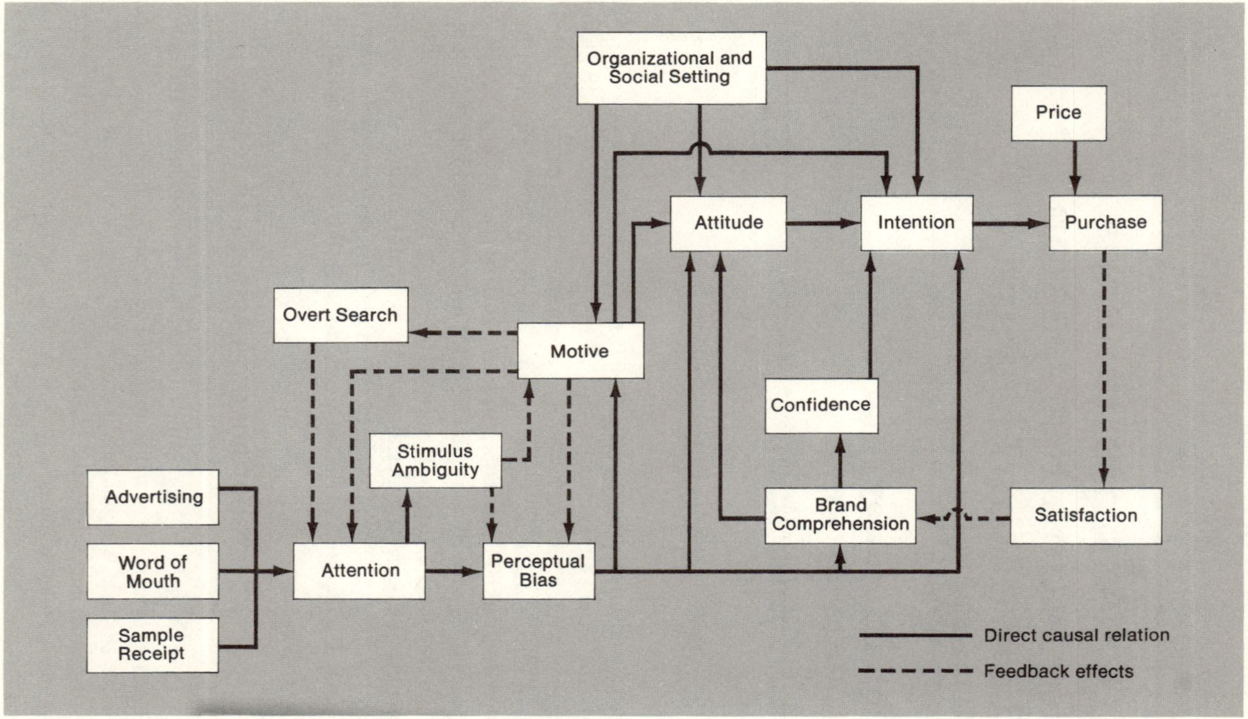

——— Direct causal relation

‑ ‑ ‑ Feedback effects

the outside environment and on which interactions within the model have very little effect (that is, the exogenous variables). This initial step is important as it establishes bases for empirical procedures to be followed. For working purposes, all variables that affect other variables *and* are themselves affected by others are endogenous. The exogenous variables, which affect the system but are not affected in return, are the components of the marketing program plus some environmental measures and some sociopsychological characteristics of the buyers. While buyers' decisions in the aggregate ultimately feed back to the firm, causing it to modify its marketing program, the data collection period is so short in this case that price, receipt of samples, advertising and display can be viewed as being determined outside the system. It is eminently reasonable to assume that no changes occur in sociopsychological variables as a result of a consumer's being aware of or being a purchaser of a product of the type under study.

In the system of relationships summarized in Figure 10.1, there are eleven endogenous measures, labeled $Y$ by convention, and a set of exogenous variables, labeled $X$. The necessary minimum number of exogenous variables will be established later.

| Endogenous | | Exogenous | |
|---|---|---|---|
| $Y1$ | Attention level | $X1$ | Advertising exposure |
| $Y2$ | Perceptual bias | $X2$ | Level of word-of-mouth activity |
| $Y3$ | Stimulus ambiguity | $X3$ | Receipt of sample or coupon |
| $Y4$ | Motive | $X4$ | Price |
| $Y5$ | Overt search activity | $X5$ | Various characteristics of the social and organiza- |
| $Y6$ | Attitude | . | tional setting |
| $Y7$ | Intention | : | |
| $Y8$ | Brand comprehension | $X(K)$ | |
| $Y9$ | Confidence | $X(K+1)$ | Prior purchase |
| $Y10$ | Purchase | | |
| $Y11$ | Satisfaction | | |

Notice that, of the exogenous variables, prior purchase $(X(K+1))$ plays a special role in the sense that it is a lagged value of an endogenous variable, $Y10$.

One of the losses of a global test of the model, relative to the partial analyses reported earlier, is richness in definition of each of the variables. In fact, for the present test, the value of each of the variables must be reduced to a single index number. (The definitions of the variables are shown in Appendix 1.) This means, of course, that a global analysis is only part of the sequence of relevant tests, and that richness, in terms of complex functional relationships, multiple-value measures, and high orders of interaction, is better contributed by various partial analyses.

## CONFIGURING THE MODEL FOR TESTING

From the point of view of empirical analysis, the distinction in Figure 10.1 between endogenous and exogenous variables is critical, but the distinction between direct and feedback effects is not important. (The latter are simply relationships among endogenous variables.) To configure the entire model in a manageable form, we consider values of each of the endogenous variables in boxes in Figure 10.1 as dependent or explained variables in an equation, and we consider the immediate flows of influence (indicated by arrows showing direction) into these boxes as explanatory variables. The goal of the empirical analysis is to evaluate the strength of these influences. To formulate the model as a series of equations, each of the connecting links in Figure 10.1 is labeled using the following conventions, subject to a minor modification indicated earlier concerned with prior purchase $(X(K + 1))$:

1.   If the link connects two endogenous variables it will be labeled $\beta$, and if it connects an exogenous variable with an endogenous variable it will be labeled $\gamma$. (The predetermined exogenous variables are not themselves dependent upon any other variables within the system.)

2.   Each of the labels bears a two-element subscript. The first element will be the variable that is being influenced, and the second will be the variable that is doing the influencing. Thus, the label $\beta_{i,j}$ represents an influence link, and the magnitude of $\beta_{i,j}$ represents the net influence on variable $i$ per unit of magnitude of variable $j$. The set of labels with subscripts is shown in Figure 10.2. For example, the endogenous variable motive $Y4$ is influenced by perceptual bias $Y2$ to the extent of $\beta_{4,2}$, by stimulus ambiguity $Y3$ to the extent of $\beta_{4,3}$ and by all the exogenous organizational and social variables to the extent indicated by $\gamma_{4,5} \ldots \gamma_{4,K}$. Motive in turn influences attention, $Y1$, as measured by $\beta_{1,4}$, overt search, $Y5$, as measured by $\beta_{5,4}$, intention, $Y7$, as measured by $\beta_{7,4}$, attitude, $Y6$, to the extent of $\beta_{6,4}$, and perceptual bias to the extent of $\beta_{2,4}$. These coefficients, called the structural parameters of the system, are to be estimated.

# Figure 10.2
## Model of Buyer Behavior Indicating Variables and Coefficients for Empirical Tests

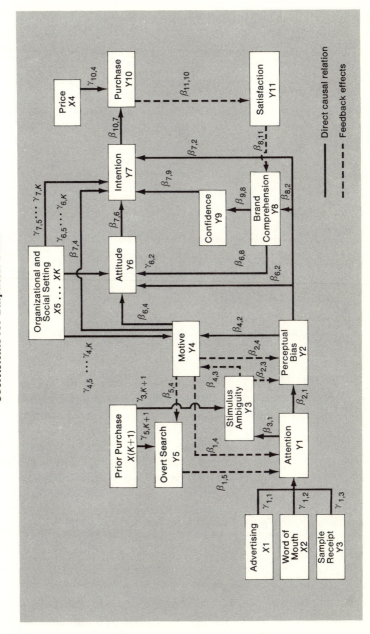

At this point, we face a major decision about what functional form to adopt for the model. The flow chart implies only general "depends on" relationships, and the choice may be very important theoretically. For example, only certain functional relationships are admissible under the general structure of demand theory for the price-income-purchase relationships.[12] The choice in this case was to use linear relationships for reasons discussed in Farley and Ring,[4] and multiple-equation regression techniques common in econometrics may provide an appropriate avenue for the empirical analysis. The model will be of the following form:

$$Y(i) = \sum_{\substack{j=1 \\ (j \neq i)}}^{11} \beta_{i,j} Y(j) + \sum_{k=1}^{K+1} \gamma_{i,k} X(k) + \gamma_{i,0} + u(i) \; ; i = 1,...,11 \quad (1)$$

Each $Y(j)$ and $X(k)$ is a single-valued observation on one variable. $\gamma_{i,0}$ is the additive constant in the $i$th equation, and $u(i)$ is an error term related to the model's ability to predict values of the endogenous variables $Y(i)$ well.

The linear system (1) has as many equations as there are endogenous variables, and these eleven equations are written compactly using matrix notation as:

$$BY + \Gamma X = u \quad (2)$$

where B is an $11 \times 11$ matrix of coefficients of the endogenous variables, $Y$ is an 11-component column vector of observations of the endogenous variables for one sample point, $\Gamma$ is an $11 \times (K+2)$ matrix of coefficients of the exogenous variables, $X$ is a $(K+2)$-element column vector of values of the exogenous variables for the same sample point (including $X(0)=1$), and $u$ is an $11 \times 1$ column vector with elements $u(i)$. The relevant elements of B and $\Gamma$ in (2) can be read directly from Figure 10.2 above, using the standard convention that $\beta_{i,j}$ is the entry in the $i$th row and $j$th column of B, and similarly for $\gamma_{i,j}$ in $\Gamma$. These two matrices are shown in Figure 10.3. All blank entries, identically zero, turn out to be very important.

## IDENTIFICATION

The B and $\Gamma$ matrices must have certain characteristics for empirical work to be feasible on the model—that is, for parameter estimation to be possible in principle. These are conditions of "identifiability"—a set of characteristics that must be met before estimation of structural parameters (the $\beta$'s and $\gamma$'s)

**Figure 10.3**

$$\beta = \left\{ \begin{array}{ccccccccccc}
-1 & & & \beta_{1,4} & \beta_{1,5} & & & & & & \\
\beta_{2,1} & -1 & \beta_{2,3} & \beta_{2,4} & & & & & & & \\
\beta_{3,1} & & -1 & & & & & & & & \\
 & \beta_{4,2} & \beta_{4,3} & -1 & & & & & & & \\
 & & & \beta_{5,4} & -1 & & & & & & \\
 & \beta_{6,2} & & \beta_{6,4} & & -1 & & \beta_{6,8} & & & \\
 & \beta_{7,2} & & \beta_{7,4} & & \beta_{7,6} & -1 & & \beta_{7,9} & & \\
 & \beta_{8,2} & & & & & & -1 & & & \beta_{8,11} \\
 & & & & & & & \beta_{9,8} & -1 & & \\
 & & & & & & \beta_{10,7} & & & -1 & \\
 & & & & & & & & & \beta_{11,10} & -1
\end{array} \right\}$$

$$\Gamma = \left\{ \begin{array}{ccccccccc}
\gamma_{1,1} & \gamma_{1,2} & \gamma_{1,3} & & & & & & \gamma_{1,0} \\
 & & & & & & & & \gamma_{2,0} \\
 & & & & & & & \gamma_{3,K+1} & \gamma_{3,0} \\
 & & & & \gamma_{4,5} & \cdots & \gamma_{4,K} & & \gamma_{4,0} \\
 & & & & & & & \gamma_{5,K+1} & \gamma_{5,0} \\
 & \gamma_{6,2} & & & \gamma_{6,5} & \cdots & \gamma_{6,K} & & \gamma_{6,0} \\
 & & & & \gamma_{7,5} & \cdots & \gamma_{7,K} & & \gamma_{7,0} \\
 & & & & & & & & \gamma_{8,0} \\
 & & & & & & & & \gamma_{9,0} \\
 & & & \gamma_{10,4} & & & & & \gamma_{10,0} \\
 & & & & & & & & \gamma_{11,0}
\end{array} \right\}$$

can proceed. These conditions generally take the form of restrictions on elements of the B and Γ matrices, usually involving some coefficients being identically zero. There are matrix conditions which are necessary and sufficient for identification and the equations in Figure 10.3 meet these conditions[4] as modified to meet the comments of Lutz and Resek.[9] All equations in (2) are identified in principle, and parameter estimation can proceed.

## TESTING THE MODEL

Parameter estimation poses some statistical problems caused by the joint causal relationships among the endogenous variables. Consider, for example, the third and fourth equations:

$$Y4 = \gamma_{4,0} + \beta_{4,2} Y2 + \beta_{4,3} Y3 + \sum_{j=5}^{16} \gamma_{4,j} X_j + u_4 \qquad (3)$$

$$Y2 = \gamma_{2,0} + \beta_{2,1} Y1 + \beta_{2,3} Y3 + \beta_{2,4} Y4 + u_2 \qquad (4)$$

The standard linear regression model is in some ways inadequate, because it is built on the assumption that the explanatory variables in the equation are independent of the error term in the same equation. But substitution of (3) into (4) for $Y4$ shows that $Y2$ is a function of $u_4$, and $Y2$ is an explanatory variable in Equation (3) containing $u_4$. There is no way to produce unbiased estimates of the structural parameters of the system, but there are several variants on ordinary regression that eliminate this bias asymptotically in probability. Examples of such techniques are two-stage least squares and limited or full-information maximum likelihood techniques.

### A. Ordinary Regression Tests

However, it is often useful to make an initial pass at estimating the parameters of a model like (2) with ordinary regression—that is, with ordinary least squares. Besides its computational simplicity, OLS has a number of virtues, particularly for exploratory analysis on large systems. OLS stands up well to multicollinearity and specification errors,[3,7] two major problems in work with equation systems.

Since the test is of the model as a whole, the relevant tests involve joint hypotheses of sets of coefficients. These fall into four categories: (1) coefficients of the endogenous variables; (2) coefficients of the exogenous marketing variables, some controllable and some uncontrollable by the firm; (3) coefficients of exogenous social and demographic variables; and (4) coefficients measuring goodness of fit. These tests are extremely harsh, as they are applied cross-sectionally to data on the behavior of individual households, rather than on aggregates of consumers, which tend to produce more stable estimates,[3,10] or on time series measures, which tend to produce better goodness of fit measures.[1]

1. *Coefficients of the Endogenous Variables.* Positive partial relationships are theoretically expected between each pair of endogenous variables. Thus, the 21 coefficients in the first 11 columns of Table 10.1 should all be significantly positive. All twenty-one coefficients are positive as expected, and nineteen of these are significant at $a = .05$ or better. Further, each of the endogenous variables enters at least one of the equations as a statistically significant predictor variable.

2. *Coefficients of the Exogenous Market Variables.* These four variables include two related to the tendency of the subject to be exposed in general to information (from media and from a general tendency to talk to other people). The other two variables measure controllable elements of the marketing program: receipt of samples and average prices paid. The results here are very disappointing, as there are no significant relationships among the four variables involved. There are at least two probable explanations.

First, the effects of these variables have historically been difficult to estimate on a disaggregated level. Second, the variables occur only in the first equation (attention), the sixth (attitude), and the tenth (purchase). The definition of attention (see Appendix 1) is unsatisfactory, but is about the best available to us. In the case of price, there was very little variability in the data series—in fact, just barely enough to permit its inclusion in the analysis.

3. *Coefficients of the Exogenous Variables.* The social and demographic variables enter the fourth (motive), sixth (attitude), and seventh (intention) equations. Eleven of the twelve variables enter at least one of these three equations significantly in two-tailed tests; fourteen of the 36 coefficients are statistically significant.

Strong motive is positively related to kitchen time, meal size, household size, and leadership, and negatively related to company at meals, to education, and to the size of the city in which the family lives. Favorable attitudes are also related to small meal groups, small meals, homemaking skill, urbanism, and the age of the housewife. Intention is related positively to household size, lack of education, and family income. Prior purchase, which plays the same role in this cross-sectional model as a lagged endogenous

## Table 10.1
### Ordinary Least Squares Estimates of Structural Parameters in Linear Formulation of Howard-Sheth Buyer Behavior Model

| Equation # | \multicolumn{11}{Endogenous Variables} | | | | | | | | | | | \multicolumn{4}{Exogenous Variables / Market} | | | |
|---|---|---|---|---|---|---|---|---|---|---|---|---|---|---|---|
| | $Y1$ Attention | $Y2$ Perceptual bias | $Y3$ Stimulus ambiguity | $Y4$ Motive | $Y5$ Overt search | $Y6$ Attitude | $Y7$ Intention | $Y8$ Comprehension | $Y9$ Confidence | $Y10$ Purchase | $Y11$ Satisfaction | $X1$ Advertising | $X2$ Word of mouth | $X3$ Receipt of sample | $X4$ Price paid |
| 1 | −1 | | | | | | | | | | | .015 | −.023 | .009 | |
| 2 | .111[b] | −1 | .048[b] | .022 | .300[a] | | | | | | | | | | |
| 3 | .369[a] | | −1 | .109[a] | | | | | | | | | | | |
| 4 | | .108[a] | .120[a] | −1 | | | | | | | | | | | |
| 5 | | | | .061[a] | −1 | | | | | | | | | | |
| 6 | | .182[a] | | .305[a] | | −1 | | .329[a] | | | | | −.006 | | |
| 7 | | .148[a] | | .146[a] | | .162[a] | −1 | | .485[a] | | | | | | |
| 8 | | .008 | | | | | | −1 | | | | | | | |
| 9 | | | | | | | .094[a] | .260[a] | −1 | | | | | | |
| 10 | | | | | | | | | | −1 | .238[a] | | | | |
| 11 | | | | | | | | | | .565[a] | −1 | | | | .140 |

[a]Significant at $\alpha = .01$

[b]Significant at $\alpha = .05$

[c]Significant at $\alpha = .10$

## Table 10.1 (Cont.)

### Exogenous Variables
### Social, Personal, Demographic

| | Company at meal (X5) | Homemaking skill (X6) | Leadership of (X7) | Household size (X8) | City, 10,000 to 100,000 (X9) | City, over 100,000 (X10) | Wife's age (X11) | Wife's education (X12) | Wife's hr/wk employment (X13) | Household income (X14) | Time/wk spent in kitchen (X15) | Size of meal eaten (X16) | Prior purchase (X17) | Constant $\gamma_{i0}$ | $R^2$ |
|---|---|---|---|---|---|---|---|---|---|---|---|---|---|---|---|
| | | | | | | | | | | | | | | .549 | .063[a] |
| | | | | | | | | | | | | | | 5.26 | .027[a] |
| | | | | | | | | | | | | | .106[a] | 5.10 | .107[a] |
| | -.201[c] | .019 | .161[b] | .075[b] | -.175 | -.212[b] | -.030 | -.267[a] | .015 | -.018 | .299[a] | .101[b] | | 1.20 | .131[a] |
| | | | | | | | | | | | | | .247[a] | .183 | .065[a] |
| | -.233 | .120[b] | .083 | -.005 | .273[c] | .372[b] | .218[a] | -.098 | .001 | .020 | .121 | -.088 | | 1.50 | .142[a] |
| | -.059 | .048 | .013 | .091[a] | -.008 | -.165 | .041 | -.200[b] | .037 | .072[b] | .010 | .040 | | -.477 | .422[a] |
| | | | | | | | | | | | | | | .672 | .028[a] |
| | | | | | | | | | | | | | | 2.927 | .017[a] |
| | | | | | | | | | | | | | | -1.142 | .153[a] |
| | | | | | | | | | | | | | | 0.0 | .252[a] |

217

variable used as exogenous in a time series model,[1] contributes significantly to the third and fifth equations under this specification.

4. *Goodness of Fit*. All eleven coefficients of determination are significantly different from zero, but most are rather small. (With almost seven hundred observations, it is hardly surprising that the $R^2$'s are significant.) Little can be done about this, but some hints are available for the design of future studies. First, the fits are particularly poor for those dependent variables that are either very difficult to measure or for which the measures available for this study are not particularly good (attention and brand comprehension, for example). The fits are relatively good when the definitions are better or the measures are more closely related to the phenomenon: attitude, intention, and purchase, for example. Second, the noise is much worse for variables early in the theoretical sequence, where interpersonal variability is particularly large. Third, relatively poor fits characterize large cross-sectional studies such as this, in which variability across subjects is to be expected and the phenomena in question are subtle.[2] Fourth, we are assuming in this first approximation that there are no significant segments in the market. That is, we are assuming that the same set of regression coefficients is appropriate for all members of the sample. Convenient statistical procedures for handling this problem are only now under development, but any significant segmentation will markedly affect the goodness of fit. Finally, there is the matter of the sharpness of the data instruments themselves. Even if the variables have been defined correctly, the measurement techniques are themselves quite blunt in several cases. For example, some measures are simply two-value dummy variables, and others are four-to-seven point category scales. Another result of the high noise level in measurement is that the noise level in pair-wise relationships made it impossible to look for nonlinear relationships in scatter diagrams.

### B. Two-Stage Least Squares Tests

The results of the OLS tests generally affirm important elements of the model, even though there is evidence of interdependence among the exogenous variables. These results encourage use of one of the more advanced estimation techniques, and two-stage least squares was chosen for computational reasons. The procedure literally involves two steps of regressions. In the first stage, regressions are run on each of the endogenous variables with all the exogenous variables as independent variables. Values of the endogenous variables are estimated from these regressions (called the reduced form equations), and are substituted for the *nondependent* endogenous variables in each of the structural relationships. This process purges the explanatory endogenous variables ($Y2$ and $Y3$ in (3), for example) of the correlation with other error terms in the sense that the resulting estimates are consistent. Consistency is a very weak statistical property, but it is a desirable one, all other things equal. There are some possible losses, though. For example, collinear exogenous variables may cause the two-stage estimates to become unstable even when OLS procedures appear to have no such problems.[3] In the present case, the extremely weak fits of OLS in some of the structural equations portend difficulties, since computer rounding errors may similarly cause stability problems.[8] Nevertheless, progress in the use of systems like the Howard-Sheth model will require more experience with various procedures for parameter estimation, and the results of TSLS estimation are shown in Table 10.2. The discussion of these results parallels that of the last section.

1. *Coefficients of the Endogenous Variables.* The results are somewhat less satisfactory than under OLS procedures. Sixteen of 21 coefficients are positive and 11 of these are significant in one-tail tests at $a = .05$ or better. This is a much better than chance performance in terms of consistency with the Howard-Sheth model, and relatively strong intercorrelations among the exogenous variables are undoubtedly part of the cause of the weakening of the results.

2. *Coefficients of the Exogenous Marketing Variables.* Results here are almost identical (disappointing) to those reported in connection with the OLS results.

3. *Coefficients of the Exogenous Social and Demographic Variables.* Signs of 29 of the 36 coefficients are the same as the OLS estimates, although the statistical strengths of the relationships are somewhat changed. The effects of prior purchase remain positive and significant.

4. *Goodness of Fit.* The coefficients of determination are displayed in Table 10.2 only for convenience of comparison to the same measures in Table 10.1. As would be expected from the differences in OLS and TSLS estimates of the structural parameters, the fits are generally weaker for TSLS than for OLS.

## DISCUSSION

As a first try at global testing of a large system of interrelationships, the results are encouraging. In concert with richer and more detailed partial analyses reported earlier, the Howard-Sheth model has been shown to be invaluable in focusing data analysis in a large-scale project such as this. In

# Table 10.2
## Two-Stage Least Squares Estimates of Structural Parameters in Linear Formulation of Howard-Sheth Buyer Behavior Model

| Equation # | Attention Y1 | Perceptual bias Y2 | Stimulus ambiguity Y3 | Motive Y4 | Overt search Y5 | Attitude Y6 | Intention Y7 | Comprehension Y8 | Confidence Y9 | Purchase Y10 | Satisfaction Y11 | Advertising X1 | Word of mouth X2 | Receipt of sample X3 | Price paid X4 |
|---|---|---|---|---|---|---|---|---|---|---|---|---|---|---|---|
| | | | | | | | | | | | | | | Market | |
| 1 | −1 | | | | | | | | | | | | | | |
| 2 | −.006 | −1 | .014 | .002 | .510[b] | | | | | | | .015 | −.034 | −.015 | |
| 3 | 1.38[a] | | −1 | .435[a] | | | | | | | | | | | |
| 4 | | .699[a] | .182[b] | −1 | | | | | | | | | | | |
| 5 | | | | .125[b] | −1 | | | | | | | | | | |
| 6 | | −.898 | | 2.86[b] | | −1 | | 1.23 | | | | | .004 | | |
| 7 | | 1.72[c] | | −3.36 | | 1.32[b] | −1 | | .707[c] | | | | | | |
| 8 | | −.058 | | | | | | −1 | | | .582[a] | | | | |
| 9 | | | | | | | | 1.660[a] | −1 | | | | | | |
| 10 | | | | | | | .129[a] | | | −1 | | | | | .117 |
| 11 | | | | | | | | | | .892[a] | −1 | | | | |

[a] Significant at α = .01

[b] Significant at α = .05

[c] Significant at α = .10

**Table 10.2 (Cont.)**

Exogenous Variables

Social, Personal, Demographic

| | X5 Meal time group | X6 Homemaking skill | X7 Leadership | X8 Household size | X9 City, 10,000 to 100,000 | X10 City, over 100,000 | X11 Wife's age | X12 Wife's education | X13 Wife's hr/wk employment | X14 Household income | X15 Time/wk spent in kitchen | X16 Size of meal eaten | X17 Prior purchase | Constant $\gamma_{i,0}$ | $R^2$ |
|---|---|---|---|---|---|---|---|---|---|---|---|---|---|---|---|
| | | | | | | | | | | | | | .938[a] | .527 | .014 |
| | | | | | | | | | | | | | | 4.74 | .029 |
| | | | | | | | | | | | | | | 4.43 | .096 |
| | -.176 | .031 | .005 | .103[b] | -.242[c] | -.266[c] | -.056 | -.111 | .004 | -.063[c] | .262[a] | .114[b] | | -2.65 | .136 |
| | | | | | | | | | | | | | .209[a] | .030 | .055 |
| | .278 | .082 | .301[a] | -.231 | .686[b] | .665[b] | .482[a] | .363[c] | .002 | .075 | -.648[c] | -.300[c] | | .626 | .198 |
| | -.289 | -.012 | .181 | .421[c] | -.908 | -1.10[c] | -.452 | -.526 | .037 | -.088 | .687 | .370 | | -5.97 | .304 |
| | | | | | | | | | | | | | | 1.02 | .010 |
| | | | | | | | | | | | | | | 1.89 | .049 |
| | | | | | | | | | | | | | | -1.13 | .088 |
| | | | | | | | | | | | | | | -.061 | .067 |

221

general, working from comprehensive general models like this one looks much more promising than extension of attempts to predict purchase directly from a large set of exogenous demographic, socioeconomic, and psychological characteristics of buyers. (See Massey, Frank and Lodahl[10] for an example of an excellent and almost definitive attempt to do the latter.)

In terms of substantive results, coefficients of structural parameters are consistent with predictions of the model (especially for the part of the structure involving endogenous variables) but weak goodness of fit measures indicate that a substantial investment in improving data collection is needed.

1.  Data collection should concentrate particularly on measuring the endogenous variables and the exogenous market variables. Even a careful survey that asks all sorts of conventional market research questions fails to provide good measures for some of the variables that are key elements of the model.

2.  Particular attention should be paid to precise definition and measurement of the exogenous marketing variables, as these will yield the key policy implications from the model. A complex structure like that implied by the theory should give a good opportunity to assess the influence of advertising, sampling, etc. When more precise estimates of the system parameters are available for forecasting, these same control variables will be of paramount importance in evaluating a firm's marketing activities.

3.  A great deal of attention should be paid to pretesting. Without aggregation, it is virtually impossible to clean up noisy data once they are collected. Careful work on data collection may mean that less data are needed than are now collected in many omnibus market research studies.

**References**

1. Bass, Frank M., and Leonard J. Parsons, "Simultaneous-Equation Regression Analysis of Sales and Advertising," in Charles Goodman, ed., *Changing Perspectives in Marketing* (Chicago: American Marketing Association, 1968), pp. 228–249.
2. Farley, John U., " 'Brand Loyalty' and the Economics of Information," *Journal of Business* 37 (October 1964): 370–382.
3. Farley, John U., "Estimating Structural Parameters in Marketing Systems," in Charles Goodman, ed., *Changing Perspectives in Marketing* (Chicago: American Marketing Association, 1968), pp. 316–321.
4. Farley, John U., and L. Winston Ring, "An Empirical Test of the Howard-Sheth Model of Buyer Behavior," *Journal of Marketing Research* 7 (November 1970): 427–438.
5. Farley, John U., and L. Winston Ring, "On L & R and Happisimm," *Journal of Marketing Research* 9 (August 1972).
6. Howard, John A., and Jagdish N. Sheth, *The Theory of Buyer Behavior* (New York: John Wiley & Sons, Inc., 1969).
7. Johnston, Jack, *Econometric Methods* (New York: McGraw-Hill Book Company, 1963).
8. Langley, James W., "An Appraisal of Least Squares Programs for the Electronic Computer from the Point of View of the User," *Journal of the American Statistical Association* 62 (September 1967): 819–829.
9. Lutz, Richard J., and Robert W. Resek, "More on Testing the Howard-Sheth Model of Buyer Behavior," *Journal of Marketing Research* 9 (August 1972).
10. Massey, William F., Ronald E. Frank, and Thomas M. Lodahl, *Purchasing Behavior and Personal Attributes* (Philadelphia: University of Pennsylvania Press, 1968).
11. Nicosia, Franco, *Consumer Decision Processes* (Englewood Cliffs, New Jersey: Prentice-Hall, Inc., 1966).
12. Russell, Robert R., "The Empirical Evaluation of Some Theoretically Plausible Demand Functions," working paper, Department of Economics, Harvard University, 1966.

## APPENDIX 1

### Definition of Variables

This section describes the variables and the stage of the data collection process in which this particular information was gathered. A number of details about variable definition, various adjustment procedures, and the like are included.

*Endogenous Variables.*

*Attention* $(Y_1)$: Recollection of seeing ads for the product. Data from second telephone interview.

*Perceptual bias* $(Y_2)$: A filter variable, related to a tendency to use new products and rate them well. Data from the mail questionnaire.

*Stimulus ambiguity* $(Y_3)$: The ability to describe the product accurately. Results from the first telephone interview. Characteristics chosen were "powdered, in a box, many flavors, drunk, and individual portions." The variable is the total number of correct identifications among the five categories.

*Motive* $(Y_4)$: A scale variable collected on the first mail questionnaire on interest in differences among brands of the product.

*Overt search* $(Y_5)$: Endogenous, experience-induced search for information by talking to someone else. Data from first round telephone interview.

*Attitude toward product* $(Y_6)$: Scaled overall evaluation of product, from mail questionnaire.

*Intention to purchase* $(Y_7)$: Answer on mail questionnaire as to likelihood of buying the product in the next month.

*Brand comprehension* $(Y_8)$: Ability to recall at least one brand of the product. Collected on first telephone interview.

*Confidence* $(Y_9)$: General confidence in ability to make judgments about such products. Scaled from "extremely confident" to "not confident at all"; data from first telephone interview.

*Purchase* $(Y_{10})$: Number of units purchased, as reported in purchase diaries.

*Satisfaction* $(Y_{11})$: Post-purchase scaled satisfaction with the product, measured in second telephone interview.

*Exogenous Variables.*

*Exposure to advertising media* $(X_1)$: Recall measure on mail questionnaire of tendency to be exposed to advertising media.

*Word of mouth conversation activity* $(X_2)$: General index based on tendency to socialize and communicate on matters concerning the home. Data from mail questionnaire.

*Brand stimulus* $(X_3)$: Receipt of sample or coupon, reported in first telephone interview.

*Prices paid* $(X_4)$: Average price reported paid for product in raw purchase data reported in diaries.

*Mealtime group* ($X_5$): Index constructed from data in mail questionnaire, involving tendencies to eat a relevant meal alone versus with others.

*Homemaking skill* ($X_6$): Self-evaluative scale rating in first mail questionnaire.

*Leadership* ($X_7$): Index constructed from self-evaluation of leadership roles described in mail questionnaire.

*Household size* ($X_8$): Number of people reported in household on screening questionnaire.

*Size of city* ($X_9, X_{10}$): Two dummy variables for cities greater than 100,000 and less than 10,000, from screening questionnaire.

*Age of housewife* ($X_{11}$): From screening questionnaire.

*Housewife's education* ($X_{12}$): Number of years of formal education, from screening questionnaire.

*Housewife's employment* ($X_{13}$): Number of hours per week that housewife works, from screening questionnaire.

*Household income* ($X_{14}$): Reported in mail questionnaire.

*Housewife's time per week in kitchen* ($X_{15}$): Reported in mail questionnaire.

*Size of meal* ($X_{16}$): Index number describing size of meal eaten when product might be consumed, from mail questionnaire.

*Past purchases* ($X_{17}$): Reported in screening questionnaire.

# V

## A Synthesis of the Results

# 11. A Synthesis of the Empirical Studies

## Morris Baldwin Holbrook

### I. INTRODUCTION

This book has presented a series of efforts to apply components of a theory of buyer behavior to specific research problems. The present chapter attempts to synthesize these results by providing a condensed but unified overview. We employ a particular integrative scheme despite the fact that the authors were in no sense working within such a specific framework and that it was, indeed, completed after the papers themselves. In fact, the framework benefited in some cases as much from the papers as the papers did from the framework.

We shall begin with a brief outline of Howard's twelve-equation model as our conceptual basis. Next, we shall review each article, indicating its relationship to Howard's theory and summarizing its methodology and findings. Finally, we shall offer an appraisal of the research within this framework.

### II. A SUMMARY OF HOWARD'S MODEL

Exhibit I lists a twelve-equation summary of the Howard-Sheth model from Chapter 1, and a set of definitions for the symbols used. Equations (1), (2), (3), (7), and (8) represent the familiar hierarchy of effects—facts exposed, facts coded, attitude, intention, and purchase (a refinement of the earlier model in which attention and brand comprehension appeared as the first two stages in the hierarchy). Equations (4), (5), (6), (9), (10), (11), and (12) deal

The author wishes to thank Professors John Farley, John Howard, and Paul Lazarsfeld for their helpful comments on an earlier draft of this paper.

with the determinants of the hierarchy variables and with feedback effects; in that sense, but in no other, they are subsidiary to the main flow of stages in the purchasing decision over time.

**Exhibit I:  Howard's Simultaneous Relationship Model of Buyer Behavior**

$$(1)\ P_x \quad\quad = f(I_x)$$
$$(2)\ I_x \quad\quad = f(F_x^C, A_x, C_x, \underline{C^u}, \underline{S^C}, \underline{S^{OS}}, \underline{T^P}, \underline{F^S})$$
$$(3)\ A_x \quad\quad = f(B_x^C, S_x, F_x^C, \underline{C^u}, \underline{S^C}, \underline{S^{OS}}, \underline{P^T})$$
$$(4)\ C_x \quad\quad = f(B_x^C, S_x, F_x^C, \underline{P^T})$$
$$(5)\ B_x^C \quad\quad = f(F_x^C, \underline{C^u}, \underline{S^C}, \underline{S^{OS}}, \underline{I^P}, \underline{P^T})$$
$$(6)\ S_x \quad\quad = f(P_x)$$
$$(7)\ F_x^C \quad\quad = f(F_x^E, A_x^n, P_x^B)$$
$$(8)\ F_x^E \quad\quad = f(O_x^S, F_{\underline{x}}^A, M^H)$$
$$(9)\ A_x^n, O_x^S = f(M^a, \underline{I^P}, \underline{P^T}, \underline{T^P})$$
$$(10)\ M^a \quad\quad = f(S_x^A, C_x, F_x^C, \underline{F^S})$$
$$(11)\ S_x^A \quad\quad = f(F_x^E)$$
$$(12)\ C^C \quad\quad = f(F_x^C, M^a, \underline{M^c})$$

where the definitions of symbols are as follows, with all terms referring to brand $x$:

| | | |
|---|---|---|
| $P_x$ | = | purchase of brand |
| $I_x$ | = | intention to purchase brand |
| $F_x^C$ | = | facts coded re brand |
| $A_x$ | = | attitude toward brand |
| $C_x$ | = | confidence in brand evaluation |
| $\underline{C^u}$ | = | culture |
| $\underline{S^C}$ | = | social class |
| $\underline{S^{OS}}$ | = | social and organizational setting |
| $\underline{T^P}$ | = | time pressure |
| $\underline{F^S}$ | = | financial status |
| $B_x^C$ | = | brand comprehension |
| $S_x$ | = | satisfaction with brand |
| $\underline{P^T}$ | = | personality traits |
| $\underline{I^P}$ | = | importance of the purchase |
| $F_x^E$ | = | facts exposed re brand |

$A_x^n$ = attention to brand information

$P_x^B$ = perceptual bias of brand information

$O_x^S$ = overt search for brand information

$\underline{F_x^A}$ = facts available re brand

$\overline{M^H}$ = media habits toward vehicles containing brand information

$\overline{M^a}$ = motive arousal

$S_x^A$ = stimulus ambiguity

$C^C$ = choice criteria

$\underline{M^c}$ = direct motives

To facilitate the discussion below, we have adopted two conventions relating to the distinctions (a) between $F_x^C$ (facts coded) and $B_x^C$ (brand comprehension) and (b) between $S_x^A$ (stimulus ambiguity) and $C_x$ (confidence).

(a)   Howard distinguishes between $F_x^C$, which contains all cognitive material concerning the brand, and $B_x^C$, a subset of $F_x^C$ that contains only denotative cognitions.

(b)   A murkier issue involves $C_x$ and $S_x^A$. We shall attempt to preserve some clarity in the dicussion by referring to all confidence-uncertainty-complexity-novelty-ambiguity-related variables as $C_x$ *except* where the author has taken pains to relate $S_x^A$ to the properties of the stimulus itself.

## III. A SUMMARY OF THE EMPIRICAL STUDIES

Our summary of the empirical studies will proceed by the analysis of each contribution in terms of the following five issues in tabular form:

(a)   how its terminology corresponds to Howard's
(b)   which of the twelve relationships are involved
(c)   how the author defines his variables operationally
(d)   methodology
(e)   findings.

In several cases, complete disclosure of all of these factors is not included in the paper here, although they are revealed in source documents mentioned in each paper.

**Lampert's Word of Mouth Study**

Lampert focused on the flow of information via word of mouth concerning a new "product" (brand B) in the tradition of research on the diffusion of innovations. From the viewpoint of Howard's theory, he deals almost entirely with the *perceptual* variables via a series of two-variable relationships that relate word of mouth to some hypothesized determining factors.

*Correspondence between Terminologies.*  Most of the terms used by Lampert correspond closely to Howard's except:

| Lampert's Term | Howard's Symbol |
|---|---|
| WOM | (one element of) $O_x^S$ |
| General Self-Confidence | (one element of) $\underline{P^T}$ |
| Information | $F_x^E$ |
| Unaided Recall | (one element of) $F_x^C$ |

*Relationships Tested.*  Lampert tested the following bivariate reductions and single multivariate form of Howard's equations:

| Lampert's Hypothesis Number | Howard's Equation Number(s) | Functional Form Tested |
|---|---|---|
| 3 (p. 75) | (9) (10) | $O_x^S = f(C_x)$ |
| 4 (p. 75) | (4) (9) (10) | $O_x^S = f(\underline{P^T})$ |
| 5 (p. 76) | (9) (10) (11) | $O_x^S = f(F_x^E)$ |
| 6 (p. 76) | (9) (10) | $O_x^S = f(F_x^C)$ |
| B (my notation) | (9) (10) (11) | $O_x^S = f(C_x, F_x^E, F_x^C)$ |

*Operational Definitions.*  Lampert based his operational definitions entirely upon data contained in the mail questionnaire (MQ) and the telephone interviews (T1–T3). The specific instruments and question numbers used appear below:

| Howard's Variable | Lampert's Measure | Instrument |
|---|---|---|
| $O_x^S$ | dichotomous (p. 71) | T–Q4 |
| $C_x$ | trichotomous (p. 75) | T–Q8 |
| $\underline{P^T}$ | dichotomous (p. 75) | MQ–Q6 |
| $F_x^E$ | index (p. 76) | T–Q5, T–Q6, T–Q1 (?), T–Q2 (?) |
| $F_x^C$ | dichotomous (p. 76) | T–Q1 |

*Hypothesis-Testing Methodology.* Lampert tested his hypothesis for brand B only, using contingency tables with synchronous data drawn from T1–T3 (except in the case of $\underline{P^T}$, based on the mail questionnaire, MQ–Q6). This procedure yielded three static group comparisons for each relationship, and these were evaluated with appropriate Chi-square tests of significance.

Those hypothesized relationships that received consistent support (in any direction) were combined and tested via multiple-regression analysis (apparently utilizing 0,1 variables).

*Empirical Findings.* Lampert defined "consistent support" for a relationship as that which held at significant levels in all three T's (a relatively strong criterion). He found such support for hypotheses 3 (in the wrong direction), 5, and 6. The ensuing multiple-regression produced statistically significant coefficients for each independent variable.

### Sheth's Attitude Study

Sheth's study, in contrast to Lampert's, concerned itself almost entirely with *learning*, focusing on the last three stages in the hierarchy of effects. He defined and analyzed the components of attitude and traced the effects of attitude upon intention and purchase via a series of two-variable relationships.

*Correspondence between Terminologies.* Terminology between Howard and Sheth diverges somewhat:

| Sheth's Term | Sheth's Symbol | Howard's Symbol |
|---|---|---|
| Affect | $A$ (p. 92) | $A_x$ |
| Total beliefs | $TB$ (p. 93) | $F_x^C$ |
| Evaluative beliefs | $EB$ (p. 93) | subset of $F_x^C$ |

| | | |
|---|---|---|
| Behavioral intention | $BI$ (p. 92) | $I_x$ |
| Behavior | $B$ (p. 90) | $P_x$ |
| Nonpredictable situation | $NS$ (p. 91) | includes $\underline{T}^P$ |
| Predictable situation | $PS$ (p. 92) | includes $\underline{F}^S$ |
| Social Factors | $So$ (p. 92) | $\underline{S}^{OS}$, $\underline{C}^u$, $\underline{S}^C$ |
| Attitude | | $A_x^*$ (my notation) |

*Relationships Tested.*  The relationships tested by Sheth relate primarily to Howard's first two equations and to the feedback effects of $P_x$ on $A_x$.

| Sheth's Section | My Number | Howard's Equations Number(s) | Functional Form Tested |
|---|---|---|---|
| III (p. 97) | III | (3) | $A_x = f(F_x^C)$ |
| IV (p. 99) | IVA | (2) | $I_x = f(F_x^C)$ |
| (p. 100) | IVB | (2) | $I_x = f(A_x)$ |
| V (p. 105) | V | (2*) | $I_x = f(A_x^*)$ |
| VI (pp. 108 ff.) | VIA | (1) (2) | $P_x = f(A_x)$ |
| (pp. 108 ff.) | VIB | (1) (2*) | $P_x = f(A_x^*)$ |
| (pp. 108 ff.) | VIC | (3) (6) | $A_x = f(P_x)$ |
| (pp. 108 ff.) | VID | (3*) (6) | $A_x^* = f(P_x)$ |

*Operational Definitions.*  In general, Sheth used T1–T3 for all measures; the key exception was his measure of $P_x$, which was based on the purchase diaries (D's).

| Howard's Variable | Sheth's Measure | Instrument |
|---|---|---|
| $A_x$ | (p. 95) | T–Q7 – scale 8 |
| $F_x^C$ | (p. 95) | T–Q10 |
| $I_x$ | (p. 95) | T–Q10 |
| $A_x^*$ | Respondent's score on a single principal component derived | T–Q7 – scales 1–7 |

$P_x$    Based on purchase diaries    D's
between one T and the next;
four categories (p. 107).

via a type of principal component analysis of seven semantic
differential scales (pp. 101 ff.).

*Hypothesis-Testing Methodology.* In testing his hypothesis, Sheth used data for all three brands in all three telephone interviews. Tests for hypotheses III–V used synchronous data in either multiple-regression (III and IVa) or bivariate correlation (IVb and V). This procedure therefore yielded nine static correlation coefficients to test each relationship.

Sheth turned to longitudinal data in bivariate regression to test hypotheses VIa–VId (that is, measures of the independent variable *preceded* measures of the dependent variable in time).

*Empirical Findings.* Because Sheth's key results take the form of correlation coefficients, we may summarize them in compact form:

| Sheth's Hypothesis and Table Number | Number of Relevant Coefficients | Significance | Strength of Association |
|---|---|---|---|
| III Table 5.1 | 9 R's | all sig. at .01 | $R^2$'s range from .41 to .71 |
| IVA Table 5.2 | 9 R's | all but one sig. at .01 | $R^2$'s range from .10 to .38 |
| IVB Table 5.3 | 9 r's | all sig. at .01 | $r^2$'s range from .06 to .40 |
| V Table 5.6 | 9 r's | not given | $r^2$'s range from .09 to .31 |
| VIA Table 5.7 | 6 r's | not given | $r^2$'s range from 0 to .07 |
| VIB Table 5.7 | 6 r's | not given | $r^2$'s range from .01 to .10 |
| VIC Table 5.7 | 6 r's | not given | $r^2$'s range from .01 to .07 |
| VID Table 5.7 | 6 r's | not given | $r^2$'s range from .02 to .07 |

(We should note that for the dynamic tests (VIA–VID) the highest reduction in variance is 10 percent. Thus, even if significant, these last relationships are very weak.)

## Pellemans' Study of Attitude and Purchase Intention

Like Sheth, Pellemans focuses on the attitude variables, extending forward to examine the effects of attitude on intention, but also extending backward to investigate the determinants of attitude (and intention).

*Correspondence between Terminologies.* Most of the terms used by Pellemans correspond to those of Howard, with these exceptions:

| Pellemans' Term | Howard's Symbol |
|---|---|
| Ad Recall | $F_x^C$ |
| Word of Mouth | $F_x^E$ |
| Usership | $P_x$ |
| Education | $\underline{S}^C$ |

*Relationships Tested.* Pellemans tested the following relationships, several of which imply the chaining together of two or more of Howard's twelve equations:

| Pellemans' Hypothesis (my notation) | Howard's Equation Number(s) | Functional Form Tested |
|---|---|---|
| I | (2) | $I_x = f(A_x)$ |
| A | (3) | $A_x = f(F_x^C)$ |
|  | (2) | $I_x = f(F_x^C)$ |
| B | (7) (3) | $A_x = f(F_x^E)$ |
|  | (7) (2) | $I_x = f(F_x^E)$ |
| D | (6) (3) | $A_x = f(P_x)$ |
|  | (6) (3) (2) | $I_x = f(P_x)$ |
| E | (2) | $I_x = f(C_x)$ |
| F | (3) | $A_x = f(S_x)$ |

$$(3)(2) \qquad I_x = f(S_x)$$

G$\qquad (3) \qquad A_x = f(\underline{S}^C)$

$\qquad (2) \qquad I_x = f(\underline{S}^C)$

H$\qquad (9)(8)(7)(3) \qquad A_x = f(\underline{I}^P)$

$\qquad (9)(8)(7)(3)(2) \qquad I_x = f(\underline{I}^P)$

II$\qquad (2) \qquad I_x = f(A_x)$

*Operational Definitions.* Pellemans' operational definitions are:

| Howard's Variable | Pellemans' Measure | Instrument |
|---|---|---|
| $A_x$ | (p. 116) | T–Q7 – scale 8 |
| $I_x$ | (p. 116) | T–Q10 |
| $F_x^C$ | (p. 118) | T–Q6 |
| $F_x^E$ | (p. 119) | T–Q4 |
| $P_x$ | (p. 120) | T–Q1 |
| $C_x$ | (p. 122) | T–Q8 |
| $S_x$ | (p. 122) | T–Q1 |
| $\underline{S}^C$ | (p. 123) | SQ |
| $\underline{I}^P$ | (p. 123) | MQ–Q15 |

*Empirical Findings.* Pellemans finds support for all the relationships tested, although he omits correlation coefficients or other measures of goodness of fit.

### Day's Study of Attitude Stability

Day's study is the third to focus primarily on the attitude variable, its determinants, and its effects on purchase. In particular, he views attitude stability as the effect of confidence. Moreover, he investigates the moderating effect of confidence on the relationship between attitude and purchase (finding that it is substantial) and examines the remaining relationship between intention and purchase with attitude held constant (concluding that it is slight). Thus, while Day's hypotheses extend beyond those immediately suggested by the Howard-Sheth theory, we may put most of them into the framework of the twelve-equation model.

*Correspondence between Terminologies.* The following terms and symbols that appear in Day's paper may require clarification:

| Day's Term | Day's Symbol | Howard's Symbol |
|---|---|---|
| Confidence (a proxy for attitude stability) | | $C_x$ |
| Involvement | | $\underline{I}^P$ (rough correspondence) |
| Attitude | $Ai$ (p. 134) | $A_x$ |
| Household Income | | $\underline{F}^S$ |
| Inhibitory Factors | Beta (p. 134) | $\underline{S}^{OS}$, $\underline{C}^u$, $\underline{S}^C$, $\underline{F}^S$, etc. |

*Relationships Tested.* Day stresses the effects of moderating variables, that is, the degree to which some relationship depends upon the level of a third variable. We may write these relationships in the form $Y = f(X \mid Z)$, "$Y$ is a function of $X$, given $Z$." Day's hypotheses thus assume the following form:

| Day's Hypothesis (Page number) | My Notation | Howard's Equation Number(s) | Functional Form Tested |
|---|---|---|---|
| (p. 133, Table 7.1) | A | (9) (8) (7) (4) | $C_x = f(\underline{I}^P)$ |
| (p. 134) | B | (2) (1) | $P_x = f(A_x)$ |
| (p. 134) | C | (2) (1) | $P_x = f(A_x \mid C_x, \underline{F}^S)$ |
| (p. 139) | D | (1) | $P_x = f(I_x \mid A_x)$ |
| (p. 139) | E | (2) | $I_x = f(C_x)$ |
| (p. 141) | F | more closely related to persuasibility literature; not discussed below | Delta $A_x = f(C_x)$ $\Delta$ |

*Operational Definitions.* Several of Day's operational definitions may be inferred from his discussion:

| Howard's Variable | Day's Measure | Instrument |
|---|---|---|
| $\underline{I}^P$ | (p. 131) | MQ—Q15 |
| $C_x$ | (p. 132) | MQ—Q16, T—Q8 |
| $P_x$ | probability of purchase brand X; given a purchase | not given (assume D) |
| $A_x$ | general-liking scale (p. 135) | MQ—Q17b—19b – scale 8 and/or T—Q7 – scale 8 |
| $\underline{F}^S$ | (p. 135) | SQ |
| $I_x$ | | not given (assume T—Q10) |

*Hypothesis-Testing Methodology.* Day tested hypothesis A by means of contingency tables, using static data (MQ—Q15 and 16) for four products (see Table 7.1).

Hypotheses B—D appear to have been tested for one brand only. To test hypothesis B, he regressed $P_x$ on $A_x$. With respect to hypothesis C, he formed six segments based on three levels of $C_x$ and two levels of $\underline{F}^S$; he then performed a regression of $P_x$ on $A_x$ for each segment. His test for hypothesis D depended on the partial correlation coefficient between $P_x$ and $I_x$ given $A_x$ ($r_{PI \cdot A}$).

Finally, Day relied on synchronous data (T1 and T3) for brands A and B to test hypothesis E; Figure 7.1 gives a graphic representation of the contingency tables based on this hypothesis.

*Empirical Findings.* Day concluded that his data supported hypothesis A; Goodman and Kruskal's Gamma ranged from .41 to .67 (see page 132). Hypothesis B yielded a correlation coefficient significant at $P = .001$ ($r^2 = .242$). In support of hypothesis C, Day found a strong interaction effect between the segmenting variables and the regression of $P_x$ on $A_x$. His analysis of this effect—based on differences in $R^2$'s and Beta coefficients between segments—notes that between the high $C_x$—high $\underline{F}^S$ and low $C_x$—low $\underline{F}^S$ groups, $R^2$'s differed by a factor of 13.2 (see page 137). The data did not support hypothesis D; $r_{PI \cdot A}$ was not statistically significant, suggesting that most of the information relevant to predicting behavior was contained in $A_x$ (page 139). Hypothesis E was supported by high Goodman and Kruskal Gammas in all four subtests.

**Perry's Simulation of Buyer Behavior**

Perry explicitly regards his work as an extended test of the Howard-Sheth model, but his methodology differs profoundly from anything else contained in this volume. Specifically, he constructed a computer simulation of the buying behavior process and evaluated the underlying model in terms of the simulation's ability to use the mail questionnaire data to generate intuitively acceptable and descriptively accurate predictions of the buyer's brand-related behavior over time.

*Correspondence between Terminologies.*  Several of Perry's symbols require specification:

| Perry's Term | Perry's Symbol | Howard's Symbol |
|---|---|---|
| Disposition | | includes: $A_x$, $C_x$, $I_x$, and $\underline{M^C}$ |
| Self-confidence | SSCO | $C_x$ |
| Attitudes | ATIT | $A_x$ |
| Intention | INTE | $I_x$ |
| Motives | | $\underline{M^C}$ (?) |
| Information | NUAD, NUCO | $F_x^E$ or $F_x^C$ |
| Purchase | BUYS | $P_x$ |

*Relationships Tested.*  The clearest statement of Perry's relationships is in Figure 8.2 from which the following functional forms are derived:

| My Notation | Howard's Equation Number(s) | Functional Form Tested |
|---|---|---|
| A | (8) | $F_x^E = f(F_{\underline{x}}^A, M_{\underline{x}}^H)$ |
| B | (7) (8) (9) (10) | $F_x^C = f(F_x^E, C_x)$ |
| C | (4) (6) | $C_x = f(F_x^C, P_x, \underline{P^T})$ |
| D | (3) (6) | $A_x = f(F_x^C, P_x, \underline{P^T})$ |
| E | (2) ($\underline{M^C}$ added) | $I_x = f(A_x, C_x, \underline{M^C})$ |
| F | (1) | $P_x = f(I_x)$ |

*Hypothesis-Testing Methodology.* Perry used the mail questionnaire to develop the simulation represented by Figure 8.3. This simulation is designed to be isomorphic with the conceptual model found in Figure 8.2 (and, hence, with the functional relationships presented in our table above). A computer run of this simulation generated printouts of predicted $F_x^C, C_x, A_x, I_x$, and $P_x$ (with $x = A$ and $x = B$) over ten cycles for each respondent. Such a procedure (incorporating lags and feedback effects more or less automatically) has the virtue of being dynamic in essence.

In general, one may argue that insofar as the simulation performs well, the model upon which it is based gains credibility (page 168). Thus a test based on simulation is, at best, an indirect test of the underlying model, as a summary of Perry's validation procedure should make clear.

(a) The *internal analysis* examines the intuitive acceptability of the simulation output.

(b) The *prediction analysis* compares the simulated purchase rates with the actual rates obtained from the purchase diaries. This analysis may proceed at the *macro-level* (comparing simulated brand-share over all ten cycles with actual brand-share) or at the *micro-level* (comparing individual period-by-period purchase predictions for each respondent with the actual outcomes). At the micro-level, Perry used a *t* test of the difference between the percentage of purchases correctly predicted and the percentage of correct predictions expected by chance; he also evaluated the proportional reduction in error attributable to the simulated predictions using Goodman and Kruskal's Tau.

(c) The *sensitivity analysis* evaluates the simulation's ability to predict process variables $(F_x^C, C_x, A_x, I_x)$ as measured by T1-T3. Perry did not compare predicted with actual by using regression across respondents (page 164), but instead relied on a qualitative comparison between average levels of predicted and actual variables at T1-T3.

*Empirical Findings.* Because Perry's test of the Howard model was indirect, we can interpret his results with respect to our ability to predict various variables, but not with respect to the relationships themselves.

(a) Perry's internal analysis concludes that the outputs shown in Tables 8.1 and 8.2 are intuitively acceptable.

(b) In his prediction analysis, Perry argues that the model performed well at the macro-level, yielding highly accurate predictions of overall brand-share (see Table 8.3 and page 160). At the micro-level, *t* tests of the degree to which predictive accuracy exceeded chance expectations found performance significantly above chance for brand B in all but one period, but not for brand A in any period (see Tables 8.3 and 8.4 and page 162). Such relationships are weak, however, with Goodman and Kruskal's Tau less than 5 percent in all cases.

(c)   The sensitivity analysis attempted only a qualitative evaluation of the accuracy of predicting average levels of the process variables in T1–T3. Perry found predicted and actual average levels "very similar except for the attitude measure of the new brand" (page 164). It should be clear, however, that these qualitative and aggregated results cannot be interpreted as supporting faith in our ability to predict the process variables at the micro-level.


## O'Brien's Cross-Lagged Correlation Study

O'Brien developed his hypotheses from the same concept of hierarchic effects that underlies the Howard-Sheth theory. The resulting predictions spanned the behavioral process from the perceptual through the learning stages. To test these hypotheses, O'Brien applied the method of cross-lagged correlation, which makes explicit use of the temporal distinctions possible with panel data. He found a set of relationships supporting the hierarchy in general, but also suggesting a complex pattern of feedback effects.

*Correspondence between Terminologies.* O'Brien's terminology closely parallels that of Howard, with the following exceptions:

| O'Brien's Term | Howard's Symbol |
|---|---|
| Stimulus Exposure (ADS, TV, WOM) | $F_x^E$ |
| Knowledge | $B_x^C$ |
| Awareness | $F_x^C$ |
| Confidence | $S_x^A$ |

*Relationships Tested.* O'Brien tested the following hypotheses, predicting monotonic relationships for hypotheses (1), (2), (4), and (5) and nonmonotonic results for hypothesis (3):

| O'Brien's Hypothesis Number | Howard's Equation Number(s) | Functional Form Tested |
|:---:|:---:|:---:|
| (1) | (7) | $F_x^C = f(F_x^E)$ |
| (2) | (5) | $B_x^C = f(F_x^C)$ |
|  | (differs) | $S_x^A = f(F_x^C)$ |
|  | (1) (2) (3) | $P_x = f(F_x^C)$ |
| (3) | (8) (9) (10) | $F_x^E = f(S_x^A)$ |
|  | differs | $F_x^E = f(B_x^C)$ |
|  | (8) (9) (4) (3) | $A_x = f(S_x^A)$ |
|  | (3) | $A_x = f(B_x^C)$ |
| (4) | (2) | $I_x = f(A_x)$ |
| (5) | (1) | $P_x = f(I_x)$ |

*Hypothesis-Testing Methodology.* O'Brien's method of cross-lagged correlation used Kendall's Tau Beta as the measure of full and partial correlation, apparently with data for all three brands in all three telephone interviews. The cross-lagged method makes explicit use of the longitudinal properties of panel data, assigning causal priority to variable $X$ over variable $Y$ if the correlation between $X$ at time 1 and $Y$ at time 2 significantly exceeds the correlation between $Y$ at time 1 and $X$ at time 2 (see page 175). Thus O'Brien earns his distinction as the only researcher in this volume to make consistent, direct, explicit use of dynamic hypotheses and longitudinal tests in a manner that allows for the presumed temporal priority of a causal variable.

*Empirical Findings.* O'Brien adopted an explicit set of criteria for judging whether a particular relationship was supported by the tests described above (see page 177).

Hypothesis 1 was supported by two out of three of the relevant relationships (namely, those relating $F_x^C$ to ADS and WOM). All three parts of hypothesis 2 received support. O'Brien found no support for the first two relations of hypothesis 3; the last two relations were upheld according to Figure 9.1, but O'Brien's discussion suggests serious reservations (page 192). O'Brien claims support for both hypotheses 4 and 5.

## Farley and Ring's Simultaneous Equation Study

Farley and Ring attempted explicitly to test the entire set of theoretical relationships postulated by Howard and Sheth and reformulated by Howard's twelve-equation model. To execute such an overall test of the buyer behavior theory, they used econometric techniques that permit dealing with simultaneous equations via two-stage least squares regression. The resulting pattern of results gives the model its most complete and isomorphic empirical test to date.

*Correspondence between Terminologies.*  The majority of Farley and Ring's terms correspond exactly to Howard's, with only a few exceptions as noted below:

| Farley and Ring's Term | Farley and Ring's Symbol | Howard's Symbol |
|---|---|---|
| Advertising | $X1$ | $F_x^A$ |
| Word-of-mouth | $X2$ | $F_x^A$ |
| Receipt of sample | $X3$ | $F_x^A$ |
| Wife's education | $X12$ | $\underline{S^C}$ |
| Wife's hours employed | $X13$ | $\underline{T^P}$ |
| Household Income | $X14$ | $\underline{F^S}$ |
| Satisfaction | $Y11$ | $S_x$ |
| Prior purchase | $X17$ | $S_x$ |

*Relationships Tested.*  Even though Farley and Ring's hypotheses correspond very closely to those of Howard, they do not explicitly test all twelve of his equations; nor do Howard's equations include all of the relationships tested by Farley and Ring. In discussing these tests, we shall continue to focus only on those hypotheses which bear directly on Howard's conceptual model.

| Farley and Ring's Number | Howard's Equation Number(s) | Functional Form Tested |
|---|---|---|
| (1) | (9) | $A_x^N = f(M^a)$ |
| (4) | (10) (7) | $M^a = f(S_x^A, P^B)$ |
| (6) | (3) (7) | $A_x = f(B_x^C, P^B, \underline{S^C})$ |
| (7) | (2) (7) | $I_x = f(P^B, A_x, C_x, \underline{S^C}, \underline{T^P}, \underline{F^S})$ |
| (8) | (5) (7) | $B_x^C = f(P^B)$ |
| (9) | (4) | $C_x = f(B_x^C)$ |
| (10) | (1) | $P_x = f(I_x)$ |
| (11) | (6) | $S_x = f(P_x)$ |

*Operational Definitions.* Farley and Ring present operational definitions in Appendix 1, page 223.

*Hypothesis-Testing Methodology.* Farley and Ring used simultaneous equation multiple-regression (OLS and TSLS) techniques borrowed from econometrics to test their hypothesized relationships cross-sectionally. While they may have made an attempt to relate independent and dependent variables consistently in order over time, some problems arise. For example, in hypothesis 4, $S_x^A$ is measured *after* $M^a$, the variable it predicts; similarly, in hypothesis 7, $C_x$ is measured after $I_x$; and in hypothesis 6, $S_x$ is measured after $A_x$.

*Empirical Findings.* We may assess the overall pattern of Farley and Ring's results by examining their $R$-coefficients (Tables 10.1 and 10.2). For OLS, all 11 $R$'s were significant at the .01 level. The relationships tended to be weak; reductions in variance range from .027 to .422 for OLS (with 5 of 11 below .10) and from .010 to .304 for TSLS (with 8 of 11 below .10).

In terms of the relationships postulated by Howard, sixteen of the coefficients in each half of the tables bear directly on those relationships. We find that, for OLS, all but four of the sixteen ($\beta_{8,2}$, $\beta_{1,4}$, $\gamma_{6,12}$, $\gamma_{7,13}$) are significant in the right direction, but that, for TSLS, eight of the sixteen fail to attain significance in the right direction ($\beta_{6,2}$, $\beta_{8,2}$, $\beta_{1,4}$, and all Gammas except $\gamma_{6,12}$).

## IV. A SYNTHESIS OF RESULTS

The above summary of results of each study, plus attempts to put the structure and notation into consistent form, allows us now to discuss the results across studies in terms of several criteria:

a.   Correspondence between terminologies and hypothetical constructs;

b.   Consistencies of hypothesized relationships;

c.   Problems in operational definition;

d.   Internal validity of hypothesis-testing methodologies;

e.   Empirical findings.


In all cases, it is important to recall that the authors did not necessarily set out to "test" the theory in any active sense, that the work described here was carried out essentially independently from study to study, that the model itself was undergoing substantial modification as the empirical work progressed, that the empirical work was done at quite different times, and that the data base used, while the same in all studies, was not ideally designed for several of the purposes for which it was used. Nonetheless, a critical summary with regard to each of the above points can be very useful both for establishing perspective and for helping design more appropriate studies and data bases in the future.

Our critical evaluation will not attempt to raise detailed criticisms of the specific studies. Such an approach would be unfair since many of these studies lack sufficient detail to serve as grist for a skeptic's mill and—more importantly—since some of the authors did not intend their work as a direct test of Howard's twelve-equation model. Rather, we shall continue to view the empirical work presented here as an overall body of research more or less pertinent to a particular theoretical perspective. Taken together, the studies found in this book, based as they are on a common body of data, represent the results to date of a broad program for research. The reader must keep in mind that it is the overall research program, not individual projects, that we wish to evaluate from a self-critical perspective that examines the extent to which this program builds toward a scientifically adequate theory in marketing.

Two circumstances inherent in the theoretical approach and research presented in this volume make it particularly difficult for these efforts collectively to attain scientific adequacy.

First, in an area such as marketing that lacks a theory of its own, one must often resort to an eclectic approach to theorizing, attempting to synthesize and integrate a wide range of micro-theories coming from diverse branches of the social sciences and attempting to relate these propositions to the domain of marketing. But such enthusiastic borrowing, no matter how carefully executed, soon encounters *the problem of eclectic inconsistency.* The resulting theory may embody variables and relationships that do not transfer comfortably from one domain to another (the transfer problem) and, worse yet, may contain propositions drawn from diverse disciplines that actually contradict one another (making for logical inconsistency).

The second problem, which we shall refer to as the *programmatic research problem,* arises when one tries to coordinate a group of fertile, but independent, minds all working in the same problem area with a common theoretical orientation—if not a common theory—as their starting point. In the present case, the phases of theory formulation, operational hypothesis specification, data collection, and hypothesis testing all proceeded simultaneously. Such jumbling of the usual temporal order serves the desirable end of bringing a wide range of capabilities to bear on a common problem, but undeniably it can result in awkward situations wherein the data are collected before the hypotheses are specified or the model is later refined in a manner that contradicts a given researcher's hypotheses.

Under such circumstances, shortcomings in the reported research appear inevitable. We shall not shrink from the responsibility of acknowledging these difficulties. Rather, we shall attempt in the following discussion to indicate how eclectic inconsistency and programmatic research problems have conjoined to provide us some grounds for disappointment without damaging our hopes for the eventual resolution of these weaknesses in future work.

### Summary of the Correspondence between Terminologies and Hypothetical Constructs

Differences in terminology present no insurmountable problems as long as the terms in question refer to the same thing. If researcher $X$ calls a variable $X1$ and researcher $Y$ calls it $Y1$, the two can converse—after a little practice—as long as the two terms refer ultimately to the same underlying constructs. Annoying though they may be to the reader, the deviations in terminology that we have encountered cannot themselves be taken as evidence of scientific weakness. There are, however, cases in which the underlying hypothetical constructs appear to differ between authors. The confusion between $S_x^A$ and $C_x$ probably results from the fact that these two constructs have been borrowed from two different research traditions. The decision-theoretic concept of confidence or certainty, which implicitly underlies the Bauer-inspired work on perceived risk, would view $C_x$ as a variable inherent in the purchasing-decision situation. $S_x^A$, on the other hand, relates to the psychologist's attempt to deal with a stimulus confronting a subject in terms of theories of motivation-conflict and bits of information.

Another inconsistency involves the fundamental concept of attitude. Sheth, for example, does not distinguish between his concepts of "affect" and "attitude," while several authors (Day, Pellemans, and Farley and Ring) use what Sheth calls "affect" as their concept of "attitude."

The programmatic research problem accounts for the less serious confusion between $F_x^C$ and $B_x^C$. The earlier Howard-Sheth model hypothesized a hierarchy of effects $(A_x^n \rightarrow B_x^C \rightarrow A_x \rightarrow I_x \rightarrow P_x)$ while Howard's revised version implies a slightly different hierarchy $(F_x^E \rightarrow F_x^C \rightarrow A_x \rightarrow I_x \rightarrow P_x)$. Some of the earlier research efforts continue to employ the $A_x^n$ and $B_x^C$ variables in place of the newer $F_x^E$ and $F_x^C$. It is not surprising, therefore, to encounter inconsistencies between empirical work and the revised versions of models, and between the empirical studies themselves.

## A Summary of the Consistency in Hypothesized Relationships

We have noted occasional logical inconsistency based on the model. Pellemans, for example, argues that since $I_x = f(C_x, A_x)$, some relationship should exist between $C_x$ and $A_x$ (page 122). More common are problems stemming from the transfer of concepts between disciplines. The best examples of these are Lampert's hypotheses 1–4 (which stem from the research on the diffusion of innovations) and Day's hypothesis F (which relates attitude change to confidence and which appears related to the Janis-inspired research on persuasibility and self-esteem, though Day doesn't say so). In both cases, the hypotheses fall rather uncomfortably within the context of Howard's twelve equations.

Even more common are logical inconsistencies resulting from the programmatic problem. In many cases, direct relationships formerly hypothesized are now hypothesized only indirectly. Thus we may require several of Howard's new equations to account for one relationship proposed by some author (see, for example, Lampert–4 and 5; Pellemans–B, D, and H; Day–A; O'Brien–3). In other words, a given author's hypothesis, even though consistent with a version of Howard and Sheth's work, may imply chaining together several of Howard's revised equations. Such logic, however, ignores the complex structural interactions and feedback loops contained in the theory. It is as if we were committing the linear-thinking fallacy inherent in the simplistic hierarchy-of-effects hypothesis all over again. Hence, some of the hypotheses listed are made illogical or naive in light of later developments.

A second type of difficulty springing from the programmatic nature of the research involves direct inconsistencies between various authors as, for example, in the case of the hypothesized relationship between attitude and purchase as mediated by intention. Probably no variable has undergone more changes in conception during the development of the theory of buyer behavior than the variable $I_x$. Thus we find Sheth arguing that predictable inhibitors intervene between $A_x$ and $I_x$ and nonpredictable inhibitors intervene between $I_x$ and $P_x$. But Pellemans assumes that $I_x$ shows the effects of all constraints; Perry views all inhibitors as acting directly on $P_x$; and Day disregards the role of inhibitors altogether (page 145). (Part of the explanation, of course, would focus on the time at which we measure $I_x$.)

### A Summary of Problems in Operational Definitions

We shall have little to say about the problems of instrument bias and measurement reliability. Yet some consideration of the validity of operational definitions appears essential because the eclectic and programmatic problems have intensified difficulties in defining the model's variables operationally.

The problem of eclecticism is most severe when variables originally formulated in an experimental setting appear in a survey-based approach. Lampert, for example, considers word of mouth a type of $O_x^S$, but few would argue that this variable bears a clear-cut relationship to the exploratory behavior investigated by experimental psychologists. Nor can we interpret Farley and Ring's definition of $A_x^n$ (ad recall–T2–Q6) as in any sense equivalent to what psychologists mean by orienting response. There are other examples of problems due to the borrowing of concepts from other disciplines, especially at the perceptual end of the model.

An even more common breakdown in operationalization stems from the programmatic research problem. As noted earlier, the authors of many of the studies presented here formulated their hypotheses only *after* the collection of the data. Thus, for example, Lampert, O'Brien, and Farley and Ring were forced to adopt extremely crude measures of the cognitive variable $F_x^C$ or $B_x^C$ based on unaided, aided, or no recall (T–Q1). Key variables were also undoubtedly omitted because of the impossibility of defining them operationally in data already collected.

### Summary of the Internal Validity of the Hypothesis-Testing Methodologies

Internal validity must stress the importance of testing procedures in survey research that take account of (a) the time-order of variables and (b) complex structural relations between systems of variables. With respect to the first requirement, one recurring theme dominates our survey of the researchers' test methodologies: the widespread failure to treat the data in the dynamic fashion that the carefully designed panel procedure would have permitted. Although panel data offer the opportunity, rare in survey research, of establishing the time-order of some variables, most of the studies are static in nature. Farley and Ring are found to employ independent variables that were in some cases measured after the dependent variables they are supposed to predict. Clearly, relationships found under such conditions are always susceptible to an increased number of skeptical interpretations such as reverse causality, acquiescence set, or self-consistency of responses within an instrument. An example of this breakdown of dynamic hypothesis-testing with static data is the "flip-flop" problem, involved in Lampert's work. Thus the dynamic hypothesis is that $C_x \rightarrow O_x^S \rightarrow$ higher $C_x$; but such a relationship through time obviously eludes the scope of static data. Of course, the longitudinal studies (O'Brien's, for example) make use of the panel design, and Perry also treats his simulation tests dynamically. Sheth's treatment of hypothesis VI also successfully overcomes the flip-flop problem mentioned above.

Second, testing procedures do not always take account of complex structural relations. Lampert, Sheth, Pellemans, and Day deal primarily with simple two-variable tests (though Day and O'Brien also employ partial correlation). Only Perry, and Farley and Ring, use methodologies that explicitly treat structural relations within a complete system of variables.

### Summary of the Empirical Findings

Exhibit II presents a summary of the empirical findings bearing directly on Howard's twelve-equation model. The key criterion for judging a relationship to be supported was the author's specific claim that it reached statistical significance in the right direction. In some cases, where no statement of statistical significance appeared, we accepted the author's conclusion, based on some reasonable set of criteria, that his data supported a relationship (e.g., O'Brien). For further details, see our discussion of the individual chapters.

The overall impression of the empirical findings is one of incompleteness. First of all, out of 37 clearly interpretable tests, only 24 and two-thirds produced evidence consistent with Howard's simultaneous equation model, although most studies dealt with only a small part of the system. Second, such support as exists is highly fragmentary, based for the most part on bivariate relations. Third, no single link in the model receives consistent support over those studies which actually deal with it. Finally, none of the studies can boast $R^2$'s consistently above 10 percent, and proportional reduction in standard error would be even smaller. It is clear that substantial problems in data and measurement of the phenomena remain.

## Exhibit II:  Summary of Results

( ) = Relationship tested
(*) = Relationship supported (author's conclusion re statistical significance)
(i) = Indirect evidence

| Howard's Equation / Form Tested | Lampert | Sheth | Pellemans | Day | Perry | O'Brien | Farley and Ring OLS |
|---|---|---|---|---|---|---|---|
| **(1)** $P_x = f(I_x)$ | | | | | | | |
| $P_x = f(I_x)$ | | | | | (i) | (*) | (*) |
| $P_x = f(I_x|A_x)$ | | | | ( ) | | | |
| $P_x = f(A_x)$ | | | (?) | | (*) | | |
| $P_x = f(A_x/C_x, \underline{F^S})$ | | | | | (*) | | |
| $P_x = f(F_x^C)$ | | | | | | (*) | |
| **(2)** $I_x = f(F_x^C, A_x, C_x, \underline{C^u}, \underline{S^C}, \underline{S^{OS}}, T^P, F^S)$ | | | | | | | |
| $I_x = f(P^B, A_x, C_x, \underline{S^C}, T^P, F^S)$ | | | | | | | (*) |
| $I_x = f(A_x, C_x, \underline{M^c})$ | | | | ( ) | | | |
| $I_x = f(F_x^C)$ | | (*) | (?) | | | | |
| $I_x = f(A_x)$ | | (*) | (?) | | | | (*) |
| $I_x = f(C_x)$ | | | (?) | (*) | | | |
| $I_x = f(F_x^E)$ | | | (?) | | | | |
| $I_x = f(P_x)$ | | | (?) | | | | |
| $I_x = f(S_x)$ | | | (?) | | | | |
| $I_x = f(\underline{S^C})$ | | | (?) | | | | |
| **(3)** $A_x = f(B_x^C, S_x, F_x^C, \underline{C^u}, \underline{S^C}, \underline{S^{OS}}, P^T)$ | | | | | | | |
| $A_x = f(B_x^C, P^B, \underline{S^C})$ | | | | | | | (*) |
| $A_x = f(F_x^C, P_x, \underline{P^T})$ | | | | ( ) | | | |
| $A_x = f(F_x^C)$ | | (*) | (?) | | | | |
| $A_x = f(F_x^E)$ | | | (?) | | | | |
| $A_x = f(P_x)$ | | (*) | (?) | | | | |
| $A_x = f(S_x)$ | | | (?) | | | | |
| $A_x = f(\underline{S^C})$ | | | (?) | | | | |
| $A_x = f(\underline{I^P})$ | | | (?) | | | | |
| $A_x = f(S_x^A)$ | | | | | | ( ) | |
| $A_x = f(B_x^C)$ | | | | | | ( ) | |

| Howard's Equation / Form Tested | Lampert | Shethmans | Pelle | Day | Perry | O'Brien | Farley and Ring OLS |
|---|---|---|---|---|---|---|---|
| **(4)** $C_x = f(B^C_x, S_x, F^C_x, \underline{P^T})$ | | | | | | | |
| $\quad C_x = f(F^C_x, P_x, P^T)$ | | | | | ( ) | | |
| $\quad C_x = f(B^C_x)$ | | | | | | | (*) |
| $\quad C_x = f(I^P)$ | | | | (*) | | | |
| **(5)** $B^C_x = f(F^C_x, \underline{C^u}, \underline{S^C}, \underline{S^{OS}}, \underline{I^P}, \underline{P^T})$ | | | | | | | |
| $\quad B^C_x = f(P^B)$ | | | | | | | (*) |
| $\quad B^C_x = f(F^C_x)$ | | | | | | (*) | |
| **(6)** $S_x = f(P_x)$ | | | | | | | |
| $\quad S_x = f(P_x)$ | | | | | | | (*) |
| **(7)** $F^C_x = f(F^E_x, A^n_x, P^B_x)$ | | | | | | | |
| $\quad F^C_x = f(F^E_x, C_x)$ | | | | | ( ) | | |
| $\quad F^C_x = f(F^E_x)$ | | | | | | (2/3) | |
| **(8)** $F^E_x = f(O^S_x, \underline{F^A_x}, M^H)$ | | | | | | | |
| $\quad F^E_x = f(\underline{F^A_x}, M^H)$ | | | | | ( ) | | |
| $\quad F^E_x = f(S^A_x)$ | | | | | | ( ) | |
| $\quad F^E_x = f(B^C_x)$ | | | | | | ( ) | |
| **(9)** $A^n_x, O^S_x = f(M^a, \underline{I^P}, \underline{P^T}, \underline{T^P})$ | | | | | | | |
| $\quad O^S_x = f(C_x, F^E_x, F_x)$ | (*) | | | | | | |
| $\quad O^S_x = f(C_x)$ | ( ) | | | | | | |
| $\quad O^S_x = f(\underline{P^T})$ | ( ) | | | | | | |
| $\quad O^S_x = f(F^E_x)$ | (*) | | | | | | |
| $\quad O^S_x = f(F^C_x)$ | (*) | | | | | | |
| $\quad A^n_x = f(M^a)$ | | | | | | | (*) |
| **(10)** $M^a = f(S^A_x, C_x, F^C_x, \underline{F^S})$ | | | | | | | |
| $\quad M^a = f(S^A_x, P^B_x)$ | | | | | | | (*) |
| **(11)** $S^A_x = f(F^E_x)$ | | | | | | | |
| $\quad S^A_x = f(F^C_x)$ | | | | | | (*) | |
| **(12)** $C^C = f(F^C_x, M^a, \underline{M^c})$ | | | | | | | |

# VI

## A Glimpse into the Future

# 12. Buyer Behavior and Related Technological Advances

## John A. Howard

"How much more will I sell if I double my advertising?" the manager asks. "How should I analyze these facts?" the market researcher wonders. "Is the concept of a marketing information system a sensible one?" many people are asking. "How do I explain to this Congressional committee that advertising will not change basic eating habits?" a company president contemplates. "Should the government provide consumer information programs?" a Congressman poses to his colleagues. "What is the process by which a buyer's attitude toward the brand causes him to buy or not buy the brand?" a university researcher muses. The solution to these and many other important marketing problems is greatly influenced by the state of our knowledge of buyer behavior.

The decade of the 1960's has been a time of rapid growth in consumer behavior research and practice. Drawing on the theoretical contributions and empirical evidence of behavioral scientists in other fields of endeavor as well as their own creative work, marketing scholars such as Bass, Bauer, Ferber, Frank, Green, Kassarjian, Kuehn, Massey, Myers, Nicosia, and Pessemier have made major contributions to our knowledge of the processes of consumer behavior. Much of this work has already resulted in substantial improvements in marketing operations.

The quantity of facts and propositions on the buying behavior of consumers accumulated by companies and researchers is enormous. However, many of these bits of information or propositions stand alone and are used in the context of a specific decision situation. What is lacking in this approach is

This article is reprinted from the *Journal of Marketing*, January 1970.

the leverage to be gained from a comprehensive structure which makes possible substantial predictions about consumer behavior. The need for such a structure to guide research and to improve marketing practice is obvious. It is this author's opinion that efforts in the next decade will be directed at the empirical validation and continuing refinement of such a theory.

Based upon the splendid work of the men cited above, a comprehensive theory of buyer behavior has been developed at the Columbia Business School. This theory integrates relevant behavioral propositions from learning theory, cognitive theory, and exploratory behavior theory, with other ideas from the behavioral sciences and systems analysis. The theory posits the nature, relationships, operating characteristics, and flows that exist in the consumer decision-making process. Given a knowledge of exogenous variables, the theory relates outputs (behavior) to inputs (internal and external stimuli) through hypothetical constructs which describe the processes internal to the consumer.

Developments such as those noted result in an operational technology which will have major impact on the science and practice of marketing. This technology represents a systems view of the market, a view which distinguishes between the controllable and uncontrollable variables that play upon the buyer, and which brings relevant factors into a quantitative, coherent, unified, operational picture.

The immediate importance of this technology is confined to the narrow topic of buyer behavior and to the interests of the market researcher. It has also far-reaching implications for the marketing manager, developer of marketing information system, company president, public policy maker, and university researcher.

### FOR COMPANY MARKET RESEARCHERS

Market researchers will collect less data but will derive more information from them. In applying these ideas they will contribute to the technology and to fitting the theory to their particular markets.

First, the question of which facts to collect will be more systematically decided, i.e., those facts specified by the theory. The researcher can be more discriminating instead of collecting facts which he hopes will be useful.

Second, collecting facts from the same person at two or more points in time—a panel—will be more common. Panels have rarely been efficiently used.

Third, more systematic data-storage procedures will be adopted. Casual observation indicates that research departments' ways of storing facts have been a serious handicap to the extensive analysis essential for adequate diagnoses. There will be, for example, greater accessibility to "marginals," which are important both in themselves and as an essential link between the questionnaire and the analyses that follow.

Fourth, statistical techniques which incorporate causality and its increased explanatory power will be more widely applied. Multi-equation models will enable us to deal rigorously with the complexity that characterizes consumer behavior in response to marketing effort. From each period's data, lagged correlation can obtain more specific information about the nature of the relations so that in the next period the multi-equation model can be more precisely specified to the particular market. In this way, the researcher can increase the precision of his methods from period to period. A goal of this technological development will be to get the "noise" level down, i.e., to reduce the unexplained variance in the dependent variable. Experience indicates that the crucially important variables of advertising, price, and selling effort are most subject to the "noise" problem, which limits linking them directly or indirectly to purchasing behavior. This linking is essential if real progress is to be made. The theory is deliberately designed to focus upon the marketing or controllable variables

Finally, in every analysis there is the task of interpretation and logical extension of the conclusions beyond the data. Systematic diagnosis is currently so severely handicapped that it is almost never done. Even if diagnosis were so highly valued that effort was assigned to it in the face of horrendous time pressures, the appropriate data are not identified, the constructs are not validated, and they are treated piecemeal instead of as parts of a system. If appropriate data were identified, adequate means of collection would not be employed because of the exaggerated fear of contamination. If appropriate data were collected, they would be stored in such a way as to render them inaccessible for further use. Assuming these data were readily accessible, current techniques of analysis would not be up to these demands. Finally, even if all prior conditions were not met, diagnosis would probably be stopped because by and large we have not had the necessary theory nor developed the practical skills to use it. This description is a bit harsh but not much.

## FOR MARKETING MANAGERS

"Marketing manager" refers to anyone who is concerned not only with marketing, but also with the total marketing picture, irrespective of his level in the corporate hierarchy. The technology will yield the marketing manager more information with less data because the system is more efficient. The systems view will lay before him a quantitative review of the consequences of his marketing alternatives.

This integrated, causal picture of the influences affecting the buyer will provide a powerful lever to the marketing manager's understanding of the market by giving him concepts which will cut through the maze of complexity and which will encourage sharp diagnoses of marketing failures and successes. These diagnoses will be adding to his comprehension of the market, enable the marketing manager to build a marketing philosophy which aids imaginative innovation and prevents him from being misled by minor aberrations of the market. More logical and elaborate control—performance measures—will be built into his marketing procedures. His observations of and conclusions about the meaning of these measures will enormously strengthen the more systematic diagnoses that follow.

Also, the premises underlying his strategy will be more explicit and articulated. These will not only guide him but also will facilitate *communication*. In relations with superiors, such as in defending his marketing plan and its supporting budget, he will be better able to secure approval because management will be in a better position to comprehend and appreciate his arguments. For the same reason, his relations with his peers will improve. His directions to his subordinates will be more explicit, better understood, and therefore better executed. Some of the differences in views about the probable effectiveness of different plans will diminish. The better communication will improve relations with the market researcher. Thus, the manager can assume leadership in identifying and designing the necessary studies instead of passively reacting to proposals from the market research department. The manager can usually better perform this role than the researcher because he is more aware of the appropriate corporate goals and of broad market issues.

A variety of operations research and management science techniques lie fallow because of the lack of behavioral input. The technology will provide this input for some of these techniques which will simplify the manager's decision making and planning. In fact, with the behavioral relations better understood, simpler optimizing techniques will suffice.

## FOR MARKETING INFORMATION SYSTEMS

The new technology will facilitate the development of a marketing information system. Such a system typically implies a commitment to collect facts on the same variables for several periods of time. The theory will assist this task (1) by specifying the facts, and (2) by suggesting ways of collecting facts. Moreover, the statistical techniques could form an essential part of such a system.

The comments made here, however, provide no answer to the central question of whether the facts or derived information will "fit the manager's head." An important but subtle phenomenon is that each experienced executive has a "model" of his market which is not only unarticulated but usually totally subconscious. Yet his "model" strongly shapes which facts he considers relevant and how he interprets them. Until we have a better understanding of what these "models" are and how the manager processes his information, our capacity to build useful information systems will be limited. Some evidence suggests that in a given type of decision situation, managers use very similar information processing approaches, but more conclusive evidence is needed.

## FOR COMPANY PRESIDENTS

The technology has implications both internally and externally for the president. Internally, the concepts will make it easier for him to communicate with his marketing personnel and because of the better communication his respect for them will be enhanced.

Equally, if not more important in this day of consumerism, company presidents will be better equipped to explain and often justify their practices to the public and to government agencies. In a recent Congressional hearing, the presidents of two large companies were asked by the chairman why they did not use their advertising funds to change the basic eating habits of the poverty-stricken. The hearing transcript indicates that the presidents did not answer the question. These very able men knew intuitively that such an approach was impractical, but they lacked the concepts to adequately articulate their experientially derived beliefs to those less versed in their particular domain of expertise. This is a problem that all experts face, but those in a theory-based field can usually perform far more effectively.

## FOR PUBLIC POLICY MAKERS

Consumer interests have become a politically relevant issue, and the many able Congressmen who are directing their energies to formulating and passing appropriate legislation will find this technology useful in developing a multi-faceted, rational consumer policy. Concepts they need for comprehending the buyer will enable them to communicate more easily with the scientists in the field, with the philosophically oriented individuals who relate the scientists' facts to social values, and with the special interest groups. The same technology but with a somewhat different orientation in study design and interpretation can provide specific data to guide their decisions. One of the questions is what kind of evidence will be accepted because there has been a growing tendency to accept statistical inference as evidence.

## FOR UNIVERSITY RESEARCHERS

In a splendid recent review of a definitive book in market segmentation, Ferber states: "It (the book) suggests in analyzing consumer purchase behavior we are still at the stage where the principal difficulty is not how to answer the questions but rather how to formulate the questions and obtain meaningful data."[3] The new technology implies that we are now ready to move beyond this stage.

One of the major tasks is to acquire a fuller understanding of the relations among the variables in the system.[1,2] O'Brien and others have shown that this can be done. Some of the relations are not only nonlinear but nonmonotonic over the relevant range. Hence, some of the relations may be too subtle for field research and the laboratory will play an essential role. The new technology too will be facilitated because testing ideas that are part of a system instead of an isolated hypothesis gives leverage in the development of new knowledge: control is easier to build in and interpretation is much more productive.

Another area of research will be directed toward reducing the high level of "noise" found in the research on the relations among the variables. Hopefully it will enable us to specify the system more precisely. The timing of changes in the variables deserves particular attention. Much of the research, however, will be methodological. For example, more refined measuring instruments and better ways of analyzing data to determine causality are essential.

## CONCLUSION

Large accretions of knowledge—often breakthroughs—seem to occur when different and often apparently unrelated strands of development begin to merge. The new technology represents one such merger, in fact, a set of two mergers. First, there is the merger in psychology. Cognitive, learning, and motivation theories have begun to come together. Second, two types of research in marketing that were largely separate in the period 1955 to 1965—the quantitative and behavioral approaches to buyer behavior—have since joined into a single stream.

Another but different kind of merger appears imminent—the manager and the market. Management science and operations research have largely been concerned with normative models. However, these models made no pretense of representing the manager's thought processes. They were substitutes for these processes: One is beginning to observe that some of the highly competent people associated with this management science-operations research point of view are attempting to build formal models that are integrated into a manager's thinking processes, which currently seem rather idiosyncratic. This view will merge rapidly with the new technology, and a most exciting period in marketing should be the consequence. The new technology can replace many of the subjective estimates with objective data. Thus, because a manager's underlying premises will be more accurate, his decision process will be more systematic.

Finally, and for the sake of perspective, we must remember that ultimately, as in all good science, the product of this merger will also carry the seeds of its own destruction and yield to still better structures than we are now capable of envisioning.

**References**

1. Howard, J. A., and J. N. Sheth, *The Theory of Buyer Behavior* (New York: John Wiley & Sons, Inc., 1969), pp. 421–429.
2. Howard, J. A., and W. M. Morgenroth, "Information Processing Model of Executive Decision," *Management Science* 31 (March 1968): 416–428.
3. Ferber, Robert, in a review of William F. Massey, Ronald E. Frank, and Thomas M. Lodahl, "Purchasing Behavior and Personal Attributes," *Journal of Economic Literature* 7 (June 1969): 483–485.
4. Little, John D. C., "Models and Managers: The Concept of a Decision Calculus," Paper delivered before the symposium *Behavioral and Management Science in Marketing*, University of Chicago, June 29 to July 1, 1969.

# Combined Bibliography

Abelson, R. P., et al., eds., *Theories of Cognitive Consistency: A Source Book* (Chicago: Rand McNally, 1968).

Allport, G. W., "Attitudes," in *A Handbook of Social Psychology*, ed. C. Murchison (Worcester, Mass.: Clark University Press, 1935), pp. 798–844.

Amstutz, Arnold E., *Computer Simulation of Competitive Market Response* (Cambridge: M.I.T. Press, 1967).

Arndt, Johan, "Perceived Risk, Sociometric Integration and Word of Mouth in the Adoption of a New Food Product," in *Science, Technology, and Marketing*, ed. R. M. Hass (Chicago: American Marketing Association, 1966).

————, "Word of Mouth Advertising: The Role of Product-Related Conversations in the Diffusion of a New Food Product," Unpublished dissertation, Harvard University, 1966.

————, "Role of Product-Related Conversations in the Diffusion of a New Product," *Journal of Marketing Research* 4 (August 1967): 291–295.

————, *Word of Mouth Advertising: A Review of the Literature* (New York: Advertising Research Foundation, 1967).

Bass, Frank M., and Leonard J. Parsons, "Simultaneous-Equation Regression Analysis of Sales and Advertising," in *Changing Perspectives in Marketing*, ed. Charles Goodman (Chicago: American Marketing Association, 1968).

Bauer, Raymond A., "Consumer Behavior as Risk Taking," in *Dynamic Marketing for a Changing World*, ed. R. S. Hancock (Chicago: American Marketing Association, 1960).

————, and Stephen A. Greyser, *Advertising in America: The Consumer View* (Boston: Division of Research, Graduate School of Business Administration, Harvard University, 1968).

Baumol, William, "Calculation of Optimal Product and Retailer Characteristics: The Abstract Product Approach," *Journal of Political Economy* 75 (October 1967): 674–685.

Becknell, James C., Jr., Warner R. Wilson, and J. C. Baird, "The Effect of Frequency of Presentation on the Choice of Nonsense Syllables," *Journal of Psychology* 56 (July 1963): 165–170.

Bell, G. D., "Self-Confidence and Persuasion in Car Buying," *Journal of Marketing Research* 4 (February 1967): 46–52.

Benson, Purnell H., "Eliminating Consumer Biases in Survey Data by Balanced Tabulation," *Journal of Marketing Research* 1 (November 1964): 66–71.

Berg, Dale H., "An Enquiry into the Effect of Exposure to Advertisements on Subsequent Perception of Similar Advertisements," *Journal of Applied Psychology* 51 (December 1967): 503–508.

Berlyne, Daniel E., *Conflict, Arousal and Curiosity* (New York: McGraw-Hill, 1960).

————, "Complexity and Incongruity Variables as Determinants of Exploratory Choice and Evaluative Ratings," *Canadian Journal of Psychology* 17 (September 1963): 274–290.

————, "Motivational Problems Raised by Exploratory and Epistemic Behavior," in *Psychology: A Study of Science*, V, ed. Sigmund Koch (New York: McGraw-Hill Book Co., 1963).

————, et al., "Novelty, Complexity, Incongruity, Extrinsic Motivation and the GSR," *Journal of Experimental Psychology* 66 (December 1963): 560–567.

————, and George H. Lawrence, II, "Effects of Complexity and Incongruity Variables on GSR, Investigatory Behavior and Verbally Expressed Preference," *Journal of General Psychology* 71 (July 1964): 21–45.

————, and Sylvia Peckham, "The Semantic Differential and Other Measures of Reaction to Visual Complexity," University of Toronto, 1968 (mimeographed).

Blalock, Hubert, *Causal Models in the Social Sciences* (Chicago: Aldine-Atherton, Inc., 1971).

Bogart, Leo, *Strategy in Advertising* (New York: Harcourt, Brace and World, 1967).

Boulle, Pierre, *Time Out of Mind* (New York: Vanguard Press, 1966).

Broadbent, Donald E., *Perception and Communication* (London: Pergamon Press, 1958).

Bucklin, Louis P., and James M. Carman, *The Design of Consumer Research Panels: Conception and Administration of the Berkeley Food Panel* (Berkeley: Institute of Business and Economic Research, University of California, 1967).

Cohen, A. R., *Attitude Change and Social Influence* (New York: Basic Books, 1964).

Coleman, J., E. Katz, and H. Menzel, "The Diffusion of an Innovation among Physicians," *Sociometry* 20 (December 1957): 253–270.

————, H. Menzel, and E. Katz, "Social Processes in Physicians' Adoption of a New Drug," *Journal of Chronic Diseases* 9 (January 1959): 1–19.

Costner, H. L., "Criteria for Measures of Association," *American Sociological Review* 30 (June 1965): 341–353.

Cox, D. F., "The Audience of Communicators," in *Toward Scientific Marketing*, ed. S. A. Greyser (Chicago: American Marketing Association, 1964).

Cox, H. B., and S. M. Cunningham, "Chicken Sara Lee Team Report," Graduate School of Business Administration, Harvard University, 1961 (Unpublished paper).

Cunningham, Scott M., "Perceived Risk as a Factor in Product Oriented Word of Mouth Behavior: A First Step," in *Reflections on Progress in Marketing*, ed. L. G. Smith (Chicago: American Marketing Association, 1965).

————, "The Role of Perceived Risk in Product-Related Discussion and Brand Commitment," Dissertation, Harvard University, 1965.

Danzig, Fred, "Ajax Market Share Improves, but White Knight Turns in His Tin Suit," *Advertising Age* (December 25, 1967): 3, 42.

Day, George S., "Buyer Attitudes and Brand Choice Behavior," Dissertation, Columbia University, 1967.

————, *Buyer Attitudes and Brand Choice Behavior* (New York: Free Press, 1970).

Doob, Leonard, "The Behavior of Attitudes," *Psychological Review* 54 (January 1947): 135−156.

Driscoll, James M., and John T. Lanzetta, "Effects of Two Sources of Uncertainty in Decision-Making," *Psychological Reports* 17 (October 1965): 635−648.

Dulany, D. E., "The Separable Effects of the Information and Affect Conveyed by a Reinforcer," Niagara Falls, 1964. (Paper presented at the annual meeting of the Psychonomic Society.)

————, "Awareness, Rules, and Propositional Control: A Confrontation with S-R Behavior Theory," in *Verbal Behavior and General Behavior Theory*, eds. T. R. Dixon and D. L. Horton (Englewood Cliffs, N.J.: Prentice-Hall, 1968).

Eckart, C., and G. Young, "The Approximation of One Matrix by Another of Lower Rank," *Psychometrika* 1 (September 1936): 211−218.

Engel, James F., David T. Kollat, and Roger D. Blackwell, *Consumer Behavior* (New York: Holt, Rinehart and Winston, 1968).

Engel, J. F., D. A. Knapp, and D. E. Knapp, "Sources of Influence in the Acceptance of New Products for Self Medication: Preliminary Findings," in *Science, Technology and Marketing*, ed. R. M. Hass (Chicago: American Marketing Association, 1966), pp. 776−782.

Farley, John U., " 'Brand Loyalty' and the Economics of Information," *Journal of Business* 37 (October 1964): 370−382.

————, "Estimating Structural Parameters in Marketing Systems," in *Changing Perspectives in Marketing*, ed. Charles Goodman (Chicago: American Marketing Association, 1968).

————, and L. Winston Ring, "On R and H and HAPPISIM," *Journal of Marketing Research* 9 (August 1972).

————————, and L. Winston Ring, "An Empirical Test of the Howard-Sheth Model of Buyer Behavior," *Journal of Marketing Research* 7 (November 1970): 427–438.

Ferber, Robert, in a review of William F. Massey, Ronald E. Frank, and Thomas M. Lodahl, "Purchasing Behavior and Personal Attributes," *Journal of Economic Literature* 7 (June 1969): 483–485.

————————, and Hugh W. Wales, *Motivation and Market Behavior* (Homewood, Illinois: Richard D. Irwin, Inc., 1958).

Festinger, Leon, "Behavioral Support for Opinion Change," *Public Opinion Quarterly* 28 (Fall 1964): 404–417.

Fishbein, Martin, "The Relationship between Beliefs, Attitudes and Behavior," in *Cognitive Consistency, Motivational Antecedents and Behavioral Consequences*, ed. S. Feldman (New York: Academic Press, 1966).

————————, ed., *Readings in Attitude Theory and Measurement* (New York: John Wiley & Sons, Inc., 1967).

————————, and B. H. Raven, "The AB Scales: An Operational Definition of Belief and Attitude," *Human Relations* 15 (February 1962): 35–44.

Gold, Jack A., "Testing Test Market Predictions," *Journal of Marketing Research* 1 (August 1964): 8–17.

Goodman, Leo A., and William H. Kruskal, "Measures of Association for Cross-Classifications," *Journal of the American Statistical Association* 49 (December 1954): 732–764.

————————, "Measures of Association for Cross-Classification," *Journal of the American Statistical Association* 54 (March 1958): 732–764.

Harris, Chester W., ed., *Problems of Measuring Change* (Madison, Wisconsin: University of Wisconsin Press, 1967).

Hermann, C., "Validation Problems in Games and Simulations with Special Reference to Models of International Politics," *Behavioral Science* 12 (May 1967): 216–231.

Hochberg, Julian E., *Perception* (Englewood Cliffs, N.J.: Prentice-Hall, 1964).

Hoeffding, Wassily, "A Class of Statistics with Asymptotically Normal Distributions," *The Annals of Mathematical Statistics* 19 (September 1948): 293–325.

————————, " 'Optimum' Nonparametric Tests," in *Proceedings of the 2nd Berkeley Symposium on Mathematical Statistics and Probability* (July 31–August 12, 1950), ed. Jerzy Neyman (Berkeley: University of California Press, 1951).

Hovland, Carl I., et al., *Communication and Persuasion: Psychological Studies of Opinion Change* (New Haven: Yale University Press, 1953).

————————, "Reconciling Conflicting Results Derived from Experimental and Survey Studies of Attitude Change," *American Psychologist* 14 (January 1959): 8–17.

Howard, John A., *Marketing Management* (Homewood, Ill.: Richard D. Irwin, Inc., 1963).

————————, "Confidence as a Validated Construct," Columbia University, 1968 (unpublished paper).

_____, "Confidence as a Validated Construct," New York, 1969 (Paper presented at the Third Annual Buyer Behavior Conference, Columbia University).

_____ and W. M. Morgenroth, "Information Processing Model of Executive Decision," *Management Science* 31 (March 1968): 416–428.

_____ and Jagdish N. Sheth, *The Theory of Buyer Behavior* (New York: John Wiley & Sons, Inc., 1969).

Insko, C. A., *Theories of Attitude Change* (New York: Appleton-Century-Crofts, 1967).

James, William, *The Principles of Psychology* (New York: Henry Holt and Co., 1890).

Johnston, Jack, *Econometric Methods* (New York: McGraw-Hill Book Co., 1963).

Katona, G., and E. Mueller, "A Study of Purchase Decisions," in *Consumer Behavior: The Dynamics of Consumer Reactions*, ed. L. M. Clark (New York: New York University Press, 1954), pp. 30–87.

Katz, Elihu, "The Two-Step Flow of Communication: An Up-to-Date Report on an Hypothesis," *Public Opinion Quarterly* 21 (Spring 1957): 61–78.

_____, and Paul F. Lazarsfeld, *Personal Influence* (New York: The Free Press of Glencoe, 1955).

Kendall, Maurice G., "A New Measure of Rank Correlation," *Biometrika* 30 (June 1938): 81–93.

_____, *Rank Correlation Methods* (London: Charles Griffin & Co., 1948).

_____, *Rank Correlation Methods*, 2d ed. (London: Charles Griffin & Co., 1955).

Kendall, Patricia, *Conflict and Mood* (New York: Free Press of Glencoe, 1953).

Kerby, Joe Kent, "Semantic Generalization in the Formation of Consumer Attitudes," *Journal of Marketing Research* 4 (August 1967): 314–317.

Kollat, David T., and Ronald P. Willett, "Customer Impulse Purchasing Behavior," *Journal of Marketing Research* 4 (February 1967): 21–31.

Kosobud, Richard F., and James N. Morgan, eds., *Consumer Behavior of Individual Families Over Two and Three Years* (Ann Arbor: University of Michigan Press, 1964).

Krugman, Herbert E., "The Measurement of Advertising Involvement," *Public Opinion Quarterly* 30 (Winter 1966-67): 583–596.

_____, "Processes Underlying Exposure to Advertising," Washington, D. C., September 1967. (Paper presented at the 75th annual convention of the American Psychological Association.)

Lampert, Shlomo I., "Word of Mouth Activity during the Introduction of a New Food Product," Dissertation, preliminary draft, Columbia University, 1969.

Lancaster, Kelvin J., "A New Approach to Consumer Theory," *Journal of Political Economy* 74 (April 1966): 132–157.

_____, "Change and Innovation in the Technology of Consumption," *American Economic Review* 56 (May 1966): 14–23.

Langley, James W., "An Appraisal of Least Squares Programs for the Electronic Computer from the Point of View of the User," *Journal of the American Statistical Association* 62 (September 1967): 819–829.

Lanzetta, John T., and Vera T. Kanareff, "Information Cost, Amount of Payoff and Level of Aspiration as Determinants of Information Seeking in Decision Making," *Behavioral Science* 7 (October 1962): 459–473.

Lavidge, Robert J., and Gary A. Steiner, "A Model for Predictive Measurements of Advertising Effectiveness," *Journal of Marketing* 25 (October 1961): 59–62.

Lawrence, Douglas H., "The Nature of a Stimulus: Some Relationships Between Learning and Perception," in *Psychology: A Study of a Science*, ed. Sigmund Koch, Vol. 5 (New York: McGraw-Hill Book Co., 1963).

Lindzey, Gardner, and Elliot Aronson, eds., *Handbook of Social Psychology* (Reading, Mass.: Addison-Wesley Publishing Co., 1968).

Lionberger, H. F., "Some Characteristics of Farm Operators Sought as Sources of Farm Information in a Missouri Farm Community," *Rural Sociology* 18 (December 1953): 327–338.

————, "The Relation of Informal Social Groups to the Diffusion of Farm Information in a Northeast Missouri Farm Community," *Rural Sociology* 19 (September 1954): 233–243.

————, and E. Hassinger, "Neighborhoods as a Factor in the Diffusion of Farm Innovation in a Northeast Missouri Farming Community," *Rural Sociology* 19 (December 1954): 377–384.

Little, John D. C., "Models and Managers: The Concept of a Decision Calculus," Chicago, 1969. (Paper presented at the symposium "Behavioral and Management Science in Marketing," University of Chicago, June 29 to July 1, 1969.)

Lubin, A., "Linear and Nonlinear Discriminating Functions," *British Journal of Psychological Statistics* 3 (March 1950): 90–104.

Lutz, Richard J., and Robert W. Resek, "More on Testing the Howard-Sheth Model of Buyer Behavior," *Journal of Marketing Research* 9 (August 1972).

Marketing Science Institute, "Communications Models of the Advertising Process," Cambridge, Mass., February 1969.

Maslow, Abraham H., "A Theory of Human Motivation," *Psychological Review* 50 (July 1943): 370–396.

Massey, William F., "Forecasting the Demand for New Convenience Products," *Journal of Marketing Research* 6 (November 1969): 405–412.

————, Ronald E. Frank, and Thomas M. Lodahl, *Purchasing Behavior and Personal Attributes* (Philadelphia: University of Pennsylvania Press, 1968).

McGuire, W. J., "Attitudes and Opinions," *Annual Review of Psychology* 17 (1966): 475–514.

————, "The Nature of Attitudes and Attitude Change," in *Handbook of Social Psychology*, eds., G. Lindzey and E. Aronson (Reading, Mass.: Addison-Wesley, 1968).

Menzel, Herbert, and Elihu Katz, "Social Relations and Innovation in the

Medical Profession: The Epidemiology of a New Drug," *Public Opinion Quarterly* 19 (Winter 1955-56): 337–352.

Moran, P. A. P., "Partial and Multiple Rank Correlation," *Biometrika* 38 (June 1951): 26–32.

Myers, J. G., *Consumer Image and Attitude* (Berkeley: Institute of Business and Economic Research, University of California, 1968).

National Industrial Conference Board, *Market Testing Consumer Products*, Experience in Marketing Management, No. 12, New York, n.d.

Nicosia, Franco, *Consumer Decision Processes* (Englewood Cliffs, N.J.: Prentice-Hall, 1966).

Norman, Donald A., *Memory and Attention* (New York: John Wiley & Sons, 1969).

O'Brien, Terrence V., "Information Sensitivity and the Sequence of Psychological States in the Brand Choice Process," Dissertation, Columbia University, 1969.

Opinion Research Corporation, "Accelerated Purchase Panels," *ORC Findings* (Princeton: Opinion Research Corporation, n.d.).

Osgood, C. E., and P. H. Tannenbaum, "The Principle of Congruity in the Prediction of Attitude Change," *Psychological Review* 62 (January 1955): 42–55.

Osgood, Charles E., G. J. Suci, and P. L. Tannenbaum, *The Measurement of Meaning* (Urbana: University of Illinois Press, 1957).

Palda, Kristian S., "The Hypothesis of a Hierarchy of Effects: A Partial Evaluation," *Journal of Marketing Research* 3 (February 1966): 13–24.

Parfitt, J. H., and B. J. K. Collins, "The Use of Consumer Panels for Brand-Share Prediction," *Journal of Marketing Research* 5 (May 1968): 131–146.

Peak, Helen, "Attitude and Motivation," in *Nebraska Symposium*, ed. M. R. Jones (Lincoln, Nebraska: University of Nebraska Press, 1955).

Pellemans, P. A., "Investigation on the Relationship Existing Between the Attitude Toward the Brand and the Intention to Buy the Same Brand," Dissertation, Columbia University, 1969.

————, "Investigations on Attitude and Purchase Intention toward the Brand," Dissertation, Columbia University, 1970.

Pelz, Donald C., "Comments on the Method of Cross-Lagged Correlation," (Michigan Survey Research Center, University of Michigan, November 1967).

————, and Frank M. Andrews, "Detecting Causal Priorities in Panel Study Data," *American Sociological Review* 29 (December 1964): 836–848.

Perry, Michael, "Measures of Association in Business Research," San Francisco, 1968. (Paper presented at ORSA/TIMS annual meeting.)

Pessemier, E. A., P. C. Burger, and D. J. Tigert, "Can New Buyers Be Identified," *Journal of Marketing Research* 4 (November 1967): 349–354.

Rickard, Stanley E., Jr., "Using Correlations to Test Causal Hypotheses," Dissertation, Northwestern University, 1967.

Ring, L. Winston, "Adjustment for Measurement Effects in Panel Data From

Test Markets," Denver, 1968. (Paper presented at the American Marketing Association Fall Conference.)

Robertson, Thomas S., "Purchase Sequence Responses: Innovators vs. Non-Innovators," *Journal of Advertising Research* 8 (March 1968): 47–52.

_____, "A Critical Examination of 'Adoption Process' Models of Consumer Behavior," New York, 1969. (Paper presented at the Third Annual Buyer Behavior Conference, Columbia University.)

Rokeach, M., *Beliefs, Attitudes and Values: A Theory of Organization and Change* (San Francisco: Jossey-Bass, 1968).

Rosenberg, M. J., "Cognitive Structure and Attitudinal Affect," *Journal of Abnormal and Social Psychology* 53 (November 1956): 367–372.

Russell, Robert R., "The Empirical Evaluation of Some Theoretically Plausible Demand Functions," Department of Economics, Harvard University, 1966. (Unpublished paper).

Ryan, B., and N. C. Gross, "The Diffusion of Hybrid Seed Corn in Two Iowa Communities," *Rural Sociology* 8 (May 1943): 15–24.

Scott, W. A., "Attitude Measurement," in *Handbook of Social Psychology*, ed. G. Lindzey and E. Aronson (Reading, Mass.: Addison-Wesley Publishing Co., 1968).

Sherif, Carolyn W., Muzafer Sherif, and Roger Nebergall, *Attitude and Attitude Change: The Social Judgment-Involvement Approach* (Philadelphia: Saunders, 1965).

Sherif, Muzafer, and Carolyn W. Sherif, *An Outline of Social Psychology*, 2nd ed. (New York: Harper and Brothers, 1956).

Sheth, Jagdish N., "How Adults Learn Brand Preference," *Journal of Advertising Research* 5 (September 1968): 25–38.

_____, "Perceived Risk and Diffusion of Innovation," in *Insights into Consumer Behavior*, ed. J. Arndt (Boston: Allyn and Bacon, 1968).

_____, "Attitude as a Function of Evaluative Beliefs." (Paper presented at the A.M.A. Consumer Behavior Workshop, August 22–23, 1969.)

_____, "Using Factor Analysis to Estimate Parameters," *Journal of the American Statistical Association* 64 (September 1969): 808–822.

_____, "Are There Differences in Post-Decision Dissonance Reduction Between Housewives and Students?" *Journal of Marketing Research* 7 (May 1970): 243–245.

_____, "Problems in Summing Beliefs Prior to Correlating With Affect." (Unpublished paper.)

Sieber, Joan E., and John T. Lanzetta, "Conflict and Conceptual Structure as Determinants of Decision-Making Behavior," *Journal of Personality* 32 (December 1964): 622–641.

Siegel, Arthur I., and J. Jay Wolf, *Man-Machine Simulation Models* (New York: John Wiley & Sons, Inc., 1964).

Siegel, Sidney, *Nonparametric Statistics* (New York: McGraw-Hill Book Co., 1956).

Sills, Davis, ed., *International Encyclopedia of the Social Sciences* (New York: The Macmillan Co. and the Free Press, 1968).

Simon, Herbert A., "On the Concept of Organizational Goal," *Administrative Science Quarterly* 9 (June 1964): 1–22.

Smirnov, N. V., "Tables for Estimating the Goodness of Fit of Empirical Distributions," *Annals of Mathematical Statistics* 19 (September 1948): 280–281.

Sonquist, John A., and James N. Morgan, *The Detection of Interaction Effects*, Monograph No. 35, Survey Research Center, University of Michigan, 1964.

Tolman, Edward C., in Talcott Parsons and Edward Shils, eds., *Toward a General Theory of Action*, Part 3 (Cambridge, Mass.: Harvard University Press, 1951).

Weiss, Robert S., *Statistics in Social Research* (New York: John Wiley & Sons, 1968).

Wells, William D., "Measuring Readiness to Buy," *Harvard Business Review* 39 (July–August 1961): 81–87.

————, and Leonard A. LoScuito, "Direct Observation of Purchasing Behavior," *Journal of Marketing Research* 3 (August 1966): 227–233.

Woolf, Harry, *Quantification* (Indianapolis: Bobbs-Merrill Company, 1961).

Zajonc, Robert B., "The Attitudinal Effects of Mere Exposure," *Technical Report No. 34*. Research Center for Group Dynamics, Institute for Social Research, University of Michigan, September 1965.

# Index